JUL 88 11 95

The Power of Genre

D1280560

Published with assistance
from the Margaret S. Harding Memorial Endowment
honoring the first director
of the University of Minnesota Press.

The Power of Genre

Adena
Rosmarin

University of Minnesota Press, Minneapolis

Copyright © 1985 by the University of Minnesota
All rights reserved. No part of this publication may be
reproduced, stored in a retrieval system, or transmitted, in
any form or by any means, electronic, mechanical, photo-
copying, recording, or otherwise, without the prior written
permission of the publisher.
Published by the University of Minnesota Press
2037 University Avenue Southeast, Minneapolis MN 55414.
Published simultaneously in Canada
by Fitzhenry & Whiteside Limited, Markham.
Printed in the United States of America.

Library of Congress Cataloging in Publication Data

Rosmarin, Adena.
  The Power of Genre.
  Bibliography: p.
  Includes index.
  1. Literary form. 2. Poetics. 3. Monologue.
4. Lyric poetry—History and criticism. 5. English
poetry—19th century—History and criticism. 6. American
poetry—20th century—History and criticism. I. Title.
PN 45.5.R67 1985   801'.951   85-8630
ISBN 0-8166-1395-8
ISBN 0-8166-1396-6 (pbk.)

Extracts from "The Love Song of J. Alfred Prufrock" reprinted by permission of Faber and
Faber Ltd from *Collected Poems 1909–1962* by T. S. Eliot. Extracts from "Gambling in
Stateline, Nevada," copyright © 1968 by James Wright reprinted from *Collected Poems* by
permission of Wesleyan University Press.

The University of Minnesota
is an equal-opportunity
educator and employer.

For Heather and Alexander

with assays of bias,
By indirections find directions out.

William Shakespeare

Contents

Preface

This book is an attempt to answer a theoretical yet pressing question: How, in the wake of deconstruction, can we make critical explanations that are at once reasoned, convincing, and self-aware? The answer is mounted in terms of genre. I begin by inquiring into criticism's traditional resistance to genre, proceed to analysis of those theories of genre that, in recent years, have been the most influential, and then propose a "corrective," a theory of genre that is simultaneously aware of itself as such and yet is designed to harmonize with its traditional antagonist, the literary text. Finally, this theory is put into practice, not by testing its premises in the old or strictly representational way, by gauging their correspondent "fit" to either the text or an *a priori* schema, but by testing them in a rhetorical and pragmatic way, by dramatizing their usefulness in performing the act of critical explanation. Specifically, I attempt to explain problematic instances of the dramatic monologue, the genre whose interpretive history, perhaps even more than that of the novel, has been obsessed with deciding its generic identity. This attempt involves not only redefining that genre but also defining another genre, the mask lyric, which enables fuller explanations of poems such as Tennyson's "Ulysses" and Eliot's "Prufrock." The book's theoretical claim is that its theory of genre is properly valued not only for its power to make sense of prior critical practice but also for its power to enable present practice. Its most general thesis, in sum, is that theory and practice are not ideally separate but pragmatically joined.

I began this study with the assistance of a grant-in-aid from the American Council of Learned Societies. An Andrew W. Mellon Faculty Fellowship at

Harvard University enabled me to complete the first draft, and a fellowship to the School of Criticism and Theory at Northwestern University provided the time and arena for rethinking. The University of Miami provided funds for summer research, duplicating, and typing. The final revisions and editing were done during my year as an Ethel Wattis Kimball Fellow at the Stanford Humanities Center. I am deeply grateful for this support.

I would also like to thank Wayne Booth, Jerome Buckley, Frederick Crews, Murray Krieger, Leonard Nathan, Ralph Rader, and Thomas Sloane for their early and continuing support. Morton Bloomfield and Seymour Chatman read the first draft, and many of their suggestions have been gratefully incorporated. A special thanks to my colleague, Steven Mailloux, who read, argued, and encouraged throughout. My greatest debt is to my husband, Peter Rosmarin, who read the manuscript not once but twice and kept us all going.

Portions of chapters 2 and 3 were originally delivered at the Victorian Division meeting of the 1981 Modern Language Association convention in New York and were subsequently published in "The Historical Imagination: Browning to Pound," *The Victorian Newsletter* 61 (1982): 6–11. Part of the introduction was published in "Theory and Practice: From Ideally Separate to Pragmatically Joined," *The Journal of Aesthetics and Art Criticism* 43 (1984): 31–40. I thank the editors of both journals for permission to reprint. The lines from the manuscript of Tennyson's "Ulysses" are reproduced by permission of the Houghton Library, Harvard University. The lines from James Wright's "Gambling in Stateline, Nevada" are reproduced by permission of Wesleyan University Press; the lines from T. S. Eliot's "The Love Song of J. Alfred Prufrock" are reproduced by permission of Harcourt Brace Jovanovich and Faber & Faber.

A.R.

The Power of Genre

A Theoretical Introduction

> Theories thus become instruments, not answers to
> enigmas in which we can rest.
>
> William James

The Dilemma of Theoretical Desire

[handwritten marginal note: basic // fundamental conflict is between theory + practice]

Like all engrossing dramas, twentieth-century criticism is fueled by conflict. For the last two decades notice of this fact has been as consequential as it is conspicuous, our repeated discussion of our critical disagreements drawing our attention "deeper" in search of their cause.[1] Thus we have turned from performing the act of critical explanation to explaining the dynamics and difficulties of that performance. This shift, however, has not resolved the troubled surfaces of our practical criticism. Rather, it has brought into being another set of conflicts, definitively "deeper" or "theoretical" and, ironically, more deeply unresolvable than those we would explain. The dramatic energy of these conflicts seems inexhaustible: the conflict between the reader and the text, perhaps the most important of contemporary struggles for interpretive authority, has plotted an entire school of criticism, that called "reader-response," and lent subplots to disparate others, including deconstruction.[2]

But in actual practice the energy or explanatory power of this and, indeed, of all theoretical conflicts is self-exhausting. The more they are used to explain, the more we "see through" them to a yet deeper conflict, which seems to ground or explain all others—that between theory and practice. One might expect this conflict also to wear out, to show itself grounded by yet another, but this is not happening. Despite the tentative emergence of what might be called a "theoretical criticism," of studies that, like J. Hillis Miller's *Fiction and Repetition*, are intricately interwoven of reading and self-reading, the antagonism between theory and practice not only persists but grows conspicuous.[3]

3

4   A THEORETICAL INTRODUCTION

This antagonism is in part a consequence of the way we have traditionally defined theory. The word itself comes, by way of late Latin, from the Greek *theoria*, which meant "a looking at, viewing, contemplation, speculation."[4] A theorist was a spectator, a looker on, and to theorize was to view or contemplate. Entering English in the Renaissance, "theory" retained its original sense, being used by Lancelot Andrewes, Sir Thomas Browne, and William Harvey to mean a "sight," "mental view," or "contemplation." John Norris in 1710 defined theory essentially as we do today: "Speculative knowledge contemplates Truth for itself, and accordingly stops and rests in the Contemplation of it, which is what we commonly call Theory."[5] Although later usage expanded the definition—theory came also to mean a system of ideas, the principles of a subject as distinguished from its practice—the basic sense has remained unchanged. Theory is something different from and apart from practice. It is distinguished by its Arnoldian disinterestedness, by its way of "keeping aloof from what is called 'the practical view of things.' "[6] Or, as Paul de Man has said, "A general statement about literary theory should not, in theory, start from pragmatic considerations."[7] The irony, of course, is that such pragmatic considerations are precisely what have kept this antipragmatic definition alive: we keep using it because it gives us a way—a deeply troubled way but nevertheless a way—of evaluating knowledge. Good knowledge is "valid," "objective," "speculative." It is uncontaminated by practice. It "contemplates Truth for itself." This study will argue the desirability of defining theory differently, but for the moment let us simply note that the traditional definition of theory as disinterested knowledge is a manifestly interested definition. Like all definitions, it is used because it is—or has been—useful.

A more complex reason for our antagonism toward theory is its increasingly obvious futility *as* a practice—a practice, moreover, that paradoxically denies its status as such. For literary theory, like the traditional philosophies upon which it is modeled, has defined itself against practice: it "sees" itself as a face-to-face confrontation with the object of knowledge. This object, of course, has itself been variously defined: in terms of the reader's experience, the author's intention, the conditions of signification, the imitated action, the text's ultimate undecidability, and so on. But what ties these definitions together is their common situation: the object of knowledge is either "buried" or, somewhat less frequently, "on the horizon." In either case, it is always just out of sight.[8] The theorist must accordingly search for it, a search conducted either in terms of the archaeological metaphor of traditional ontology, by digging ever deeper in quest of bedrock, or in terms of the visual metaphor of traditional epistemology, by polishing what Richard Rorty has called "the mirror of nature."[9] When firm ground has been reached or, alternatively, when the mirror has been polished to perfection, the theorist stops and rests in the contemplation of truth. And this contemplation, when penned or represented in words, is what we call valid cri-

'ie, criticism c/n seem motivated by finding a particular theory –
it must be unbiased.

A THEORETICAL INTRODUCTION   5

ticism. The problem with this program is that the search—whether for the perfectly solid ground or for the perfectly reflective medium—is never ending.
More precisely, it is always reachable in theory but never reached in practice.
Thus does the theorist-would-be-critic define himself into the quintessential
Romantic dilemma: that of Endymion, or the lover on the Grecian urn, or Tennyson's Ulysses, a "gray spirit yearning in desire/ To follow knowledge like a
sinking star,/Beyond the utmost bound of human thought."

This infinite regress and its consequences for critical practice are increasingly
apparent. Hence Michael McCanles:

> In attempting to think himself back into the perspective of the Renaissance
> the historicist commits himself either to an infinite regress or to a method-
> ological contradiction. Since on the one hand all such texts and the codes
> that fund them are no more "natural" and intuitively intelligible than
> denser texts like Shakespeare, Spenser, or Milton they are adduced to il-
> luminate, the historicist can never rest finally with a text that interprets
> without itself requiring interpretation. On the other hand, the more usual
> method is to find a group of texts that present themselves as ultimate and
> natural. In order to use them as such the historicist must take them "at face
> value"; and to do this he must also, in however covert and undisclosed
> a manner, interpret them to find if they are such. In other words, the whole
> process of seeking out lexicons and codes as prolegomena to interpretation
> necessarily commits the investigator to interpretation as a prior step in his
> investigation.[10]

The traditional critic, that is, gives himself two choices: either enact his theoretical program consistently, in which case he continues searching forever, or
make a "methodological contradiction," in which case he can start writing.
McCanles calls the latter "the more usual method," but in fact it is the only
method possible when practicing criticism in traditional terms. For it is only by
deciding upon a set of "lexicons and codes" (or, what is effectively the same,
a "group of texts" that seem their transparent embodiment) that the theorist-
would-be-critic can give himself a way of doing criticism. The problem, however, is that validity has its own conventions, all of which require the studied
implicitness of this decision: the critic's starting place must seem coincident with
the theorist's ending place; it must seem found or discovered, not made or
chosen; it must be buried, out of sight, "covert and undisclosed." Valid reading
is reading that starts with solid ground and unbiased vision, not with "pragmatic
considerations." Particularly inimical to validity is the open declaration of such
considerations.

Hence our current impasse. Of the two alternatives open to theory and criticism as traditionally defined, one is unworkable and the other undesirable. On
the one hand is an ideal practice, which is impossible to perform, and on the

one strategy — collapse T+P into one; or accept it as inevitable part of language

big prob going from exp of rdng to attempt to classify — + distort to

other a possible practice, which contests not only this theoretical ideal but also the topics and texts that it proposes to serve, namely, literature itself. The first alternative leads to Steven Knapp's and Walter Benn Michaels' argument "Against Theory" (*Critical Inquiry*, Summer 1982). Their strategy is to define theory in terms of practice, collapsing and thereby ending the conflict.[11] Their minor premise is that theory is "the name for all the ways that people have tried to stand outside practice"; their major premise is that "no one can reach a position outside practice"; and their conclusion is that "the theoretical enterprise should therefore come to an end."[12] The deductive rigor is unimpeachable, but the many theoretical responses to this argument, itself conspicuously theoretical, cast doubt on one or the other of their premises and thereby on their conclusion, suggesting that theory, despite its traditional definition, is itself a practice and likely to do anything but end. This suggestion points to the other alternative, laid out by de Man in the same issue of *Critical Inquiry*. His thesis is that the conflict between literary theory and literary practice is inherent in the nature of human language and that we must, therefore, continue to enact this self-defeating drama.[13] He first states the conflict: "Most of us feel internally divided between the compulsion to theorize about literature and a much more attractive, spontaneous encounter with literary works."[14] Then the impossibility of its resolution: theory is "inherent in language, in the necessity, which is also an impossibility, to connect the subject with its predicates or the sign with its symbolic manifestations . . . [it] will always . . . manifest itself as soon as experience shades into thought."[15]

The Question of Genre

De Man's Romantic portrait of man as trapped between the practical futility of his theoretical desire and his recognition of its inevitability presents the conflict between theory and practice on its "deepest" stage: to think is to use language, and to use language is to separate ourselves from what we think about. The object of our reading can never be fully and transparently present to our thought or theorizing because all conceptual languages, as Kenneth Burke has said, select and deflect their topics.[16] But de Man also presents this conflict on the distinctive stage of our discipline: our notion and experience of the literary text seem inherently at odds with the procedures and goals of its explanation. We typically strive both to unfold the unique and unmediated particularity of the text or our reading experience and to generalize this particularity, phrasing its explanation in terms not its own. The resulting reduction and distortion has proven always undesirable and frequently untenable: "All books dealing with classifications and systems of the arts," wrote Benedetto Croce, "could be burned without any loss whatsoever."[17]

But as Richard Rorty has observed, "the universal-particular distinction is

But, that is our only method of understanding — to group things. If we do not generalize, we can't discuss

universal-particular is center of T-P conflict

But genre is very much out of favor — it is seen as denigrating the text

A THEORETICAL INTRODUCTION   7

the *only* metaphysical distinction we have got."[18] If we fulfill Crocean desire by obliterating this distinction, we obliterate as well the very possibility of reasoned discussion about literature. Burke argues similarly, observing that there are two kinds of terms: "terms that put things together, and terms that take things apart."[19] If anything, Burke's claim is more radical than Rorty's: he is saying that we cannot talk or think or write at all without using terministic screens, that refusing to use terms that make the universal-particular distinction obliterates not only reasoned discussion but all discussion. The refusal is tantamount to silence.

The general-particular debate is literary criticism's most precise staging of its most profound conflict: between the individual reading and its generalization, between practice and theory. My concern in this study, however, is with a distinct staging of this debate, one that increasingly compels our attention and whose resolution is meant to suggest a way of resolving this larger conflict. My concern, in short, is with the question of genre. It is a question that has multiple phrasings. Does genre constitute the particular or do particulars constitute the genre? Are genres found in texts, in the reader's mind, in the author's, or in some combination thereof? Or are they not "found" at all but, rather, devised and used? Are they "theoretical" or "historical"? Are they "prescriptive" or "descriptive"? Are they used deductively or inductively? Can we "see" them or do they hover on the hermeneutic "horizon," always potentially but never actually in view? Is their use in literary explanation inevitable? If so, should it be foregrounded? Can genres be used to explain "literariness"? Or are they the enemy of all that makes literature seem "literary"? Might they be the enemy of the reader as well, a too rigorous constraint on the interpretive act? How many genres are there? Where do they come from? How, exactly, do they work? And change?

After having been not only ignored but mocked by generations of Croceans and formalists, these questions have been asked with growing frequency and urgency. Like other shifts in an "age of theory," this one is both cause and consequence of our increasing awareness of the constitutive power of our interpretive strategies, even when, as is particularly the case with genre, we deny that very power.[20] The dissolution of genres, we repeatedly say, began with the Romantics and has been going on ever since.[21] To be a modern writer and to write generically is a contradiction in terms. Genre works against the text's exalted stature and, what is much the same, its power to inquire into the stature and dynamics of its own writing. Hence Maurice Blanchot:

> The book alone is important, as it is, far from genres, outside rubrics—
> prose, poetry, the novel, the first-person account—under which it refuses
> to be arranged and to which it denies the power to fix its place and to deter-
> mine its form. A book no longer belongs to a genre; every book arises

from literature alone, as if the latter possessed in advance, in its generality, the secrets and the formulas that alone allow book reality to be given
to that which is written. Everything happens as if, genres having dissipated, literature alone were affirmed, alone shined in the mysterious light
that it spreads and that every literary creation sends back to it while multiplying it—as if there were an "essence" of literature.[22]

But "in reading those very writings of Blanchot," as Tzvetan Todorov has
observed, "one sees at work categories whose resemblance to generic distinctions is difficult to deny."[23] Indeed, is not Blanchot's "literature" itself a vast
genre, one whose "generality" is paradoxically hidden by its very vastness?
And is his "book" the natural or self-evident "particular" that it seems?[24] What
is most interesting about Todorov's observation is that it states what is everywhere apparent but virtually nowhere said: that we often feel the practical and
theoretical need to deny the constitutive power of genre in literary explanation.
This denial takes place in two ways, which are frequently joined. The critic may
explain a text as if its writing had proceeded without generic constraints, or he
may explain a text as if his own writing is proceeding without generic constraints, in particular those that he himself has chosen or defined in order to explain. The former denial leads him to explain "Ode to a Nightingale" not in
terms of its "odeness" but in terms of its imagery, its "form," its speaker's
act, or whatever. The latter denial may or may not entail the former. Thus the
critic may acknowledge that Keats wrote with generic consciousness and that
any good explanation of the ode includes discussion of its "odeness" while
simultaneously denying, whether implicitly or explicitly, that he has in any way
shaped the generic definition that he is using to explain. It is primarily this
second denial that will interest us here, the denial that is a special case of criticism's more general denial of the premises and purposes that serve the pragmatic
ends of critical explanation and, thereby, shape the text explained. Why we routinely make this denial is, of all the questions asked about genre, the first that
requires answering.

Resisting Genre

To choose or define a genre in order to explain seems counterintuitive. We are
so accustomed to discussing explanation in representational rather than pragmatic terms, in terms of what mirrors rather than of what works, that doing
otherwise seems strange if not wrong. Indeed, to discuss explanation in terms
of terms seems itself counterintuitive, for description, which is another name for
valid or representational reading, traditionally works to conceal and deny whatever terminology is used. Of course, representation itself uses terminological
screens or metaphors, particularly those drawn from archaeology and optics, but

explanation has been largely representational, not pragmatic;
it has become a process of discovering. Metaphor of rep.
on language of explanation. Fits b/c we have desire to know what
"is really there" - has to be uncovered. Main problem is seeming to be
objective (Truth exists, not created)

with repeated usage these screens have grown transparent. As metaphors, they have died, becoming so deeply "buried" in both our philosophical discourse and our language that even recent attempts to awaken them have created only momentary signs of life.[25]

It has come to seem natural, in other words, to understand understanding as the result of "going under" to "stand" on the bedrock of truth rather than as something that happens when we write or listen well. We habitually discuss explanation *as* excavation, as the removal of obfuscating layers so as to confront the thing or text or, to take Blanchot's interpretive "ground," the "literature" from which all else "arises." And when we perform this excavation well, we habitually discuss our reward in terms of representation's other metaphor: we say that the newly uncovered ground sheds light on (explains) all that was previously dark (unexplained) and that we, its spectators, are thus enlightened. Thus Blanchot imagines his "literature" as if it "alone shined in the mysterious light that it spreads and that every literary creation sends back to it while multiplying it."

With long and almost exclusive use, the metaphors of representation have proliferated into a conceptual vocabulary so extensive that, for this reason alone, it is difficult to talk otherwise. When we "know" we say that we *see, see through, spot, discern, recognize,* have it *dawn* on us, have our *eyes* opened, and, in a phrase that bespeaks the essential mysticism of this Platonic language, go from *seeing through a glass darkly* to *seeing face-to-face.* Alternatively, we say that we have gotten to the *root* or *bottom* of things, that we have staked out a *territory* or mastered a *field.* We like to have things or texts *illuminated* or *elucidated.* We value arguments insofar as they are *brilliant, clear,* and *lucid.* Alternatively, we value them insofar as they are *basic, underlying, deep, well grounded,* and, at times, *radical.* We dislike having matter beyond our *ken,* our range of vision, but, significantly, we do not want it in *plain view* either. Challenge or, as I have been saying, conflict is necessary to explanation, even when defined representationally, in terms of seeing and confrontation, rather than rhetorically and pragmatically, in terms of saying and justification. The *horizon* and *bedrock* are thus the ideal hermeneutic *sites,* the *places* where the most potentially *illuminating* or *solid* knowledge dwells.[26] And what is desirably "on" the horizon is an *idea,* a most valued feature of the representational landscape whose etymological *roots* extend to the Greek verb *ideîn: to see.*

The language of representation also seems natural because its grammar is *grounded* in our *deep-rooted* desire to know what is "really there." It promises to fulfill metaphorically our reflex need for *support,* for being on *firm ground,* and it capitalizes, again metaphorically, on our highly developed capacity for visualization. But the difficulty of thinking and talking in other than representational terms is finally and most significantly due to representation's strategy of self-erasure. In order to create the illusion of an unbiased and unmediated encounter with truth, representation denies both its conceptual medium and its pragmatic purpose. This denial—which is the denial of genre writ large—has been so unremitting that to think of it as being itself conceptual and strategic seems counterintuitive. But our intuition acquires the assistance it needs if, as is suggested by the most prominent of representation's two metaphors, we turn from criticism to painting. E. H. Gombrich's analysis of the techniques of making and reading visual representations will not only help us to "see" our guiding metaphor for knowledge but, more importantly, to "understand" why we so frequently deny genre's constitutive power, even genre's relevance in critical explanation, and why, on those occasions when we do admit the power of genre into criticism and theory, we so carefully "ground" it in either prior historical use or a prior conceptual system.

The Rhetoric of Visual Representation

Because we dwell on the near side of what Gombrich calls the "Greek Revolution," the fifth-century B.C. awakening of Greek sculpture and painting from the conceptual rigors of its "unnatural sleep," visual representation seems not only natural but easy.[27] In actuality it is neither, for, as Gombrich emphasizes, "what is normal to man and child all over the globe is the reliance on schemata, on what is called 'conceptual art' " (p. 118). What needs explanation is not how and why painting, sculpture, and thought become conspicuously conceptual or schematic but how and why they become otherwise: how and why interpretation of any kind goes to the great and subtle trouble of attempting to conceal its conceptual origins and suasive purpose. A child's drawings are, we like to say, products of what he knows rather than what he sees. Eyes are placed near the top of a circle and hair sticks out from its edge—not because they are visually thus arranged but because the child *knows* that eyes occupy the top of the face and hair grows outside the skull. These conceptual facts precede and dominate our later knowledge: that the face occupies only part of the circle, that hair is not confined to its edge. This second set of facts comes into play only when we try to create an illusion or *trompe l'oeil*. But despite their "grounding" in appearance these facts are no less conceptual or schematic than the first set—they are simply less obviously so—and as the illusionistic sophistication of our audience increases they themselves require refinement, as will those refinements, and so on toward the infinitude of particulars that even the most verisimilar representation can no more than suggest. To think of painting hair or the leaves on a tree or the crowd on Derby Day is to recognize that incompleteness is a condition of visual representation, not a consequence of its failure.

Both individually and historically, then, we *learn* to draw illusionistically, and the lesson is difficult.[28] The convincing illusion—whether of hair or the moving spokes of a spinning wheel or water in a glass or depth itself—is an achievement not of nature but of technique. It requires strategies that, like perspective, may take centuries to "discover" but that also, precisely because they are strategic rather than intuitive, may themselves be taught and learned. The history of art, however, shows that what is arduously learned can also be forgotten. The Romans painted "realistically," even water in a glass, but subsequent centuries unlearned this lesson, thereby teaching another: that it is in actual practice easier or more natural to draw or sculpt *without* attempting illusion. Gombrich calls this unlearning a "natural pull to the minimum stereotype" (p. 144). If artists are not obliged to create an illusion, to persuade the beholder that what he sees mirrors what is, the schema rapidly returns to its natural or "conceptual" resting place and, as in Byzantium, becomes itself visible, even conspicuous.

The history of art teaches, in other words, that visual representation is like all other suasive enterprises in that it begins with a schema or premise that the painter modifies to meet the demands of his purpose and audience. The schema differs only in the nature and extremity of its distinctive demand: that it be erased or hidden behind a seeming infinitude of "accurately" represented particulars, that the artist strive for the *trompe l'oeil*. Because we are children of the Greeks and Romans, this striving strikes us as natural, even necessary, but in practice—or in theory—it is neither. The Egyptians are our most striking counterexample, for, as Gombrich observes, they were manifestly at home with the schematic: "The Egyptian statue does not represent a man standing rigidly or a man standing at ease—it is concerned with the what, not with the how. To ask for more might have struck an Egyptian artist as it would strike us if someone inquired the age or mood of the king on the chessboard" (p. 124).

But the history of art also teaches another and complementary lesson: that no effort of erasure or addition of detail can hide the schema, that no representation, however close its approach to ideal duplicity, can completely and tracelessly capture what it represents. The symptoms of this schematic incompletion and error always betray the schema "under" or "behind" the illusion and, whether in painting or in literature, are what we call "style." And this betrayal, which enables us to plot a history of art and, by analogy, a history of critical readings, marks not only conspicuously schematic art but also the most "ideal" of realisms, that of the Greeks: *style always exists*

> Even in the portrayal of man it remained wedded to types. This does not apply only to the idealized type of physique which we all associate with Greek art. Even in the rendering of movement and drapery the repertoire of Greek sculpture and painting has turned out to be strangely limited. There are a restricted number of formulas for the rendering of figures standing, running, fighting, or falling, which Greek artists repeated with relatively slight variations over a long period of time. Perhaps if a census of such motifs were taken, the Greek vocabulary would be found to be not much larger than the Egyptian. (P. 142)

(critic)
Representation trad ignores any purpose, the creator + medium unimpt. This
ignores choosing & techniques according to purpose + aud

The history of illusionism, in sum, tells us that our intuitions about illusion are wrong: that "naturalness" is a compliment paid to the successful illusion rather than an insight into its working; that even the denied schema has tremendous and finally ineradicable constitutive power; that even the most "realistic" art remains "wedded to types." This power is most visibly documented by the portraits of the sixteenth through eighteenth centuries, which even at their most specific and illusionistic show the generic heads and bodies of the patternbooks. Thus Rubens' portraits of children—even his own—repeat the generically swollen cheeks of the patternbook *putti*. But literature analogously and no less strongly documents this power. Thus the verbal portraits called "dramatic monologues," perhaps the most specifically illusionistic of literary texts, remain thoroughly wedded to types. As does their explanation, which is wedded to the type we call "genre."

A Three-Way Conflict

The critic traditionally speaks of representation—whether it be visual, as in a painting, or poetic, as in the dramatic monologue, or critical, as in the monologue's explanation—as if it in theory happened by itself: as if its creator were a copyist, the enactor of an act so minimal it ideally goes unmentioned, and its medium a transparency, a presence so minimal it also goes unmentioned—or is mentioned only as a flaw. The purpose of this conceptual phrasing is to keep the object known "pure" or "valid," uncontaminated by our schematic touch. But a rhetoric of visual representation knows better. Like all rhetorics, it offers a compendium—of schemata, premises, strategies, or, as they were anciently termed, schemes and tropes—from which makers may choose according to their purpose and audience. It is interested in the analysis of previous texts and techniques and, simultaneously, in the genesis of new. And it specifically teaches that illusionistic texts, far from simply happening, are in practice extraordinarily difficult to make. My explanations of dramatic monologues will display and, indeed, turn on this traditionally ignored difficulty. But a rhetoric of visual representation also teaches that the explanation of such texts, like their making, is more fruitfully termed a knowing-how rather than a knowing-that: it happens better when we talk in terms of doing rather than of seeing, of defining and justifying rather than of grounding and validating.[29] As Gombrich explains, "Painting is an activity, and the artist will therefore tend to see what he paints rather than paint what he sees" (p. 86).

Gombrich generalizes this counterintuitive observation as "making comes before matching" (p. 116). This, his central thesis, unites three notions that, given the predominantly representational context in which we currently think, seem incompatible: 1) that knowledge is schematically determined or constituted; 2) that knowledge is what happens when we act or, specifically, "make";

!, genres d/n just happen, unsig happenstance — they arise out of context

for him to be valid, must reject criticism as passively finding what is "out there" and instead see critic as acting. Explanation is active ... rhetorical + pragmatic A THEORETICAL INTRODUCTION   13

3) that knowledge "matches" or reflects that which is not itself. Gombrich's painter is at once empowered to make and yet is doubly constrained, on the one hand by the schema's constitutive power and on the other by the object that the schema is modified to match. These constraints conflict both with each other and with the notion of the painter or critic *acting*. Whether we imagine the knower as passively reflecting something "really out there" or as reflexively carrying out the dictates of his mental schema, the thought of his acting or, more precisely, acting on his own casts doubt on the validity of his knowledge.

Criticism has repeatedly dramatized this three-way conflict. The "matching" position is exemplified by Hume, who in attempting to arrive at a "standard of taste" postulated a *tabula rasa* reader, one "cleared of all prejudice."[30] E. D. Hirsch, some two hundred years later, argues similarly: that "The interpreter's aim . . . is to posit the author's horizon and carefully exclude his own accidental association."[31] As does Barbara Johnson: "If the deconstructive impulse is to retain its vital, subversive power, we must . . . become ignorant of it again and again"; we can repeat its "surprise" only by "forgetting what we know how to do, by setting aside the thoughts that have most changed us."[32] However great their differences in other respects, Hume, Hirsch, and Johnson similarly reject the reader-critic who is other than pellucid or passive. This rejection, which is a way of deciding the reader-text conflict in favor of the latter, is based on the primary defensive assumption of representational criticism: that the more active the reader-critic, the less accurate his representation of the text.

Of course, the reader is not always the loser. But even when the decision is in his favor, more frequently than not it is immediately reversed in favor of the schema that governs *him*:

> It looks as if the text is about to be dislodged as a center of authority in favor of the reader whose interpretive strategies make it; but I forestall this conclusion by arguing that the strategies in question are not his in the sense that would make him an independent agent. Rather, they proceed not from him but from the interpretive community of which he is a member; they are, in effect, community property, and insofar as they at once enable and limit the operations of his consciousness, he is too.[33]

Stanley Fish here emphasizes the constitutive power of the "interpretive strategies," which are congeneric with Gombrich's "schemata," McCanles' "lexicons and codes," and, ultimately, Kant's "categories." He also, however, emphasizes their independence from the reader. The reader is defined as neither choosing them nor using them. He is their instrument, not the other way around.

In other words, the reader-critic is traditionally constrained either by what he reads (the "realist" constraint) or by how he reads (the "idealist" constraint).[34] Neither way does he act rhetorically and pragmatically, in terms of his audience and purpose. This three-way conflict—between the authorities of

*must have starting place = rhetorical */e is not an object of knowledge or a medium,*
begin w/schema which constitutes the rep.
we think deductively—begin w/categories + fit things into them.

the object represented, the terms of its representation, and the maker of the representation—maps our present impasse. Gombrich does not address the conflict,
and, had he done so, important inconsistencies in his argument would have
dropped away. But his theses can nevertheless be corrected into compatibility,
into a coherent and consistent sense that, in turn, will yield our theory of genre.

Let us begin with Gombrich's thesis that all art, even that which strives to
conceal this fact, begins with a schema. Thus when we make a snowman we
"work the snow and balance the shapes till we recognize a man. The pile of
snow provides us with the first schema, which we correct until it satisfies our
minimum definition" (p. 100). The point, repeated throughout *Art and Illusion*,
is that images are not made from nothing: one has to begin somewhere, with
something. More than anything else, this emphasis on starting places, particularly on their pragmatic definition, signals Gombrich's rhetoricity.[35] Rather than
beginning with an object of knowledge and a transparent medium, Gombrich's
maker begins with a mound of snow, a blot, a circle, a patternbook *putto*, or,
as Gombrich generally terms the starting place, a "schema." The maker then
"proceeds through the rhythms of schema and correction" (p. 74), working to
match or fit this beginning to something not itself. The "distinctive features"
of this something "are entered, as it were, upon a pre-existing blank or form-
ulary. And, as often happens with blanks, if they have no provisions for certain
kinds of information we consider essential, it is just too bad for the information"
(p. 73). Here as virtually throughout *Art and Illusion* Gombrich grants constitutive power to the schema.

Our intuitive sense, of course, is not schematic but *a posteriori* or inductive.
We seem always to be responding to the particulars before us: any generalization
seems to be caused by those particulars and to happen after our response. The
attraction of the representational language is in large part due to its "fit" with
this intuition. But Gombrich here joins many post-Kantian thinkers in arguing
that we actually begin with the schema or generalization and then perform its
"correction": "Neither in thought nor in perception do we learn to generalize.
We learn to particularize, to articulate, to make distinction where before there
was only an undifferentiated mass" (pp. 100–101). Indeed, "All thinking is
sorting, classifying" (p. 301). The idea is counterintuitive, deductive,
pragmatic, and, in a word, rhetorical. It is no accident that I. A. Richards in
The Philosophy of Rhetoric argues the same thesis: "a rhetorical theorem of
meaning holds that we begin with the general abstract anything, split it . . .
into sorts and then arrive at concrete particulars by the overlapping or common
membership of these sorts."[36] Nor is it accidental that this thesis condenses to
the same words: "all thinking . . . is sorting."[37]

The explanatory power of the schema, of thinking by sorting, is enormous:
it enables the art historian to plot a history of art, even illusionistic art. Analo-

all constitutive power in schema d/n explain the how + why about them so ?. is - is there something more basic? (dp would answer yes w/ metaphors)

A THEORETICAL INTRODUCTION   15

gously, it enables the literary critic to plot a history of critical readings. In the case of any particular text, it enables him to give reasoned accounts not only of our disagreements (the critics have used different schemata) but of that more elusive phenomenon, our agreement (they have used the same schemata).[38] But placing constitutive power in the schema alone always leaves us unable to explain why one schema is used and not another. It also leaves us unable to explain how and why schemata change over time, and how and why the schema is changed in the process of making a particular painting or explanation, how and why it is "matched" to the not-itself. The important question raised by this explanatory muteness is whether there is something yet more powerfully determining than the schema, a yet more basic *a priori* something that determines *its* choice and use. The representational thinker would answer "yes" to this question, but Gombrich answers pragmatically and rhetorically. We begin, he tells us, with a purpose or, in his word, a function. And just as making comes before matching, function comes before form—not, as our intuition tells us, the other way around. According to Gombrich, the painter's eye is first on his audience and what he would convince them of, then on his schema, and only finally on his object. A rhetoric of visual representation imagines him as asking himself: What do I want my beholder's experience of this landscape to be like? What schema will best enable me to create this experience? How and how far shall I modify it? And just as the maker of a snowman does not make from nothing, Gombrich's painter does not answer his questions in a vacuum. He answers in a context: choosing from among the various received schemata at his disposal, calculating where what Hans Robert Jauss calls the "horizon" of reception lies, deciding how far he can and would move it with his particular design.

But doesn't this answer beg the question? Does it not simply replace a precise schema with the amorphous schema currently called "context"? Only if we fail to recognize that "context" is itself a terminological tool, which serves a distinct but limited critical purpose: it tells us what is or was possible, not what is or was done. Put otherwise, it is an effective way of reminding ourselves that in any given situation the so-called determining variables number themselves into indeterminacy, that the painter and the critic alike have innumerable topics to paint or say and innumerable ways of painting or saying them. "Context" is not, however, an effective way of discussing either choice of topic or choice of terms: why, for example, Picasso painted the bombing of Guernica or Miller wrote about *Wuthering Heights*, why one painted in cubist terms or the other wrote in deconstructionist terms.[39] What we explain and how we explain it are always contextual questions, but they are questions that can only be asked by context, never answered. In part this is so because "context" can never be sufficiently specified to compose an answer with power to persuade.[40] More importantly, it is so because the answer is made by a person, not by an essence or schema.

schema is chosen according to purpose

This point raises the second constituent of Gombrich's three-way conflict: the painter's or critic's act. A rhetoric of visual representation would reconcile a powerful schema with an active interpreter thus: by conceiving that interpreter as knowingly choosing his schema and conceiving that choice as determined by his painterly or critical purpose, as is his subsequent modification of the schema, his "matching" it to the not-itself. His choice is constraining, but it is itself constrained by this purpose rather than by an essence or schema below or beyond. And if his text is rigorously reasoned from a powerful premise, his painting or argument will strike us as true. In other words, this truth, which is another name for our conviction, is less a consequence of a text's actual correspondence to or grounding in the not-itself than of its maker's reasoning being both consistent and comprehensive. In Gombrich's words, the "correct portrait" is like the "useful map": "It is not a faithful record of a visual experience but the faithful construction of a relational model" (p. 90). In literary studies this truth amounts to the critical text's dramatized capacity to solve an interpretive problem, to construct a "relational model" that works. It is a "useful map" that gets us to our goal. But because the goal of criticism so frequently involves laying out the literary text's particularity, this map must meet not only the requirement of coherence but the additional requirement of complexity. That is, we value the critical or explaining text much as we value the literary or explained text: in terms of its order, which, as is increasingly noted, may be a calculated or "uncanny" disorder, and its richness of substance, its power to make us "see" matter to which we were previously blind.

But does not such "seeing" imply the prior existence of this matter, whether it be in the text or in its interpretive history? This question raises the third constituent of the conflict, namely, "matching," and a rhetoric of visual representation answers—or should answer—that the priority of the represented matter is not actual but apparent, an appearance that is a triumph not of antecedent matter but of suasive technique. Yet this answer, despite its obviousness, has in theoretical practice proven exceedingly difficult to give. The Kantian tradition provides a way of defending the schematic nature of interpretation, and the rhetorical tradition, beginning with Aristotle's premise that "rhetoric may be defined as the faculty of observing in any given case the available means of persuasion," provides a way of defending the pragmatism of interpretation.[41] But the theoretical defense of representation for its own or pleasure's sake must always, at least implicitly, do battle with Plato.

For this reason but also because it seems to fit our inductive intuition, the notion of "matching" presents the greatest obstacle to a three-way reconciliation. Demystifying this intuition requires prolonged analytic attention, as does replacing this intuition with another: that all representation is inevitably incomplete and trace-laden, that the face made with pencil and paper can never repeat the face matched because we can neither eliminate the trace of the very pencil

"seeing" is not only "true" but also persuasive

success is in being mistaken

used to draw, nor add the dimension of depth, nor repeat each of thousands of hairs and pores. The "made" face must always in practice be trace-laden ("pencilish" and "paperish") and incomplete (too flat, lacking in some of all possible detail). And if we think about it, this "made" face must even in theory be a "mistake." While it would seem that the more perfect a representation the less its ambiguity, in actuality the perfection of representation constitutes not the elimination of ambiguity but its guarantee: to take a painting of a particular face as that face is to mistake it for that face. As Gombrich notes, the successful *trompe l'oeil* is "the height of visual ambiguity. It is a multicolored canvas that we can interpret as a dining table" (p. 276). And the successful verbal representation is no less a triumph of ambiguity: when we read Browning's "My Last Duchess" we seem to hear the Duke speaking and tend to forget that he and his speech are themselves spoken or, to be precise, written. The words on the page have convinced us, however provisionally, that they are what they seem. We "mistake" them for what they are not.

Thus does the unexpected deviousness of theoretical fulfillment (the better the representation, the greater its ambiguity) join the manifest impossibility of practical fulfillment (the representation is always imperfect) to suggest that the illusionist's goal is never actual matching but always apparent matching. Always gesturing toward the not-itself and striving to convince its audience that that gesture is a grasp, visual representation is asking its audience to entertain a paradox: that the face beheld or the text read is simultaneously itself and not-itself, both what it is and what it seems. This paradox creates problems even for the realist, who places constitutive power in the face: achieving his goal is impossible practically and self-subverting theoretically. But the problem of the idealist, who places constitutive power in the schema, is worse: if his matching is actual then some or all of that power must reside not in the schema but in the particular.

Gombrich's rhetoric of visual representation wrestles with and very nearly resolves this conflict. He explains that while the schema can never be perfectly corrected to match the particular, it can be *sufficiently* corrected. The painter thus corrects his beginning schema until, as in Courbet's *Man with the Leather Belt*, his painting looks like a face, the poet his couplets until, as in Browning's "My Last Duchess," his poem sounds like someone speaking, the critic his premises until, as in Miller's reading of *Wuthering Heights*, his explanation convinces us that it is a more "total accounting" of that novel than is any previous explanation.[42] A representationalist would in theory argue that we stop correcting only when a full and trace-free representation has been achieved, when solid ground has been reached. Even in theory, however, a rhetorician readily acknowledges that this contextless goal is impossible and that this impossibility is finally beside the point. For the stopping place depends not upon the image's accuracy but upon its function, upon what it would do or how it would affect its audience. An anatomy drawing accordingly requires much correction of the beginning schema, a voodoo doll very little: "The test of an image is not its likeness but its efficacy within a context of action" (p. 110).

To be sure. But "context," once again, is a term more useful for questioning than for answering: it casts doubt on the pretensions of visual representation but cannot explain how it works. Gombrich, however, mounts just such an explanation by positing "the beholder's share," the interpretive work done by the beholder as he mentally erases traces of the schema he expected to see and completes the incompletions he expected to find. Thus, when "reading" a pencil-drawn face, the beholder attributes neither leaden color nor two-dimensionality to the face but, rather, corrects for both. The immediate implication here, which Gombrich states, is that the processes of painting and of reading paintings are closely analogous: "the very process of perception is based on the same rhythm that we found governing the process of representation: the rhythm of schema and correction" (p. 271). But the further implication is that we are persuaded to have an illusion in large part by our own effort, by the interpretive work of reading or correcting, work that quite literally makes our conviction ours. And the yet further implication is that the illusion becomes convincing not despite but because of its schematic presence, because the schema's reduction and distortion of the gestured-toward particular so strongly demand our completion and correction. The suasive power of visual representation and, indeed, of all representation turns out to be the power to schematize in a way that works.

Resolving the Conflict

These implications resolve the conflict between a prior or constitutively powerful matter and a prior or constitutively powerful schema: they show that matter's priority or power to be gestural only, to be fully strategic, not intrinsic. But Gombrich leaves this resolution implicit and, perhaps for this reason, in one place contradicts his own thesis, speaking as if constitutive power does indeed inhere in the "information" or "facts," not in the schema:

> Without some starting point, some initial schema, we could never get hold of the flux of experience. . . . Paradoxically, it has turned out that it matters relatively little what those categories are. We can always adjust them according to need. . . . An entirely fluid system would no longer serve its purpose; it would not *register facts* because it would lack pigeon holes. But how we arrange the first filing system is not very relevant. (P. 88, emphasis added)

Although the notion of "matching" does in itself suggest a pliant schema, an interpretive medium that can be fitted to the world beyond, Gombrich has so strongly argued the tool-like power of the schema, the fact that its "fit" with the world is not actual and natural but seeming and technical, that one must ques-

[handwritten margin note at top: "genre is not used b/c it reflects truth", but because it fits explanatory function"]

tion this isolated but nevertheless important denial of his own argument. The answer, I propose, lies in the order in which he has conceived his interpretive processes: that of schema and correction. Given his decision to grant constitutive power to the schema, the decision to place the schema first must have seemed natural. But it is precisely this placement that creates Gombrich's unadmitted self-contradiction, for he now has to posit something that has the power to cor- rect the schema. And the most obvious "something" is the particular worldly "fact" that the schema would match. *[margin notes: "problem's"; "correction comes from 'facts'"]*

But if Gombrich had reversed the order of "schema and correction," the problem would have dropped away. This reversal places the beginning of either making or matching in the interpreter's purposeful act, what Gombrich calls the text's "function." The maker begins, in effect, by asking a question—What do I want to do and how may I best do it?—and answers himself by choosing, cor- recting, or, to use the traditional rhetorical term, inventing a schema. Gombrich has throughout argued that form follows function; this reversal pushes his thesis to its logical and pragmatic conclusion. It is also a rhetorical conclusion: as in Aristotle's definition of rhetoric, making is preceded by the maker's analysis of previous makings, and this analytic prelude is given primary if not exclusive importance. The painter or critic is "knowing" insofar as he knows previous usage, insofar as he knows how to assess the suitability of extant schemata for his present purpose, and, having adopted a schema, insofar as he knows how to correct or modify this schema for that purpose. *[margin note: "instead, sh'd come from function"]*

The claim is obviously intertextual—that each visual text, like each verbal text, is a rewriting of previous texts—but what makes it rhetorical as well is its placement of power in the interpreter's purposeful act rather than in those texts (which would be a variant of the "realist" solution) or in some underlying "con- dition" (which would be a variant of the "idealist" solution). For although previous usage of a schema is temporally prior, it is no more necessarily deter- mining than is the schema used or the topic painted. Just as Picasso need not have painted the bombing of Guernica nor have painted in cubist terms, he need not have chosen to correct a particular previous usage of those terms, whether Braque's or his own. Topic, schema, previous usage, audience, suasive pur- pose—all are constraining but none are necessarily so. All may be temporally prior to the act of making, but this priority does not make them either logically prior or pragmatically necessary. It simply makes them available for the inter- preter's knowing use. Of course, by explicitly correcting previous usage he implicitly invites correction of his own. But the rhetorician readily extends this invitation, recognizing not only that his own solution of a problem must be pro- visional but also that the process of correction is the birthing place of thought and, yet more precisely, texts. *[margin note: "use of a genre not inevitable"]*

The implication is that each painting interprets not only the particulars with which it "matches" but also previous paintings of such particulars. Manet's

Olympia is not only a painting of a nude but also a repainting of Titian's *Venus of Urbino*. Analogously, each critical reading interprets both the text read and what I will here call its "interpretive history," the communal text composed of previous readings.[43] The two temporally prior texts interface with the critic's present text in a process that leaves none unchanged and, moreover, that undoes the conventional bond between temporal and logical priorities. Hence Harold Bloom's argument that the "strong" reading is always a "misreading" that need not respect unidirectional chronology; hence de Man's argument that the sign's connection with its "symbolic manifestations" is as impossible as it is necessary.[44] The rhetorician acknowledges the inevitability of "misreading," but he not only makes this acknowledgement without gloom, he understands this "error" to be as potentially purposeful and fruitful as it is necessary.[45]

This point has been most forcefully made by Hans Vaihinger in *The Philosophy of "As If."*[46] In his correction of Kant's categories, which he calls "fictions" in order to emphasize their inventional and heuristic nature, Vaihinger anticipates this resolution of the three-way conflict by both granting the schema full constitutive power and showing it to be fully pragmatic: it is defined in order to serve the purposes of thought, not the other way around. He also shows that it necessarily contradicts or "speaks against" the topic of that thought, so that our choice is never between more or less "valid" interpretations, but between those that are more or less useful: "what we call truth, namely a conceptual world coinciding with the external world, *is merely the most expedient error.*"[47] Vaihinger here, *avant la lettre*, pushes Gombrich's notion of "the faithful construction of a relational model" to its logical fruition, showing that "faithful" finally if subtly begs the question by throwing the basis for evaluation back into the "realist" camp. It is only by recognizing the inevitability of the model's *correspondent* imperfection that its *pragmatic* perfection can be evaluated and, indeed, devised. But Vaihinger also shows that it is only when this necessary error is made explicit that it becomes useful, even engendering: "*contradiction*," the interpreter's purposeful *speaking against* that which has gone before, "is the driving force of thought."[48]

The interpreter begins, then, by correcting or speaking against previous texts, and it is this beginning that effectively constitutes the theoretical moment of his discourse. Whereas traditional or representational theory conceives of itself as happening after the practice of criticism is finished, a rhetorical and pragmatic theory conceives of itself as a practice that initiates and informs the practice of criticism. Its goal is not the visualization or unearthing of something that already if only "in theory" exists but, rather, the performance of an act: the defining of a critical problem in such a way that its significance becomes obvious and its solution possible. Rather than arguing its validity, its mirror-like correspondence to the not-itself, a rhetorical and pragmatic theory seeks to justify its value as an argument. It presents itself not as an after-the-fact contemplation but as *how to get from schema to text 'is essential? if genre*

an ongoing inquiry into what works. Far from being disinterested, ideally separate from practice, it is manifestly interested in its practical or critical consequences, in articulating the ways in which theory and practice are and may be pragmatically joined.[49] The pragmatic "ideal," in other words, is a theoretical criticism: a practice that explicitly argues the power of schemata or premises of its own devising to serve purposes of its own choosing. And its "ideal" practitioner is not a passive and pure reflector of the topic discussed but, rather, the knowing agent of that discussion, a thinking being whose choosing, mediating, and reasoning activities are emphasized, not denied.

But how, exactly, are the arguments of a theoretical criticism made? How do we get from here to there, from the purpose and premise with which we begin to the literary text with whose particularized unfolding we end? The question is generic in the largest sense—it asks how we move from the general assertion or schema (the painter's "circle") to the particular text and point (the painted face)—and its answer is, in effect, this study. For "schemata" or "premises" or "models" are general terms for what in literary studies we call "genres." Or: a genre is a kind of schema, a way of discussing a literary text in terms that link it with other texts and, finally, phrase it in terms of those texts. More specifically, then, how can we explain texts that are different—"Composed upon Westminster Bridge" and "The Windhover"—as if they were the same kind of thing, namely, a sonnet? The "as if" construction suggests, and Vaihinger confirms, that we do so by performing an act of conceptual supposition, by proceeding as if one thing were another. And we can do this, Gombrich explains, because we are "prone to extend classes of things beyond their rational groups," because we "react to minimum images" (p. 102). This propensity is not confined to humans. Gulls, for example, will react to egglike objects as if they were eggs.[50] That they do so does not, however, mean that the gull has generalized the common ovoidness of eggs, rocks, and potatoes but, rather, that it has made a mistake: "Its filing system is a little too wide, which makes errors possible, but not likely, in its wild state" (p. 101).

But humans not only err, they often err willingly and explicitly, for both pleasure and edification. We accordingly "find" faces everywhere: in pansies, in the moon, in knockers on doors, and, most frequently, in the "faces" in paintings. And if we look at stars, clouds, and shadows we can find anything we want to find, so great is the indeterminacy of such finding places and so willing are we, for certain purposes, to accept the most minimal likenesses as "like." Such experiences substantiate Gombrich's thesis that "all thinking is sorting, classifying." They show that anything can be taken for anything else if our purpose is sufficiently compelling and our standards of acceptance sufficiently tolerant. They show, in other words, that we can always choose, correct, invent, or define a class wide enough to make the desired mistake possible.

We are able, then, to read texts that are different as if they were similar because we are able and willing to make the edifying mistake of classification. We seem "naturally" to "extend classes of things beyond their rational groups," reading portraits as if they were people, dramatic monologues as if they were real-life utterances, different poems as if they were instances of the same genre. Less often but more noticeably, we "unnaturally" and deliberately break or change classes, reading novels as if they were poems, dramatic monologues as if they were lyrics.[51] These self-conscious mistakes tend to be the most edifying, simultaneously teaching us about the text read and the procedures of that reading. The initial thesis of a rhetorical and pragmatic theory of explanation, then, is that the inevitability of making mistakes is not the bane of criticism but, rather, its enabling condition. It makes classification possible, and classification enables criticism to begin.

Chapter 1
Defining a Theory of Genre

Metaphysical systems . . . are
intrinsically metaphorical systems.

M. H. Abrams

We reason about them with a late reason.

Wallace Stevens

Similitude and Difference

Our word "genre" comes from the Greek *genus*, meaning "kind" or "sort."
To argue, as do Richards and Gombrich, that "all thinking is sorting" is to
argue that thought habitually begins with the generic or general: it defines
similarity; it repeats in spite of difference.[1] The argument, which is characteristically modern, is also ancient: Aristotle in his *Poetics* argues that "the greatest
thing by far is to have a command of metaphor. This alone cannot be imparted
by another; it is the mark of genius, for to make good metaphors implies an eye
for resemblances."[2] It implies, that is, the power to see similarity in difference,
to define the general in a multitude of particulars. And this power is no less primary for the critic or theorist than for the poet. Aristotle thus begins his own
treatise generically and, what we shall find to be much the same, deductively:
"I propose to treat of poetry in itself and of its various kinds, noting the essential
quality of each."[3]

But it is mainly under the name of "repetition" that "resemblance" or what
Shelley called "similitude" enters modern poetics.[4] In his brilliantly suggestive
"Lexicon Rhetoricae" Kenneth Burke argues that "repetitive form, the restatement of a theme by new details, is basic to any work of art, or to any other kind
of orientation, for that matter. It is our only method of 'talking on the subject.' "[5] Barbara Herrnstein Smith argues similarly in *Poetic Closure*, dramatizing at length the explanatory power of her primary premise: "Repetition is the
fundamental phenomenon of poetic form."[6] But even such straightforward affirmations of the general are twisted into paradox by the presence of the particular:

23

"repetitive form" is "the restatement of a theme *by new details.*" We name something a "repetition" when it reminds us of something else so strongly that it seems to be that something else, to be not itself but a repetition of a prior self. Yet what makes us attend to that reminder and, indeed, perceive it *as* a reminder is precisely if paradoxically these "new details," the ways in which its restatement or present self seems to differ from the prior statement that these details paradoxically enable us to infer. Thus in *Wuthering Heights* Hareton reminds Heathcliff of Catherine because he simultaneously repeats and fails to repeat Catherine, because his face at once resembles and differs from the face that is primary among that novel's multiple and unrecoverable origins.

The previous chapter stated the paradoxical dynamics of repetition in terms of visual representation: the illusion is always striving to convince its audience that it is what it seems. Cubism has critiqued visual representation by forcing the members of this paradox apart: it deconstructs or "unbuilds" this seeming by issuing conspicuously representational invitations that it no less conspicuously refuses to make good. These refusals, what Gombrich calls "reversals," force the beholder's "attention to the plane" (p. 284), making him see not only a guitar but also a painting of a guitar. Cubism thus builds its contradiction of its topic *into* its topic, accomplishing what Gombrich says is "strictly" or representationally speaking impossible: it makes our illusion conscious. It simultaneously gives the painting a substance and stature of its own. A mere copy no longer, it becomes a creation.

The procedures and consequences of deconstructing writing have proven closely analogous. The representational seemings of literary and critical texts alike have also been undone, their constitutive metaphors unbuilt, brought to light, unearthed, or, to use the textual metaphor itself, unraveled. The critical text has been shown to repeat the literary text and, as well, to display the "new details" that inhabit that repetition. As in painting, this display makes the criticism self-conscious or theoretical. It is what gives the critical text substance and stature, making it "visible" in its own right or, what is the same, in its own terms. Any convincing attempt to paint illusionistically or explain representationally in the wake of such undoings must somehow contain those undoings within itself, must somehow, as the Israeli painter Avigdor Arikha has said, perform "both the transgression and the inclusion of doubt."[7]

We shall find that an expressly deductive genre criticism is just such a performance. It would make its reader aware of its premises and, simultaneously, convince him of their explanatory power. It achieves both ends by interweaving two quite different repetitions: by repeating in its own text particulars of the text explained; by repeating the "new details" of that repetition when explaining a different literary text.[8] This second or terminological repetition, the aforementioned "display," is the traditional self-validating procedure of genre criticism and, unlike the first repetition, which is the traditional self-validating procedure of "literary" or covertly generic criticism, is itself infinitely repeatable. An expressly deductive genre criticism, however, refuses the choice between these two traditional routes and instead proposes a way around. This way is marked out or constrained by the critic's suasive purpose and constructed by his simultaneous and overt use of both repetitions. It is, in other words, fully pragmatic and rhetorical, deliberately argued from purpose to premise to particular text. It is also explicitly critical: it places constitutive or constructive power in the genre, and defines the genre neither "historically" nor "theoretically" but in terms of its use in critical explanation. The genre is the critic's heuristic tool, his chosen or defined way of persuading his audience to see the literary text in all its previously inexplicable and "literary" fullness and then to relate this text to those that are similar or, more precisely, to those that may be similarly explained.

Because it seeks to convince its reader of the explanatory power of genre, an expressly deductive genre criticism can readily acknowledge what more traditionally conceived genre criticism, whether "historical" or "theoretical," must conceal or deny. That an eye for resemblance is always also an eye for difference. That not only is perfect repetition impossible—to repeat is always also to differ—but that similarity or the general becomes convincing only when embedded in difference or the particular. That explanatory power, like affective power, tends to be greatest when the affinities are surprising, when the yokings unite seemingly incongruous matter across seemingly unbridgeable gaps. That likening evening to "a patient etherized upon a table" surprises more than likening it to a "nun breathless with adoration" precisely because Eliot's repetition is more crossed by contrast than Wordsworth's, because we have had to work harder to "find" the similarity. That this interpretive work, what Gombrich calls "the beholder's share," commits us to our finding, engendering our belief or conviction. That if "trace" is the presence of difference in similarity, it is also and simultaneously the presence of similarity in difference.[9] That reason may respect difference and imagination similitude (as Shelley said) or vice versa (as Plato might have said), but this respect is always relational, the degree of difference always being just that: a matter of degree. That once genre is defined as pragmatic rather than natural, as defined rather than found, and as used rather than described, then there are precisely as many genres as we need, genres whose conceptual shape is precisely determined by that need. They are designed to serve the explanatory purpose of critical thought, not the other way around.

A Dissonance of Theories: Genre and Representation

Genre theory, however, has traditionally chosen just this other way around. With few exceptions criticism has treated genre not as the critic's explanatory tool but as a hypothesis, a probable stab at the truth, something whose inherence in a particular literary text or whose independent existence as a schema is potentially verifiable or, at least, refutable. The characteristic treatment, in other words, has been either to naturalize or historicize the genre by retrospectively "finding" it in the literary text or to hypostatize it, making it "theoretical." But this treatment, which is in either case representational, is neither necessary nor ultimately persuasive, for both historicized and hypostatized genres similarly lose credibility as their unacknowledged definitional nature becomes increasingly obvious with increasing use. Whereas in either case the critic presents himself as describing or representing what antecedes his text—the historical genre being derived from observation of preexisting literary facts, the theoretical genre being deduced from a preexisting theory of literature—in both cases the genre is actually conceptualized, textualized, and justified by the critic's present-tense act, by his writing of the genre's definition.[10]

Although it is commonly assumed that making the critic's act explicit weakens criticism, undoing its transparence or "validity," in actuality the attempt to conceal this act is what ultimately proves weakening. This is particularly so when, as in genre criticism, the schemata or premises are conspicuous. Genres, in other words, are always and obviously open to question, and this questioning inevitably discovers the inconsistency between the critic's descriptive claim and his constitutively powerful premises. This vulnerability, however, is a consequence not of genre per se but of trying to write genre criticism while simultaneously making representational claims. It is a consequence of denying not only genre criticism's deductiveness but also its pragmatism, of denying not only the premises and procedures of its reasoning but also their origin in the critic's explanatory purpose and their present-tense existence in his explaining text.

The weakening consequences of this denial are most easily seen in E. D. Hirsch's *Validity in Interpretation*.[11] In his earlier study, "Objective Interpretation," Hirsch had constrained the potential indeterminacy of literary meaning by defining it as the author's, but in *Validity* he refines this definition, arguing that the author's most determining act is his choice of type or genre, that this genre constitutes or determines the text's meaning, and that reconstructing or inferring this genre makes possible the representation of that meaning.[12] The argument is a typical post-Kantian blend of induction and deduction, of media used as if they were powerless or "descriptive" on one level (here meaning "theory") and powerful or constitutive on another (here meaning "criticism").[13]

"All understanding of verbal meaning," Hirsch begins, "is necessarily genre-bound" (p. 76). This does not mean that we never change our minds about which genre is "right"—we obviously can and do replace old genres with new—but "ultimately everything we understand will have been constituted

. . . by the new generic conception'' (p. 76). He goes on to explain that ''this description of the genre-bound character of understanding is, of course, a version of the hermeneutic circle, which in its classical formulation has been described as the interdependence of part and whole: the whole can be understood only through its parts, but the parts can be understood only through the whole'' (p. 76). Like Karl Viëtor, René Wellek, and others, Hirsch here treats one of genre study's most frequently asked questions as a special case of the hermeneutic circle.[14] It is a question that has been most clearly posed by Wellek: ''How can we arrive at a genre description from history without knowing beforehand what the genre is like, and how can we know a genre without its history, without a knowledge of its particular instances?''[15] Wellek's answer necessarily begs the question—''It can be solved in the concrete dialectics of past and present, fact and idea, history and aesthetics''—because the question is, as Wellek himself points out, paradoxical or unanswerable.[16] Indeed, as Gustavo Pérez Firmat observes, the question is not even properly asked of genre: ''a work does not belong to a genre as a part belongs to a whole . . . since not every feature of a work is genre-bound. . . . Unlike the whole, it is less than the sum of its parts; and what is equally important, it is not simply less, it is also *different* from its parts.''[17]

But the hermeneutic circle, despite its increasingly recognized difficulties, has continued to be used, primarily because it gives us a way of articulating the problem of ''grounding'' or ''validating'' interpretation. Increasingly many of those who use it, however, recognize that it also perpetuates that problem. Hirsch's next words accordingly come as no surprise:

> This traditional formulation, however, clouds some of the processes of understanding in unnecessary paradox. It is true that an idea of the whole controls, connects, and unifies our understanding of parts. It is also true that the idea of the whole must arise from an encounter with parts. But this encounter could not occur if the parts did not have an autonomy capable of suggesting a certain kind of whole in the first place. A part—a word, a title, a syntactical pattern—is frequently autonomous in the sense that some aspect of it is the same no matter what whole it belongs to. (Pp. 76-77)

Hirsch here reduces the paradox of the hermeneutic circle by defining the independence and priority of the part: it has the *''autonomy* capable of suggesting a certain kind of whole *in the first place.''* But if Hirsch has just asserted the constitutive power of genre, how can he now assert that the text has the power to ''suggest'' or constitute the genre? He can do so because he defines the genre as ''intrinsic,'' as a concealed given or ground that is contained *within* the text and that will accordingly remain ''the same no matter what whole it belongs to.'' This conclusion phrases in generic terms Hirsch's more sweeping claim in *Aims of Interpretation*: that stylistics is the enemy of synonymity, that "an absolutely identical meaning" can survive its translation into different linguistic and conventional forms, and that upon this synonymity "genuine knowledge" and our discipline depend.[18]

As his argument proceeds, Hirsch sharpens both his claim and the paradoxical dilemma of traditionally conceived genre criticism. Interpretation begins, he tells us, with the interpreter's "guess about the kind of meaning he confronts" (p. 78). (This dilemma is prefigured in Hirsch's phrasing: he yokes the interpreter's guess, which is a conjectural or propositional act, with a confrontational metaphor, which denies that very action.) This guess or genre has "a necessary heuristic function in interpretation, and it is well known that heuristic instruments are to be thrown away as soon as they have served their purpose" (p. 76). So far Hirsch reads like Vaihinger, for whom the conceptual fiction has a purely pragmatic existence, its proper use being to be "used up." But because Hirsch has committed himself to the premise that "understanding is itself genre-bound," he also argues that "a generic conception is not simply a tool that can be discarded once understanding is attained" (p. 78). He thus concludes that "the generic conception serves both a heuristic and a constitutive function" (p. 78).

This contradiction, however, could be transformed from a logical weakness to an argumentative strength by adapting Vaihinger's thesis: by arguing that genre is heuristic when we explicitly use it pragmatically and suppositionally, *as if* it constituted the text. Indeed, if read carefully, most criticism, even that which professes its disinterest in the generic and the suppositional alike, reveals that it is already both. Let us, for example, recall the exact words of Blanchot's disclaimer: "A book no longer belongs to a genre; every book arises from literature alone, *as if* the latter possessed in advance, in its *generality*, the secrets and the formulas that alone allow book reality to be given to that which is written. Everything would happen *as if*, genres having dissipated, literature alone was affirmed, alone shined in the mysterious light that it spreads and that every literary creation sends back to it while multiplying it—*as if* there were an '*essence*' of literature" (emphasis added).[19] Nor need *we* always add the emphasis. Kenneth Burke, for example, has argued "that one can, at times, most clearly indicate the structure of a work by treating it *as if* it were designed to point a moral."[20]

But Hirsch refuses the pragmatic and suppositional in hope of finding the certain or, at least, the probable: "To know the intrinsic genre is to know almost everything" (p. 88). This refusal initiates the traditional and endless search for the "natural" stopping place, the ground that will interpret without itself needing interpretation: "An extrinsic genre is a wrong guess, an intrinsic genre a correct one. One of the main tasks of interpretation can be summarized as the critical rejection of extrinsic genres in the search for the intrinsic genre of a text" (pp. 88–89).[21] This concern with the right or wrong of a genre, with whether it is the one the author intended (intrinsic) or the one the critic intends (extrinsic), is a purely representational worry. It equates the genre's "rightness," its correspondence to the author's intention, with its power to explain the text. But this equation, perhaps the most basic assumption of genre theory, is both unwarranted and, in actual critical practice, tacitly ignored. Thus even the rare genre of whose authoritative rightness we are assured can fall before a genre of superior pragmatic virtue. Henry Fielding, to take but one example, defined the genre of *Joseph Andrews* in his preface, but critics have nevertheless felt free to replace the "comic epic poem in prose" with genres of their own devising.[22] It is the *theorist* who typically insists on the critical genre's authoritative rightness, even when, as is most often the case, that authority is impossible either to confirm or refute. It is the *critic* who in any case insists on the genre's pragmatic power.

R. S. Crane seems to argue an even more purely inductive or *a posteriori* line than Hirsch, but when he moves from "practical" genre theory to critical theory, from proposing a critical language to discussing critical languages *as* languages, the deductiveness of his argument or, to be precise, of one of his arguments becomes obvious. This inductive-deductive ambivalence typifies neo-Aristotelian or "Chicago" criticism, the theory and practice of which has most thoroughly explored the explanatory power of deductive genre and, simultaneously, has most firmly "grounded" that power in the text. Throughout "Towards a More Adequate Criticism of Poetic Structure," Crane explicitly argues that an inductive poetics is not only desirable but possible, that a transparent or constitutively powerless medium for criticism exists, and that this medium is the proper "language of criticism."[23] He accordingly attacks critics for their deductiveness, for unwittingly letting their languages or genres determine their reading:

It is fatal therefore to think that we can know the shaping principle of any poem in advance or, what amounts to the same thing in practice, that we can get at it in terms of any predetermined conception or model of what structure in poetry or in this or that special branch of poetry in general either is or ought to be. Yet this is exactly what most of the critics who have concerned themselves with questions of structure in practical criticism have attempted to do. They have come to poems equipped, so to speak, with paradigms of poetry, or of epic, tragedy, lyric, and so on, and hence with more or less definite specifications concerning the nature of the structural patterns they ought to look for; and they have as a consequence been unable to see any structural principles in poems except those already contained in their preferred definitions and models. (P. 146)

Crane uses Robert Heilman's formalist reading of *Othello* to exemplify this attack on the powerful paradigm: whereas "the question of the structure of *Othello* could surely be approached inductively," Heilman's argument is "a simple application of this paradigm to the facts of the text which it enables him to select as significant data" (p. 147). This exposé of deductive criticism is meant to convince us both that Heilman's paradigm has indeed powerfully constituted his explanation and that it shouldn't have, that that power wrongs the text. And these convictions are meant to engender another: that we need "a language in which we can envisage our questions as questions of fact rather than of relations of ideas" (p. 149). What we need, in short, is a transparent language.

Crane proposes that Aristotle's *Poetics* offers just such a language. It perfectly reflects what he defines as the essence of the literary text: "the most important thing about any poetic production is the characteristic power it has to affect us in this definite way rather than that" (p. 179). And its procedures are self-effacing: it allows us to conduct "inquiries of an *a posteriori* type which move inductively . . . from particulars to the universals they embody" (p. 155). We need criticize neither Crane's choice of language nor his superlative use of that language, as in "The Concept of Plot and the Plot of *Tom Jones*,"[24] in order to note, first, that his language seems transparent to its object because his definitions of the literary text and of his language share a common origin in the *Poetics* and, second, that his attitude toward this transparency depends upon whether he speaks as a theorist or as a metatheorist. When speaking as a theorist, as one concerned with ways of explaining literature, he values transparency or powerlessness in critical languages: "if we are to allow the facts to speak for themselves, we must in some fashion supply them with a language in which to talk" (p. 174). But when in "The Multiplicity of Critical Languages" he moves one "level" up and speaks as a metatheorist, as one concerned with ways of explaining criticism, he values those same languages for their opacity or power:

> Literary criticism is not, and never has been, a single discipline, to which successive writers have made partial and never wholly satisfactory contributions, but rather a collection of distinct and more or less incommensurable "frameworks" or "languages," within any one of which a question like that of poetic structure necessarily takes on a different meaning and receives a different kind of answer from the meaning it has and the kind of answer it is properly given in any of the rival critical languages in which it is discussed.[25]

Crane, then, mounts two distinct and contradictory arguments, one from the theorist's point of view, the other from the metatheorist's. When the critical language is the interpretive medium, he argues that it, like all perfect representational media, should be transparent, fully deferential to the object or text described. But when it is the interpretive ground, itself the object of description, he argues that it, like all perfect grounds, should be powerful or opaque, something to be looked at, not through. Representational theory desires only commensurable languages, those whose overlappings "imply" or make visible the literary ground they represent in common. Incommensurable languages are undesirable because they defeat synonymity of meaning or, rephrased in pluralist terms, the argument that there are many different and "valid" ways of representing the same text. Incommensurable languages leave their traces or "new details" in the text explained. They make their power "visible." In Gombrich's terms, they force our attention to the critical plane, making us "see" not only *Othello* but the paradigm that selects the "significant data" of *Othello*.

Of course, it is precisely the inscribing power of Heilman's paradigm that enables him to write his reading. This power is also what makes the reading "visible" to Crane, what gives it sufficient substance and stature to make it a fit topic for metacritical analysis. In other words, to inscribe the "significant data" of *Othello* is to explain the significance of *Othello*, and to reinscribe that inscription is to explain the significance of Heilman's reading. The importance of Crane's work for contemporary genre studies is that it lets us see this common ground, the way in which the practical critic's use of the powerful medium is linked to the metatheorist's recognition of that power. But Crane's work is also important because it simultaneously displays the stance of the traditional theorist: his built-in antagonism to both critical practice and its explanation, his preference for a medium distinguished by neither its usefulness nor its visibility but, rather, by its disinterestedness and invisibility. Crane as theorist, in sum, denies the very power that, when writing as a practical critic, he uses and, when writing as a metatheorist, he describes.

Even the most conspicuously schematic of genre theorists, one whose openly deductive premises and procedures lead us to expect a similarly open acknowledgment of those premises and procedures, makes a point of their denial. Northrop Frye opens his *Anatomy of Criticism* by arguing that "the first thing the literary critic has to do is . . . to make an inductive survey of his own field and let his critical principles shape themselves solely out of his knowledge of that field."[26] Moreover, this critic should in good inductive fashion keep his values from contaminating that knowledge: "Value-judgments are founded on the study of literature; the study of literature can never be founded on value-judgments" (p. 20). Such professions of inductiveness not surprisingly prove short-lived, the force and visibility with which Frye wields his schemata quickly forcing him to concede their existence: he has, he tells us, "proceeded deductively" (p. 29). But he also tells us that he has done so in order "to keep the book within the bounds that would make it possible to write and publish it" and that "the deductiveness does not extend further than tactical method" (p. 29). In other words, Frye admits his deductiveness but insists on its superficiality, an admission that, given his conspicuous schemata, must be more feint than finesse. But his opening gestures to induction are nevertheless important—not because they argue the inductiveness and thus the "validity" of his theory but because they instance the institutional sway of inductive pretense, its power to turn even a conspicuously deductive theory of genre against itself, making it vulnerable to the charges of inconsistency and self-ignorance.

Not surprisingly, Frye's inductive gestures have done little to deflect his critics, who, while routinely remarking Frye's "brilliance" and "scintillating erudition," no less routinely find his overt schematism to be too much of an already dangerous thing. Correcting Frye has accordingly become a creative first step for subsequent theories of genre, a theoretical practice that works according to the theoretical "rhythm" defined in the preceding chapter: that of correction and schema.[27] We thus find Tzvetan Todorov, in the opening chapter of *The Fantastic*, strongly faulting Frye's deductiveness.[28] But the strength of Todorov's faultfinding is less interesting than its obliquity, than the way representational pressure once again skews toward induction even those arguments that announce their deductiveness. For Todorov begins as a champion of deduction—or so it seems:

> One of the first characteristics of scientific method is that it does not require us to observe every instance of a phenomenon in order to describe it; scientific method proceeds rather by deduction. We actually deal with a relatively limited number of cases, from them we deduce a general hypothesis, and we verify this hypothesis by other cases, correcting (or rejecting) as need be. (P. 4; p. 8)

The inductive-deductive ambiguity of this passage depends upon semantic slippage in the word "deduce": Todorov uses it not in its logical or rigorous sense, meaning to argue from a premise, from general statement to particular instances, but in its colloquial or Sherlock Holmesian sense, meaning to move inferentially from particulars to generality. The former sense lingers, giving the semblance of neo-Kantian self-awareness and explanatory power to an otherwise traditional argument for representational validity. Todorov's inductiveness, however, is all but explicit by the essay's end: "The genres we deduce from the theory must be verified by reference to the texts: if our deductions fail to correspond to any work we are on a false trail" (p. 21; p. 26). His concern with falsity, verification, and correspondence is purely representational, as is his censure of Frye's categories.

But it is, of course, precisely these censured characteristics that distinguish Frye's genres. Todorov shows that these genres are purposefully defined by Frye rather than "discovered" in the text, that they contradict the text's literariness, that they usurp its autonomy and constitutive power. Any traditional theorist would fault Frye in just this way, if not this astutely. But Todorov's argument, because of the semantic slippage on which it is built, has paradoxically purchased the power to reflect on itself and discover its own impossibility:

> No observation of works can strictly confirm or invalidate a theory of genres. If I am told: a certain work does not fit any of your categories, hence your categories are wrong, I could object: your "hence" has no reason to exist; works need not coincide with categories, which have merely a constructed existence; a work can, for example, manifest more than one category, more than one genre. We are thus led to an exemplary methodological impasse: how to prove the descriptive failure of any theory of genres whatever? The reproach we made to Frye appears to apply to any work, ours included. (P. 22; p. 26)

As indeed it does. But the reproach becomes necessary only within a purely representational theory of interpretation. Because the procedures of genre criticism are ineluctably deductive—always in however concealed a fashion, moving from general to particular—and because representation only tolerates the reverse movement, genre criticism and representational theory are inherently at odds, their attempted union an inevitable embarrassment. Hence Todorov's reproach and self-reproach. Only when using a rhetorical and pragmatic language, whose grammar and vocabulary allow us to explain the constitutive power of genre as instrumental to critical thought, do such reproaches become themselves unnecessary.

Todorov's "impasse" is remarkable not only for its self-awareness but for its clear outline. In his second chapter, entitled "Definition of the Fantastic," Todorov states the premise from which he will deduce specific instances of the genre, thereby explaining them: "The fantastic is that hesitation experienced by a person who knows only the laws of nature, confronting an apparently supernatural event" (p. 25; p. 29). The explanations that follow are powerful and, as such, fully justify his definition or chosen premise. But they cannot, as critical practice more generally cannot, validate this or any definition. Theory's desire for the explaining text's complete and traceless grasp of the explained must remain unfulfilled, as must practical criticism's inductive desire for constitutively powerful textual particulars, those capable of announcing their "correct" or "intrinsic" genre. Taken together, the practical strength and conceptual candor of *The Fantastic* enact our most open staging of representation's linked dilemmas: the theoretical and practical impossibilities of its self-defined fulfillment. But a complex and concealed staging would prove yet more instructive, and for this we turn to Hans Robert Jauss's "Theories of Genres and Medieval Literature."[29] Jauss's theory, like Todorov's, is justified by a powerful practice, but, once again, this justification wears a mask of validation, a mask whose conspicuous and unavoidable slippage sets the theory's articulation at odds with its premises.

The complexity of Jauss's theory of genre is in part due to his use of not one but many schemata, in part to their location on different "levels," in part to his repeated gesturing toward a real-world context, in part to his alternating display and denial of his own interpretive act. Jauss's theory, in other words, stages the three-way conflict analyzed in the previous chapter: constitutive or explanatory power is in rapid and alternating succession located in genres, in the particulars of the historical text and context, in the theorist's "envisioning" of those genres and particulars. But Jauss, despite his proclaimed interest in the world from which literature arises and in which it is "received," is far less interested in the particulars of that world than in its literary genres and the theoretical schemata that will best "illuminate" or explain them for his present-day audience.

Jauss's argument, in other words, is fully if not quite admittedly pragmatic, carefully argued from purpose to premise to particular text. Indeed, Jauss begins by explicitly stating his purpose: "it seems worthwhile to develop a theory of literary genres within a field of inquiry that lies between the opposites of singularity and collectivity, of the artistic character of literature and its merely purposive or social character" (p. 76). Also in beginning, he defines the present-day context of genre study, thereby opening a conceptual space for his own theory: "The theory of literary genres is at the point of seeking a path between the Scylla of nominalist skepticism that allows for only *a posteriori* classifications, and the Charybdis of regression into timeless typologies, a path along which the historicization of genre poetics and of the concept of form are upheld" (p. 78). Jauss then proposes as a first step in his theory's justification the correction of a previous theory: "To initiate a justification of this path with a critique of Croce recommends itself not merely on the grounds of an interdisciplinary discussion. For Croce pushed to an extreme the critique of the universal validity of the canon of genres, a critique that had been growing since the eighteenth century, so that the necessity of founding a historical systematics of literary genres once again becomes apparent" (p. 78).

Jauss defines the "relationship between the individual text and the series of texts formative of a genre . . . as a process of the continual founding and altering of horizons. The new text evokes for the reader (listener) the horizon of expectations and 'rules of the game' familiar to him from earlier texts, which as such can then be varied, extended, corrected, but also transformed, crossed out, or simply reproduced" (p. 88). This "rhythm" is essentially that of Gombrich's "schema and correction," and, like Gombrich's, is both an aesthetic model and a critical model. Its explanatory power, that is, operates on more than one level, its ambidexterity enabling the critic to explain a text in terms of its historical reading and that reading in terms of the text. Quoting J. G. Drosen on literary genres, Jauss says as much: "they transform themselves to the extent that they have history, and they have history to the extent that they transform themselves' " (p. 89).

In one of the distinguishing leaps of his theory, Jauss now defines aesthetic value in terms of this transformation: "the more stereotypically a text repeats the generic, the more inferior is its artistic character and its degree of historicity" (p. 89). But this definition, given more fully in his earlier "Literary History as a Challenge to Literary Theory," is not an altogether happy one.[30] Although texts that challenge the norm are frequently, even usually, the ones esteemed, they are not necessarily esteemed, either at the time of their writing or later, nor are texts that do not challenge the norm necessarily not esteemed, either at the time of their writing or later. Jauss emphasizes both this "later" and these "necessities," implying that even within the ranks of genius a Stravinsky necessarily outranks a Mozart and that the subsequent reception of a text is more self-evident, stable, and unambivalent than its original reception.[31] But "conventional" texts are not infrequently valued over "challenging" texts, a valuation that is itself always open to reevaluation and in need of interpretation. Moreover, at any point in its interpretive history a text can be simultaneously valued and not valued. Most importantly, however, that point is always itself interpreted from within what Jauss himself calls the "perspective" of the present interpreter. In other words, the correlation between aesthetic value and "challenge" is always in practice a matter of the present interpreter's purpose, as in his own essay it is for Jauss. But despite its problems, Jauss's reciprocal definition of genre and aesthetic value is important, for assignation of genre, as I shall argue, is invariably a valuative act on the part of the interpreter. This act, however, involves deciding not whether genre is connected to aesthetic value but how.

Jauss in part "solves" his three-way conflict by positing a "ground" that constitutes both the text's genre and its reception:

A theory of genres grounded in an aesthetics of reception necessarily will add to the study of the structural relations between literature and society, work and audience, where the historical system of norms of a "literary public" lies hidden in a distant past; there it can most readily still be reconstructed through the horizon of expectations of a genre system that pre-constituted the intention of the works as well as the understanding of the audience. (P. 108)

But placing his "ground" on the "horizon," where it is definitively and forever just out of sight, defers rather than solves the problem of defining the site of constitutive authority. This deferral, of course, is precisely what enables Jauss to claim both social significance and generic rigor for the ground and to present it as not defined but "discovered" or, more precisely, discoverable. But the deliberate vagueness of this ground is too obvious for its authority to be convincing, and the conflict of its presentation with Jauss's repeated acts of terminological definition further weakens the argument.

Its most serious weakness, however, lies in Jauss's repeated denial of this conflict: "the modern theory of genres can proceed only descriptively, and not by definition" (p. 95); genres "cannot be deduced or defined, but only historically determined, delimited, and described" (p. 80). Whether or not we agree with these claims, Jauss's own practice could not be in fuller or more explicit disagreement, whether he is, as in his "Literary History" essay, announcing the "premises" from which he will "develop the principle of representation of a literary history" (p. 38), or whether he is, as in the following, unfolding his generic premises and the act of their definition:

> If one follows the fundamental rule of the historicization of the concept of form, and sees the history of literary genres as a temporal process of the continual founding and altering of horizons, then the metaphorics of the courses of development, function, and decay can be replaced by the nonteleological concept of the playing out of a limited number of possibilities. In this concept a masterwork is definable in terms of an alteration of the horizon of the genre that is as unexpected as it is enriching; the genre's prehistory is definable in terms of a trying and testing of possibilities; and its arrival at a historical end is definable in terms of formal ossification, automatization, or a giving-up or misunderstanding of the "rules of the game," as is often found in the last epigones. But the history of genres in this perspective also presupposes reflection on that which can become visible only to the retrospective observer: the beginning character of the beginnings and the definite character of an end; the norm-founding or norm-breaking role of particular examples; and finally, the historical as well as the aesthetic significance of masterworks, which itself may change with the history of their effects and works, and thereby may also differently illuminate the coherence of the history of their genre that is to be narrated. (P. 94)

The act of terminological definition could hardly be made more explicit, nor could its metaphoricity, nor could the emplotting or constitutive power of the "retrospective" observer's vision, nor could the narrative nature of that "vision." But it is important to recognize that Jauss's difficulty in consistently conceptualizing the emplotment or writing of literary history is less a particular difficulty than one built into the genre of "history" itself, at least as it is traditionally defined. As Hayden White has shown, the very beginning-middle-endness that gives histories their plot and thereby their appeal and significance is precisely what endangers that appeal and significance.[32] The problem, which looks philosophical but is actually rhetorical, results from the contradictory demands made by the audience of a history, whether it be literary or otherwise: we desire it to have both the feel of reality and the finish of the ideal. When Jauss insists that he is not defining but describing, he is attempting to fulfill the former desire. When he insists, as here, on the coherence of his "narrated" history, he is attempting to fulfill the latter. The two fulfillments are logically incompatible, but the appearance of their compatibility is at least provisionally achieved by the historian's strategic use of either or both of representation's traditional metaphors, preferably in "dead" form. He can present himself as "seeing" the history's coherence, as Jauss does here, or he can, as White explains, present it as "found," as a product of archaeological search and discovery:

> The historical narrative, as against the chronicle, reveals to us a world that is putatively "finished," done with, over, and yet not dissolved, not falling apart. In this world, reality wears the mask of a meaning, the completeness and fullness of which we can only *imagine*, never experience. Insofar as historical stories can be completed, can be given narrative closure, can be shown to have had a *plot* all along, they give to reality the odor of the *ideal*. This is why the plot of a historical narrative is always an embarrassment and has to be presented as "found" in the events rather than put there by narrative techniques.[33]

It is not necessary to deny—nor am I doing so—that the poet or novelist knew his genre in order to accept that our narrations of his generic manipulation are nevertheless informed by our present-tense explanatory purpose. Nor should the occasional coincidence of a critical genre with a genre similarly named in history confuse the issue by leading us either to naturalize or to hypostatize that genre, concealing thereby its definitional nature and the deductively unfolded knowledge that it enables. Even less should we be tempted to hypostatize a posited generic model or to claim its "intrinsicality" when, as is the case with the dramatic monologue, it did not as currently named exist for the writers who used it. Whether "theoretical" as in the passage above—"the genre's prehistory is definable in terms of a trying and testing of possibilities"—or "historical"— "there were in the Middle Ages basically four schemata of division at one's disposal that could, in varying degrees, serve the explanation of genres" (p. 95)— the genres that Jauss chooses or defines are similarly "grounded" in explanatory purpose. That they succeed pragmatically, that they fulfill this purpose by proving useful in making explanations, is their only possible justification. It is also the only "proof" that we, in this or in any other case, should demand.

Ralph Rader's work is a rare instance of explicitly purposeful and deductive genre criticism. Consider this passage, which follows Rader's definition of the "realism-plot-judgment form," as exemplified by *Pamela*:

I will call this conception and others to be developed later *models*, in order to emphasize their hypothetical character and their function as artificial similitudes of independently cognitive form. The model is a revision of the R. S. Crane-Sheldon Sacks concept of represented action designed to make it meet clearly the condition just mentioned, namely to define the principle of the realism-plot-judgment class and to exclude *Moll Flanders*. I should say that the models are deductive models; that is, they are meant to define the most general differentiating principle of a work's form in such a way that its more particular aspects can be rigorously deduced from it.[34]

Rader is proceeding in explicitly deductive fashion. He is defining, not discovering, and he is defining with an explicit purpose: to exclude *Moll Flanders* from the set of literary texts called "novels" and thereby to purchase greater explanatory power and precision. He emphasizes the model's pragmatism, its definitional and purposeful nature, and openly deduces particulars from this model— not the other way around.

The strength of Rader's criticism is a function of the strength of his premise or model and of the rigor or consistency of its unfolding. The suasive force of this consistency, however, depends upon its explicitness, upon his premise and procedures being explicitly acknowledged and justified. Hence the theoretical justification that opens "Fact, Theory, and Literary Explanation":

Hypothesis—interpretive assumption—does not follow from the observation of fact but necessarily precedes and structures it, so that agreement between hypothesis and fact is to some degree foreordained. The implications of this relationship have been powerfully developed in the philosophy of Sir Karl Popper, who argues that all our knowledge is inherently and permanently hypothetical, that knowledge can never begin with "the facts" but only with a conjecture about the facts, and that the test of a conjecture (read hypothesis or theory) is not the degree to which it finds confirmation in facts—the significance of which it effectively constructs—but the degree to which it risks refutation by independent facts which it does not have immediately in view. In this conception knowledge is not built up inductively from local fact to gradually justified generalization, but deductively, by extending a strong generalization over the widest possible range of fact toward potential refutation.[35]

A rhetorical and pragmatic theory of explanation welcomes this powerful argument for the deductive nature of critical thought. But Rader, like Gombrich, is arguing according to the "rhythm of schema and correction," and, like Gombrich, he therefore needs a "correcting" tool. Hence the "independent facts" to which he grants a special constitutive power, that of "refutation." But if hypothesis "necessarily precedes and structures" facts, how can these facts have the power to refute the hypothesis? Rader answers this version of the hermeneutic-circle question by stipulating that these particular facts be not "immediately in view," by placing them on the hermeneutic "horizon." But by the logic of his own theory this answer will not do. It defers rather than solves the problem, leaving the theory vulnerable to further questioning: What is the hypothesis or model that will let us "see" these correcting facts? What are the facts that will in turn provide *its* correction? The questions are infinitely regressive or, what is the same, ultimately unanswerable.

But this inconsistency, the inevitable and potentially devastating by-product of attempting to unite the theories of genre and representation, is, once again, unnecessary. One solution to Rader's problem would be to retain the "independent fact" but emphasize its definitional and pragmatic nature. Kant himself remarks the heuristic function of the *ding an sich*—for that is what Rader's "fact" actually is—and Vaihinger insists on its fictionality, arguing simultaneously that the fictional is useful only insofar as it is explicitly presented as such.[36] A related solution would be to follow through on the reversed "rhythm," that of "correction and schema," which Rader himself articulates in the first quotation. There he explicitly "grounds" his model in explanatory purpose—"to define the most general differentiating principle of a work's form in such a way that its more particular aspects can be readily deduced from it"— and locates its origin in his revision, "correction," or, more precisely, rewriting of the Crane-Sacks model. Rader could, that is, consistently treat his models or genres as the pragmatic and deductive beginnings he posits them to be, as chosen or defined to serve the purposes of our critical thought and, particularly, to begin the processes of that thought. Such a correction would make possible the fully pragmatic theory of genre to whose statement we now turn.

Syllogism, Metaphor, and the Logic of Criticism

Genre is the most powerful explanatory tool available to the literary critic. It is our most reasoned way of talking about and valuing the literary text. When both genre and its definitional nature are made explicit rather than denied, our explanations acquire the defensive strengths of self-awareness and internal consistency. They thereby reduce their vulnerability to ironic discounting or extramural deconstruction, although they, not inconsistently, welcome revision or rewriting by explanations yet to be written. But a knowing use of genre generates a constructive strength as well: it is the way of talking that, despite our traditional opinion to the contrary, most fully unfolds the characteristics that make the text seem valuable to us *as a literary text*. We value the explanation that appropriates both these defensive and constructive strengths, that can make sense both in the explanation's own terms, meaning that it is closely and consistently reasoned, and in terms of its topic, meaning that it unfolds the literary text's value as a literary text. And we value most highly the genre that helps us to make such explanations.

These valued or "literary" characteristics are, of course, themselves definitional rather than natural. Most obviously in modern poetics, they are defined aesthetically: in terms of the text's "feel" of uniqueness, particularity, and richness; in terms of an indwelling order, which is itself variously defined, being at times an "organic" unity, at times a syllogistic logic, at times an "uncanny" illogic. But these characteristics have also been defined ethically, although less in the traditional mimetic sense, in terms of the real-world value of a represented content, than in the Romantic or Shelleyan sense, in terms of the text's heuristic power, which is primarily a power to make the reader better than he was when he began to read.[37] He becomes expert in recognizing and negotiating the difficulties of reading and writing texts, particularly the textualized selves manifest in those texts. And he learns the prodigious significance of rewriting those texts, an act commonly termed "judgment" but more usefully termed "correction" and "completion." The good literary text, that is, has been most successfully defined as a text that is well made *and* as a text that makes well. And the good critical text, I am suggesting, is in this manner also well defined, particularly in terms of genre.[38]

The primary act of the generic critic is suppositional and metaphoric: let us explain this literary text by reading it in terms of that genre. Just as the painter manipulates his schema until he thinks that his audience will "recognize" a particular face, so this critic proceeds to manipulate his genre, to deduce particulars from it until he thinks that his audience will "recognize" a particular text. The "stopping place" of his schematic correction will vary from text to text, depending on its interpretive history and his audience. For some texts he will need to correct or specify at length, for some very little. But in each case his purpose or goal is to convince his audience that the posited genre is more "like" the text than the genres used to carry on previous critical discussions of the same text, that this genre, in other words, is the vehicle that most fully and precisely captures the tenor or text.[39]

When defined thus—pragmatically and rhetorically rather than "naturally" or representationally—this conviction happens without the critic's concealing the fact that the genre can no more be perfectly like that which is not-itself than can any medium. He acknowledges and builds upon the fact that it will always leave its trace in the text and always be blind to many particulars. But how, then, can the reading convince? It convinces because it takes place in an intertextual world, in which readings are expressly conscious not only of themselves as readings but also of previous readings, all of which have been generic but not all of which have used the same genre. A text's interpretive history, which is a textualized pastiche of the many genres that have "read" the text, is recalled by the critic to his audience. It thus becomes itself a suasive instrument, its various successes and failures becoming available for the critic's present suasive use. When recalled and themselves "read," they give the critic a way of substantiating and, finally, justifying his procedures of correction and construction, procedures which, when sufficiently substantial and justified, write an explanation that we call convincing or true.

I have been talking of "deducing" a text from a genre, but what exactly does this mean? Most generally, it means asserting particular instances of the traits stated or implied by the posited genre. This assertion, however, proceeds not randomly but rigorously, indeed syllogistically:

> All men are mortal.
> Socrates is a man.
> Socrates is mortal.

The first or major premise of the classical syllogism asserts that all members of one class belong to a second class. (The classes may be the same size and in generic syllogisms typically are.) The minor premise asserts that an entity belongs to the first class, and the conclusion states that it therefore belongs to the second class as well.

Let us exemplify this reasoning with a particular genre:

> Dramatic monologues invite their readers to distinguish the characterized speaker's meaning from the poem's.

> "Andrea del Sarto" is a dramatic monologue.

> "Andrea del Sarto" invites its reader to distinguish its speaker's meaning from the poem's.

The major premise asserts that all members of the genre "dramatic monologue" belong to the class of poems that invite their readers to distinguish the characterized speaker's meaning from the poem's. The syllogism then concludes that if a particular poem belongs to the first class it therefore belongs to the second class as well. All generic criticism proceeds thus, although the syllogistic pattern not only varies greatly in its explicitness but is usually abbreviated as an enthymeme (" 'Andrea del Sarto' invites its readers to distinguish its speaker's meaning from the poem's because it is a dramatic monologue") or as an "if-then" assertion ("If 'Andrea del Sarto' is a dramatic monologue, then it invites its readers to distinguish its speaker's meaning from the poem's").

The syllogistic pattern, however, does not merely begin the critic's argument. It is repeated throughout the explanation, the conclusion of the opening syllogism becoming the major premise of the next, whose conclusion in turn is always potentially and perhaps actually yet another major premise. Thus the above conclusion will in the next chapter be followed by a minor premise ("The reader makes this distinction when the speaker seems to understand his discourse less well than the reader does"), which leads to another and more specific conclusion ("Andrea seems not to 'see' his discourse, in particular his tropes, as clearly as he might"). This sorites or series of syllogisms forms the conceptual skeleton of all well-reasoned critical explanation. And it often, as it does throughout this study, takes the shape of a question-answer series, which is a version of the "correction-schema" series, the revised "rhythm" proposed in the last chapter. We accordingly ask: How do we learn that Andrea's "seeing" is faulty, that his insight is clouded by blindness? Because, we answer, he himself repeatedly corrects his vision, thereby displaying the fact that he uses tropes much as he uses his painter's "faultless" brush: to close rather than to open meaning, to achieve limited perfection rather than limitless imperfection. But if Andrea's correction of his vision is what teaches us to see its faults, how, then, does our vision come to surpass his? Because our repeated views of his tropological misuse tutor us in its recognition, so that when he seems suddenly to go blind to the damning implications of his "faultlessness," that blindness becomes itself visible to the reader. The reader thus achieves an insight denied the speaker, although the process of its achievement warns that that insight contains within itself a yet-to-be-discovered blindness.

I would emphasize, therefore, not any particular phrasing but rather a pattern of reasoning that explicitly moves from definition of genre to defining specific instances of that genre and then to the unfolding of that specificity, an unfolding structured by the sorites and fleshed out by citations from the poem itself. These citations fuse the poet's text and the critic's text, a conflation that brings the sorites to a close and, simultaneously, convinces the reader of the genre's power to "reveal" the text. This reasoning pattern, moreover, is just that: a conceptual model for the way critical argument effectively moves. It is not an attempt to imitate a "horizonal" historical reality, an "intrinsic" textual reality, a "theoretical" genre, or the process by which the critic actually "discovered" his argument. The priority of the premise is purely logical, as Kenneth Burke in the opening paragraph of his essay, "Definition of Man," points out:

> First, a few words on definition in general. . . . when used in an essay, as with Aristotle's definition of tragedy in his *Poetics*, a definition so sums things up that all the properties attributed to the thing defined can be as though "derived" from the definition. In actual development, the definition may be the last thing a writer hits upon. Or it may be formulated somewhere along the line. But logically it is prior to the observations that it summarizes. Thus, insofar as all the attributes of the thing defined fit the definition, the definition should be viewed as "prior" in this purely nontemporal sense of priority. (P. 3)

The reason for this reasoning, moreover, is purely pragmatic: it is justified wholly insofar as it helps us make better or more convincing critical arguments, those that acknowledge their premises and whose reasoning is consistent with those premises. And this pragmatic reason or purpose is what decides both the sorites' beginning point or premise and its stopping point or conclusion. It will be instructive here to consider Paul de Man's observation on the sorites or its various phrasings: "The question-and-answer structure, like the foreground-background or the conscious-preconscious structures, are abyssal frames that engender each other without end or *telos*. In the process, however, they create a sequence of apparent syntheses that convey an impression of methodological mastery."[40] While agreeing that there is no "natural" end to these procedures and that their display does indeed create an impression of methodological mastery, we should also recognize that the sorites does in fact always have a beginning and an end, as is shown, for example, in the above analysis of Jauss, whose practice de Man is here discussing. The notion that the "frames" are "abyssal" and self-engendering is a belated representational notion, one developed from our increasing awareness that the representational search for the "natural" beginning and end, traditionally termed either "bedrock" or the "horizon," is always infinitely regressive. A rhetorical and pragmatic theory of explanation has no need to place beginnings and ends "out of sight" because it locates them in the interpreter's suasive purpose, which in large part is the creation of that very "impression of methodological mastery" remarked by de Man, an end that in a representational theory must remain an incidental by-product of the interpreter's philosophic questing.

The overtness of its premises and the consistency of its reasoning endow an explanation with defensive strength, the power of prolepsis. By acknowledging rather than concealing its constitutive metaphors, it anticipates and thus defends against their extramural deconstruction or "unbuilding." But an explicitly generic criticism generates constructive strengths as well. Perhaps the most straightforward benefit of making our use of genre explicit is the greater conversational range and economy of the resulting criticism. Recall that traditional formalist criticism, fascinated with the unique and multifarious verbal surface, tends to move from particular text to particular text. This restricted and local movement, which characterizes even the best formalist criticism, even, for example, Cleanth Brooks's *The Well Wrought Urn*, both requires and is required by the denial of genre. Speaking generically, however, enables us to exemplify many texts in a single discussion. Thus Rader's reading of *Pamela*, explicitly and consistently deduced from his model of the novel, not only explains *Pamela* but by extension enables him to explain all novels like *Pamela*. Thus the generic explicitness of the following readings makes it possible to explain deduced texts in varying detail and length, the extension of the early readings enabling later abbreviation. But such synecdochic explanation is not only more economical, it is also more suggestive and, thereby, more powerfully convincing. Because we normally assume, as Gombrich has noted, "that to see a few members of a series is to see them all," because we expect to contribute our "beholder's share," critics, like painters, can invoke the "etc. principle" to suggest completion from very little indeed (p. 220). And it is the interpretive work necessary to complete this suggestion that works to make the conviction ours.

Genre, in other words, is a finite schema capable of potentially infinite suggestion. It is a special case of what Douglas Hofstadter calls a "strange loop": "what else is a loop but a way of representing an endless process in a finite way?"[41] But how does a "strange loop" differ from "normal" representation, which also seeks to capture the infinite in the finite? By making its beholder or reader aware of the "gaps" that he must fill or bridge in order to make sense. A strange loop calls attention to itself or, more precisely, to its finitude, and by so doing makes us attend to the dynamics of our attention itself, to the ways in which we accomplish the interpretive work of making sense. This redoubled attention is what makes it "strange." Put otherwise, normal and strange loops differ in the same way that illusionism differs from cubism: the one tries to conceal its difference from what is represented, the other uses, even flaunts its difference in order to convince us of the value of the representing text.

A strange loop, then, is not simply a suggestively incomplete series but one that explicitly turns back on itself, remarking its own incompletion. This turning, which is a kind of tropological maneuver, is what closes the infinite regress of representation, making the series seem complete. In the special case of genre, this illusion of completion is created when the literary text is incompletely represented (which always happens) and when attention is explicitly drawn to that incompletion (which happens only when genre is used rhetorically and pragmatically). This theoretical paradox, in other words, proves a powerful practical logic, for it is precisely the explicit incompletion of the explaining text that creates the seeming completion or fullness of the text explained. It makes the literary text seem to elude us, to contain more than we can know. And if we examine the notion of genre in terms of its other and no less inevitable representational failing—the trace or error it injects into the literary text—we end with a similar and similarly useful paradox. For no genre can represent its texts without reordering, reemphasizing, or in some way leaving its schematic imprint. There is *always* a difference between the universal and the particular, and this difference is a consequence not only of leaving something out but of putting something in. Once foregrounded, the latter proves no less useful in explanation than the former, for just as incompletion leads us to complete, difference (or, as we more usually and less precisely say, "error") leads us to "correct," to define similitude. And the activity of this "correction," no less than the activity of completion, commits us to its product, to the literary text that we have "made."

If, as Vaihinger observes, "what we generally call truth, namely a conceptual world coinciding with the external world, *is merely the most expedient error,*"[42] then what the critic seeks is not a "fit" but the most suggestive "misfit," the most expedient "error" or, as we have been saying, difference. And what is most expedient in literary criticism? We have already discussed the benefits of economy and range in explicitly generic explanation. But what about "literariness"? Genre criticism, of course, is the traditional enemy of the literary text as it has been most frequently defined and valued since the Romantics: as aesthetically rich and heuristically potent. However, if "fit" is acknowledged to be philosophically impossible but pragmatically possible, if our purpose is not finding accurate comparisons but, in Gombrich's words, "inventing comparisons which work," then we are free to define "work" as we will (p. 301). We can define it as the suggestion of just these characteristics.

One way to make this suggestion, to accomplish this simultaneously critical and "literary" purpose, is to refine our genres: "Whenever the difference between species matters, the schema is modified to meet the distinction" (Gombrich, p. 121). The distinction made in the following chapters between dramatic monologues and mask lyrics is just such a refinement, one that allows us to justify more fully the aesthetic and ethical value of such poems as "Prufrock." But a total refinement is neither possible nor desirable. Genres can never be perfectly coincident with texts unless we posit as many genres as texts—at which point we fall back into a Crocean world, into treating each text in isolation. Nor is sensitivity an absolute good. For certain conversational purposes we may want to *de*sensitize a given genre, making it less aware of differences, more emphatic of similarity. But whether we move toward greater or lesser sensitivity is, once again, not a philosophic but a pragmatic question. Just as Wordsworth's likening of the evening to a nun's breathless adoration was more apt for his meditative purpose, despite its being less surprising than Eliot's contrast-crossed metaphor, so it happens that likeness will work better than difference for certain explanatory purposes and not for others. Structuralism's search for the ever more basic underlying structures, the elemental likenesses that explain the greatest set of differences and, thereby, "define the conditions of meaning," is our boldest enactment of such a critical purpose.[43] It is also and not incidentally the least "literary" of contemporary critical languages, the least interested in saying how any particular text is just that: particular, inexplicable in general terms alone.

I have been discussing generic argument as syllogistic, as a reasoned way of discovering or, more precisely, defining the particular in the general, but the preceding remarks remind us that speaking generically is also metaphoric, a way of defining likeness in difference.[44] This kinship of syllogistic and metaphoric reasoning can be made explicit by revising our model thus:

> Let us define dramatic monologues as poems that invite their readers to distinguish the characterized speaker's meaning from the poem's.

> Let us discuss "Andrea del Sarto" as a dramatic monologue.

> Let us discuss "Andrea del Sarto" as inviting its readers to distinguish the speaker's meaning from the poem's.

The movement remains the same—from general to particular—but the asserted relationship between the two has become explicitly definitional rather than implicitly intrinsic or "natural." No longer claiming that "Andrea del Sarto" *is* a dramatic monologue, that there is some intrinsic or natural connection between the two, we now propose a pragmatic thought-experiment: let us explore what "Andrea del Sarto" is like when we read it in terms of the genre here defined as "dramatic monologue." The syllogistic process of deducing the poem from the genre is now refined—and redefined—as the unpacking of metaphoric equivalences.

But because metaphors are as crossed by contrast as they are confirmed by similarity, the process is ultimately an unpacking of difference as well, and it is here that the gap between literature and our thought about literature is finally closed. For genre, like metaphor, is powerfully persuasive not only because it leads us to perceive similarity but because it leads us to perceive that similarity in the midst of and in spite of difference. Like all metaphor, it is a way of talking "about things in terms of what they are not."[45] Like all metaphor, it perpetrates a contradiction in terms or, more precisely, in texts. For genre is not, as is commonly thought, a class but, rather, a classifying statement. It is therefore itself a text. It is writing about writing, distinguished by its topic and its way of handling that topic, the way it takes a set of literary texts and defines their relationship. This definition yokes it to its topic, the text it writes about, but it also sets it apart from that topic, articulating their difference, what Hofstadter would call the strangeness of the "loop." The text called "genre" is always different from the text it writes about.

Yet our perception of the genre's difference from the literary text leads not to suasive failure—the explicitly deductive critic defends against this failure by foregrounding the constitutive power of his genre—but to an impression of that text's value, of its particularity and power. For when the genre's trace and incompletion are acknowledged, their discovery "in" the text does not so much impugn the genre as create an impression of a distinctly *literary* text, one that seems infinitely particular and heuristically powerful precisely because it eludes our generalizing grasp. But the use of explicitly deductive genre reconciles the poem to its poetics in another way as well: by starting with the general we can deduce the most minute and numerous particulars, whereas when we purportedly start with those particulars we commit ourselves to moving away from them, to reducing them to the general. Thus does the very direction of explicitly deductive argument encourage "discovery" of an *ir*reducible text, one capable of being indefinitely because never conclusively unfolded.

But certain combinations of similarity and difference are more persuasive of this literariness than others, and those that create affinities at once surprising and profound are most persuasive of all. We shall find, for example, that it is neither surprising nor useful to connect two recognized dramatic monologues because they possess in common the use of a characterized speaker. This trait is too obvious: the similarity it remarks has, with repetition, come to seem superficial, powerless before increasingly noticed difference. It is an explanatory metaphor that has died. But to connect two monologues, as Robert Langbaum did, because they generate a common effect, is to construct a similarity that surprises us with its capacity to subsume those increasingly noticed and hitherto inexplicable differences.[46]

When the critic asserts that a particular genre is like a particular literary text, he makes a conceptual promise to his reader. He fulfills this promise by displaying both the *extensiveness* of his metaphor's power, showing how it subsumes surprisingly many poems, and its *intensiveness*, showing how it unfolds a given poem in surprising detail. Using the sorites, he reasons his way from generic premise to actual citation—in poem after poem, novel after novel. But the critic also and effectively displays how the texts of a given genre are *unlike* each other. This display, which bears a paradoxical relationship to the first, creates both the impression of each individual poem's literariness, thereby confirming its power to resist generalization, and the impression of an irresistible genre, thereby confirming its power to define difference in the midst of similarity. Taken together, these displays suggest that the "best" or most explanatorily potent genre to use for any particular discussion is the one that will extend what seems a profound similarity over a wide range of difference and that is capable of dramatizing this extension by "discovering" that difference intensively.

This extension, however, is not limitless, nor is it desirable that it should seem so. To explain everything by something is a purely representational ideal, a performance whose practical and theoretical impossibilities have been repeatedly dramatized in modern poetics. But were the performance possible, would it be desirable? Would it enable us to make better explanations of literary texts? In his analysis of poetic form Burke notes that "the peril of power is monotony,"[47] and, we might answer, so it is in critical explanation as well. The attempt to explain all or even many poems in terms of a single similarity or genre is a false economy: it would purchase extensive power by sacrificing the explanatory powers that are of particular importance in literary studies, those of subtlety and intensity.

Moreover, such an attempt would be inconsistent with a knowing use of genre. Once we define genre as constitutively powerful, we commit ourselves to the logical consequences of that definition, one of which is the recognition that a genre can no more be perfectly coincident with the literary text than it can be perfectly transparent or constitutively powerless. There are always, in other words, *two* "as if" or suppositional decisions made in generic criticism. One is obvious: we will discuss a group of poems as if they are *like* each other and their genre. The other is not: we will discuss a group of poems as if they are *unlike* each other and their genre. Moreover, we will discuss them as if they were *unlike* poems not included in the group. This display of difference is no less necessary to critical explanation than the display of similitude. Each implies the other, and each uses the other to do its interpretive work. The terms of difference are precisely what create the possibility of talk about similitude—and vice versa.

All of which means that a generic explanation best persuades not only by displaying its power to explain a great many poems in great detail but also by pushing itself to its explanatory limits. This last act both sharpens the explanation's metaphoric program—by showing us how *Moll Flanders* is not like *Pamela*, Rader shows us more clearly what *Pamela* is like—and constructs the credibility or defensive strength of that program. But it is also a creative strength, the process of completion and correction being the most suggestive of all knowledge-making processes. As our rigorous use of the genre pushes it to its explanatory limits and quite literally uses it up, its disintegration yields a hermeneutic detritus that has the "feel" of interpretive fact: what remains when the genre has been exhausted seems nothing other than the poem itself.[48] The following discussion of dramatic monologues, here defined as poems that are like "Andrea del Sarto," gradually gives way to discussion of Frost's "A Servant to Servants" and Browning's "Fra Lippo Lippi," which are less like dramatic monologues, and finally to discussion of Tennyson's "Ulysses," Browning's "Childe Roland," and Eliot's "Prufrock," which are defined to be unlike dramatic monologues in a distinctive way. The distinctiveness of this way defines a new similarity or genre, the "mask lyric," which "corrects" previous readings of these poems by making these newly defined poems seem more like each other and less like those with which they were previously said to be congeneric. But this genre also has its distinctive and acknowledged limits and, like all explanatory definitions, fully anticipates and welcomes its own future redefinition.

What, then, is a genre? The preceding pages have answered this and the other opening questions by arguing that genre is most usefully defined as a tool of critical explanation, as our most powerful and reasoned way of justifying the value we place or would place on a literary text. But to argue thus is not to claim that one of the most repeated questions of contemporary genre studies—Are genres "historical" or "theoretical"?—can only have wrong answers but, rather, is to suggest that the question is not very useful to ask. It leads us to treat as "real" a conflict that is itself invented, a terminological definition made to serve philosophical purposes that have largely passed into history. And its either-or terms effectively keep us from answering the question that compels the attention of contemporary literary studies: How can we make explanations of the literary text that are at once reasoned and yet distinctly "literary"? The answer here proposed is that we make such explanations by explicitly choosing our premises and deducing our texts. The argumentative energy of these explanations goes not into concealment but into reasoning, not into denials of the premise and the critic's act but into justifying his chosen premise by the consistency and richness of the reasoning that follows.

The critic, of course, may and often does argue the value of his genre in "historical" terms. He may, for example, argue that Browning intended us to read "Andrea del Sarto" as a dramatic monologue as here defined. But the value of such argument nevertheless remains a pragmatic rather than a "realistic" question: How well does this genre explain the poem? More precisely: How valuable is this poem when explained in terms of this genre? What makes a genre "good," in other words, is its power to make the literary text "good"— however that "good" be presently defined by our audience. Similarly, the critic may and often does argue the value of his genre in "theoretical" terms. But however laudable the internal rigor and scope of his theoretical system, any genre within the system nevertheless needs to justify itself pragmatically, by justifying the literary value of the text explained. Even Frye's strongest advocates accordingly fault him for not "practicing" the genres he preaches.

Several theorists of genre have recently observed that the historical-theoretical distinction is another way of making the inductive-deductive distinction and that the "historical" genre is a masked "theoretical" genre. The "historical" critic has simply—or not so simply—concealed his first or *a priori* step.[49] I agree with these observations but would take them one step further by noting that the "theoretical" genre is itself a mask. Like the "historical" genre, it is a way of "grounding" critical discourse in the not-itself, of displacing constitutive power from the critic's explanatory purpose and textualized act. Criticism, however, does not derive power from what it is not—whether a text or schema. Rather, it engenders power by what it does. Therefore, it is by *explicitly* returning constitutive power to the place where it in practice always resides—in the purpose and act of criticism—that we fully realize the power of genre. The questions of origin and change are answered by this "return." As exemplified by my use of the mask lyric, a genre is chosen or defined to fit neither a historical nor a theoretical reality but to serve a pragmatic end. It is meant to solve a critical problem, a problem that typically involves justifying the literary text's acknowledged but seemingly inexplicable value. The critic accordingly "finds" his genre by correcting a previous genre, in this case the dramatic monologue, a genre that is erroneous not because it is inherently wrong but because for certain poems it explains insufficiently well.[50] And the new genre is correct not inherently but pragmatically: because it explains sufficiently well, the power to explain being identical with the power to correct the old genre, to remedy its deficiencies, to make it workable. Like the "theoretical" genre, this chosen or defined genre constitutes the poem, causing us to "see" it in the genre's terms. It can and does constrain interpretation. But unlike the "theoretical" genre, its choice or definition is not itself constrained by a "deeper" ground, whether it be an entity or a category. It is always constrained pragmatically and rhetorically, by the critic's suasive purpose and audience.

This last point raises the "descriptive or prescriptive" question. As any reader of genre theory quickly learns, "descriptive" and "prescriptive" are themselves prescriptive terms, not neutral or descriptive but judgmental: a "good" genre describes, a "bad" genre prescribes. The judgment is Crocean. It is the way genre theory has played out the role of theory per se: to "look at" practice, not to affect it. Hence René Wellek and Austin Warren: "Modern genre theory is, clearly, descriptive. It doesn't limit the number of possible kinds and doesn't prescribe rules to authors."[51] Hence Paul Hernadi: "It seems to me that the better part of modern genre criticism has been more philosophical than historical or prescriptive: it has attempted to describe a few basic types of literature that *can* be written, not numerous kinds of works that *have* or, in the critic's view, *should have* been written."[52] Wellek and Warren are claiming descriptive validity for their definition of genre, but Hernadi is claiming both this validity and prescriptive power: his ideal genre *describes* the types of literature that *can* be written. This descriptive-prescriptive contradiction is yet another phrasing of the contradiction that always occurs when genre theory is yoked to a traditional or representational theory of knowledge. As in Crane and Jauss in particular, the descriptive claim is meant to mask and launder the prescriptive, but, again as in Crane and Jauss, it can't. For even as Hernadi is claiming the prescriptive powerlessness of his ideal genre, its inability to map literary practice, he is claiming that it has the power to do just that. The dilemma, however, drops away once we construe this mapping as not literary but critical.

In other words, the rhetorical and pragmatic answer to the "descriptive or prescriptive" question is that the critical genre is prescriptive, but what it prescribes is not literary but critical practice. The critic who explicitly uses his genre as an explanatory tool neither claims nor needs to claim that literary texts should be or will be written in its terms but that, at the present moment and for his implied audience, criticism can best justify the value of a particular literary text by using these terms. As shown above, this end is in part accomplished by the critic's manipulating the genre to the point at which it is used up or deductively exhausted. He thus justifies the value of his explanation by justifying the value of the poem. But he also justifies his explanation by showing it to be knowing, to be both self-aware and closely reasoned. Both justifications are finally one, similarly made possible by the explicitness of his premise and procedures, similarly concluding in the citations that conflate his text with the poet's. But his explanation's awareness of its provisional and pragmatic nature also leads to a further and paradoxical claim: that it is powerful because it has not only the power to correct previous readings but also the power to inspire the future readings that constitute its own correction.

Chapter 2
The Dramatic Monologue

A story I could body forth so well
By making speak, myself kept out of view,
The very man as he was wont to do,
And leaving you to say the rest for him.

Robert Browning

Browning was the first to be *called* difficult.

T. S. Eliot

Dramatic Monologues and the Problem of Genre

Dramatic monologues are interesting poems. Uniting the emotive intensity and formal tautness of the lyric with the inferential openness and immediate presence of the drama, they are both superficially easy and profoundly difficult to read. The problems of explaining dramatic monologues thus seem inextricable from their art. For this very reason, however, the agonistic drama of their interpretive history—the discrepancy between the value placed on these poems and our power to explain or even articulate that value—is uniquely instructive. It teaches that the monologue's paradoxical allegiances—to spontaneity and premeditation, to verisimilar disorder and artful design, to *res* and *verba*—have repeatedly defeated the mimetic language traditionally used to define and discuss the genre. Frequently noticed, they are no less frequently dismissed as anomalous. But these very paradoxes also suggest the grammar of a more powerful critical language, one able to explain the previously inexplicable.

Because the dramatic monologue has always been recognized as a distinctive yet hybrid form—like the lyric, like the drama, and thus unlike either—its interpretive history has been obsessed with deciding its generic identity.[1] Since the nineteenth century, critics have proposed a succession of rules and matrices, worrying in particular the form's distinction from the traditional lyric. Ina Beth Sessions' "The Dramatic Monologue" (1947) at once typifies and culminates these proposals, isolating, as do virtually all earlier studies, the poems that are at once undisputed and superior instances of the form—"Andrea del Sarto," "My Last Duchess," "Fra Lippo Lippi"—and defining a generic ideal in their terms.[2] The result is a descending hierarchy—"Perfect," "Imperfect," "Formal," "Approximate"—whose valuative rationale proves as mechanical as it is obvious. A dramatic monologue is "that literary form which has the definite characteristics of speaker, audience, dramatic action, and action which takes place in the present,"[3] and the monologues that inspire this definition are, not unexpectedly, judged "perfect." But the rather too obvious inevitability of this judgment does not impugn her reasoning as much as the fact that this reasoning consigns to imperfection many monologues deemed successful by their interpretive histories. To take one example, her definition demotes "Soliloquy of the Spanish Cloister" because the audience does not hear the speaker. A moment's consideration of the dramatic occasion, however, shows this supposed generic flaw to be the imaginative condition necessary to the speech of a paranoid and unwittingly self-cloistered speaker. "Ulysses," to take a quite different example, also falls victim to this literalizing or purely mimetic language: it is condemned for the deliquescent lyricism that is perhaps its most remarkable and remarked-upon strength.

Sessions' generic grammar has been routinely mocked for its rigidity, but I would suggest that our dissatisfaction is more properly directed toward its tendency to fault the many monologues that are as highly esteemed as they are consistently perplexing. When a postulated genre is too often either mute or at odds with a poem's received value and, worse, yet, with the received value of many similar poems, we traditionally question either its "rightness" (its inductive "fit" with the poem) or its rigor (the internal consistency of the explanation).[4] But the deficiencies of Sessions' criticism cannot be phrased in these terms: as long as her mimetic language remains confined to articulating the "perfect" monologues, those whose dramatic situations and actors seem unequivocably "real," it seems both adequate (it "fits" its topic) and consistent (it does not contradict its own premises or grammar). Rather, it is the narrowness of her discussion, its false conceptual economy, that should make us suspicious—not of the poems whose greater imaginative ambidexterity has exiled them to critical limbo but of a critical language that leaves so much unsaid.

The cautionary example of Sessions notwithstanding, the elusive complexity of the monologue has continued to tempt even reluctant critics into defining its generic essence. Park Honan's exemplifies those definitions that would cleanse themselves of all prescriptive or deductive stigma: "A single discourse by one whose presence is indicated by the poet but who is not the poet himself."[5] Realizing that his definition, which like Sessions' is mimetic, embraces all poems with characterized speakers—Ovid's *Heriodes*, Chaucer's "Wife of Bath's Prologue," Marlowe's "The Passionate Shepherd to His Love," Pope's "Eloisa to Abelard"—Honan defends its latitude by arguing its correspondent truth: "If it implies that many poems might be considered as both lyrics *and* dramatic monologues, it seems to reflect a truth. Is *Evelyn Hope* or is *Porphyria* not a dramatic monologue? Is either one not a lyric . . . no injustice will be done . . . by a definition of the dramatic monologue which 'overlaps' the lyric one."[6]

Given a choice between the "injustice" of too much mechanical discrimination and the "justice" of little or none, students of the form welcomed Robert Langbaum's alternative in *The Poetry of Experience*:

> We see, on the one hand, that the dramatic monologue is unprecedented in its effect, that its effect distinguishes it, in spite of mechanical resemblance, from the monologues of traditional poetry; and on the other hand, we welcome as particularly illuminating just those "approximations" that distress the classifiers. We welcome them because, having without the mechanical resemblance the same effect as the so-called "typical" monologues, they show us what the form is essentially doing.[7]

Defining this effect as "the tension between sympathy and moral judgment" (p. 85), Langbaum places the reader's experience at the center of explanatory attention. The importance of this innovative placement is undeniable, but the old problems remain—in particular, the problem of classifying poems superficially similar in form and radically different in effect. Attempting to treat the lyrical "Ulysses" and "Prufrock" as monologues, Langbaum not only reads these poems in terms of the "moral judgment" used to explain the reader's response to such poems as "My Last Duchess," he simultaneously reads them in terms of their "lyrical element." He thus modifies his initial generic assertion—the dramatic monologue is an invitation to judge its speaker—by asserting that a monologue is also the speaker's gratuitous and lyrical expression. This modification commits Langbaum to talking as if the speaker were the sufficient cause of his own words and, thereby, of the poem. Preferring verisimilitude to artifice and sincere spontaneity to devious design, Langbaum's language falls selectively mute: it cannot say that these poems are made and only seem to be said, that their speakers are not real but only seem to be real. It accordingly cannot say that the distinctive art of the genre is best defined by its capacity to heighten and wield just these paradoxes, which are endemic to all literary utterances but of paramount importance to these. Explained in Langbaum's terms, the poems seem less wondrously wrought than readers have found them to be. Their art has been simplified, made to obey the essentially Platonic rule that governs all mimetic languages: the rule that, as E. H. Gombrich has said, "we cannot, strictly speaking, watch ourselves having an illusion."[8]

Responding to its partiality, Ralph Rader has complemented Langbaum's "naturalistic" grammar with Elder Olson's "aesthetic" grammar, which emphasizes the "madeness" of the monologue. "These poems," Rader thus argues, "are most adequately seen as both determinate artistic constructs and as embodiments, in different senses, of real experience," and they are most adequately distinguished from similar poems by "the way in which the poet is related to the figure given in the poem."[9] Rader's definition, more complex and powerful than Langbaum's, is compatible with my argument that these poems are most fully explained in terms of conscious illusion: that in reading we understand them as both made and said, as both like art and like life. Put otherwise, we see the paradoxical bond between the speaker who made the poem, whom we take as more "real" if less present, and the speaker he made, whom we take as less "real" if more present. Rader's advance over Langbaum lies precisely in his recognition of this ontological ambidexterity: while agreeing with Langbaum that we think of the speaker as if he were a real person, he also agrees with Olson that we simultaneously recognize that person's "madeness." Phrased in terms of our argument here, Rader faults Langbaum's critical language for lacking the conceptual grammar needed to articulate the "as if"-ness of our reading experience.

The speaker's ambidexterity, in short, has been given a critical voice. Nevertheless, because Rader's language remains centered on that speaker and his seeming autonomy from the poet who made him, his explanations must remain fundamentally if complexly mimetic, and the oft-remarked but persistently inexplicable tropological density of these seeming "natural" utterances remains undiscussed.[10] Thus, while Rader does note the couplets of "My Last Duchess," astutely observing that they signal the poet's designing presence, this insight is not elaborated. Artifice is a topic about which the mimetic language has little or nothing to say. To achieve a fuller explanation of the monologue we need to replace this critical language, used so long it seems intrinsic to the monologues themselves, with a strategic or rhetorical language. To do so is not to discard the invaluable insight of mimesis—that we respond to the speaker as if he were real—but, rather, to subsume it, to gather the speaker's seeming reality along with his actual artifice into our larger recognition of the *poem*'s ambidexterity. The reader would still, as in Rader's language, distinguish the speaker from the poet, but rather than concentrating on the speaker's distinction from the poet, our explanation will concentrate on the reader's distinguishing activity.

This shift requires a more complex conceptual grammar, one that will enable us to attend more precisely to the dynamics of our reading response. The most systematic attention of this kind is found in Wayne Booth's *A Rhetoric of Irony*, where the grammar of "stable irony" enables explanation of such poems as "Soliloquy of the Spanish Cloister" in terms of four acts performed by the reader: a rejection of literal statement; a search for alternative positions; a decision about the position of the implied author; a reconstruction of meaning in line with this decision.[11] But Browning's conspicuous aesthetic and ethical preference for things incomplete, a preference repeatedly noted in the interpretive history, asks us to discuss not only the reader's final decision and the successful procedures that lead to that decision but also his various and incomplete *attempts* to decide.[12] The conceptual language of "affective stylistics," most fully defined and "spoken" in the early works of Stanley Fish, will give us a way of doing just this: of discussing "the making and revision of assumptions, the rendering and regretting of judgments, the coming to and abandoning of conclusions, the giving and withdrawing of approval, the specifying of causes, the asking of questions, the supplying of answers, the solving of puzzles."[13] To take such explanatory notice of the fact and dynamics of incompleteness, however, is to say neither that certain monologues do not "slam shut"—"Cleon," for one, does just that—nor that monologues do not characteristically achieve closure. They typically do. Rather, it is to argue for the importance of discussing the reader's process of making meaning as well as the meaning he finally if provisionally makes. And I say "provisionally" because, as we shall see, not only does the repeated "coming to and abandoning of conclusions" in any particular monologue cast residual doubt on any conclusion we finally come to, but each reading of each monologue is also a rereading of those that have come before. This is obviously so for those monologues in *The Ring and the Book*, whose common title proclaims their explicit intertextual kinship. But it is also the case for those monologues that, despite their seeming separateness, dwell in the larger intertextual world marked out by their critical reading.

My particular definition of the monologue—"dramatic monologues are poems that invite their readers to distinguish the poem's meaning from that of its characterized speaker"—is adopted for a purpose. Like all generic definitions, it is meant to enable discussion of a group of poems as if they were like each other and unlike poems not in the group. Discussion begins with poems, like "Cleon" and "Andrea del Sarto," that directly "fit" the definition and then proceeds to poems, like "Fra Lippo Lippi" and "A Servant to Servants," that "fit" indirectly. It stops short of poems, like Tennyson's "Ulysses" and Eliot's "Prufrock," that "fit" not at all and thus call for the definition of a new genre. The issue of "fit" or "misfit," however, is not representational but pragmatic, raised not to validate but to explain. The aim is to construct a relational system that works, that allows us to tell each other how the poems we value are simultaneously like and unlike each other, and how our valuations are themselves like and unlike. The aim, that is, is to make a reasoned and self-aware sense not only of the poems but also of previous attempts to make such a sense, attempts that, taken together, compose what I am calling the interpretive history.

In the preceding chapter I argued that any particular text can be made to seem more or less like any other particular text, that similarity can always be "discovered" no matter how distinctive the individual members of any group of poems. Which genre we choose is accordingly a question not of intrinsic rightness but of pragmatic purpose: What is our suasive goal? The answer traditionally and currently given by our discipline is readily at hand: to make a reasoned sense of the text and, what is in effect the same, to justify or raise its value. I am proposing that we can best accomplish this end with the poems traditionally called dramatic monologues by discussing them in terms of their affective design. The aim is to show them to be more artful and more profound than they have seemed in the readings already recorded in their intepretive history. Paradoxically, the following discussion will attempt to do this by adopting Browning's valuative criterion of imperfection, by arguing that monologues invite us to fault their speakers for refusing to know and use the vital open-endedness of their imaginations. I will simultaneously argue that this act of finding fault is what engenders both our edification and pleasure.

We can summarize this generic redefinition by joining the following two insights, penned a century apart. First, Walter Bagehot in 1864:

> It takes the type, so to say, *in difficulties*. It gives a representation of it in its minimum development, amid the circumstances least favorable to it, just while it is struggling with obstacles, just where it is encumbered with incongruities.[14]

Second, Hazard Adams in 1963:

> I think it unlikely that sympathy is at all an adequate word for our relation to, say, Browning's Duke. We may be fascinated by the size of his ego, by his gross materialism, by his utter coldness; but our whole tendency is, I think, to struggle out of his perspective into some other. It is this tension between encasement in the form and our desire to escape to a position of vantage which strikes us so intensely.[15]

The monologic speaker, in other words, fails precisely where his reader succeeds: in achieving a separate perspective on himself, in "putting the infinite within the finite," in structuring a "strange loop." In the preceding chapter, we discovered that self-reference necessarily makes the text referred to seem incomplete: it conjures up an image of the text as less than fully knowing. But we also discovered that this image simultaneously implies the fullness of the text that "knows" it, that the illusion of imperfection feeds a subsuming illusion, one that seems less imperfect precisely because it recognizes imperfection elsewhere. The reader of a dramatic monologue thus struggles out of the speaker's struggle by taking a perspective on it even as he paradoxically continues to dwell within it. This hermeneutic struggle will be found to enhance the poem's aesthetic value: it leads us to read a poem as well as a speech. The struggle also enhances its ethical value: the difficulty of extricating ourselves from the speaker's perspective is precisely what exercises our capacity to read and, what may finally be the same, to empathize.

The readings from "Cleon" to "A Servant to Servants" are ordered to display the increasing difficulty of such extrication and to place increasing strain on the generic model. The two orderings are coincident, implying that the great monologues teach and please by pushing the form to its limits. This is why we read and reread them even as we relegate "purer" generic efforts to the unread recesses of literary history. But the increasing strain on the model is also meant to argue a theoretical thesis: that genres, like all conceptual and pragmatic inventions, invite perpetual "correction" or, what is the same, new thought. Like the monologues read, their "imperfections" tempt us to a critical perfection, but as correction follows correction we learn that this temptation is as permanently provisional and open-ended as this "perfection" is infinitely elusive. We also learn that both are valuable precisely insofar as they are so.

Because the best dramatic monologues we have are Browning's and because Browning's best poems are dramatic monologues, study of the form traditionally and appropriately centers on his poems. But the disappearance from view of the hundreds of other monologues written in the nineteenth century has made it easy to forget just how good Browning's are. Most of the major Romantic poets wrote a few, but because the form's dramatic potential all too readily actualizes as melodrama, the dramatic monologue before Browning was distinctly the province of the minor poet.[16] The prolific and forgotten Felicia Hemans invariably showcases an exotic, insane, or wildly distraught speaker in a crisis. Southey's five monologues or, as they are sometimes called, monodramas, do likewise: in "Sappho" the speaker throws herself from a precipice at poem's end; in "Ximalpoca" a Mexican king speaks while awaiting his sacrifice; in "The Wife of Fergus" the speaker stabs herself; in "Lucretia" the violated speaker stabs herself while her husband and father watch; in "La Caba" yet another violated speaker prepares to leap from the castle battlements while the father who permitted her violation looks on.[17]

Against such routine if spectacular exploitation of the grisly, lurid, and pathetic, the oft-remarked restraint and psychological complexity of Browning's monologues emerge as all the more remarkable. Nevertheless, critics typically value his monologues for the same reason nineteenth-century readers valued those of Hemans and Southey: they represent interesting speakers in interesting situations. The interest of the poems, in short, inheres in their content. The valuation is thoroughly mimetic, as is the language used, the ongoing critical question being neither "Is this an interesting poem?" nor "How does it affect the reader?" but "Does this poem represent interesting matter and how accurately does it do so?" The following analyses will attempt to break into criticism's ongoing absorption with the monologic speaker, arguing that while verisimilitude is an undeniable and powerful factor in these poems, it is most profitably discussed not as an end in itself but insofar as it serves a different and expressly strategic end: the poem's design on its reader.

So as to enable deduction of the multiple and designed paradoxes of the monologue, its design is defined as being itself paradoxical, as involving both affective intent and formal structure. Our dissatisfaction with previous explanation is a consequence of its refusing just this paradox: of privileging the reader over the text or vice versa; of privileging ethics over aesthetics or vice versa. Criticism of the dramatic monologue thus concisely enacts contemporary criticism's repeated stagings of the reader-text agon—a drama enacted primarily by J. Hillis Miller, Norman Holland, Stanley Fish, and Wolfgang Iser—and its paradoxical resolution here is meant to suggest the possibility of a more general solution.[18] In the following pages I will accordingly argue the case for both the reader and the text by unfolding in terms of particular monologues our beginning generic assertion: that the value of the monologue is best served by discussing the reader-critic's attempt to make a sense that is both aesthetic and heuristic, a sense that, in this particular genre, is woven of his attempts to distinguish the poem's meaning from that of its characterized speaker.

Disbelief and the Well Wrought Urn: "Cleon" and "Karshish"

Even as "Cleon" typifies the genre, its criticism typifies the genre's criticism: routinely read as a dramatic monologue, the poem is just as routinely read as a display of its speaker.[19] The fact that Cleon is a man of complexity and stature, a "Plato, a Leonardo and a Goethe all in one," seems to invite and certainly rewards such a reading.[20] The epitome of Hellenistic culture as it verges on the Christian era, he is a man who has everything and knows it—everything but the hope of salvation. This qualification proves of the essence, and the poem turns on its elaboration, dramatizing Cleon's despair and then his pride, showing him doomed and then diminished.

Because Cleon is undeniably an interesting man in an interesting situation, reading the poem as a vehicle for his display very nearly satisfies. The long first part before Cleon's rejection of Christianity can be explained as the virtuoso unfolding of a complex man, and the rejection itself can be explained as further display, pride and foolishness being interesting complications of greatness. But such reading remains disturbingly mute to questions about order and proportion. Why, we would like to know, are the first 335 lines devoted to a subtle, empathetic, and lyric-like delineation of Cleon's greatness and the last 18 to the caricature of a fool? The portrait, if that is what it is, is conspicuously skewed. The proportions are noticeably disproportionate, the emphases oddly placed, the manner incongruously mixed. A Daumier nose on a Dürer face. But the inexplicability of the epigraph—"As certain also of your own poets have said"—is particularly distressing to the mimetic reading. Indeed, the explanation commonly given—that it "is taken from Acts 17:28 and is part of the address of St. Paul to the Greeks from the Areopagus in Athens"—emphasizes rather than remedies its seeming superfluity.[21]

But if we read "Cleon" as a poem that has designs on its reader, the epigraph immediately becomes functional: because it is spoken by Paul and because it is Paul's message that Cleon rejects, this rejection prefigures—and ultimately guards against—a similar rejection by Browning's contemporaries. As it happens, we know that shortly before writing "Cleon" Browning read "Empedocles on Etna" as well as Arnold's justification of his poem's withdrawal due to its Hellenistic despair (Preface to the 1853 edition of *Poems*). The issues, then, were still fresh when "Cleon" appeared two years later in *Men and Women*. Thus do literary history and explanatory power converge, suggesting that the poem does more than picture its intramural or Hellenistic time, that behind the seemingly natural and anomalous lies a presence that is designing, even devious.

Such questioning of order, proportion, manner, and epigraph weakens the "portrait" or mimetic language of explanation and argues the explanatory superiority of a language that articulates Cleon's complexity as a necessary but insufficient cause of the poem's formal complexity and suasive power. Perhaps the greatest challenge for this language, as for any critical language, is justifying the long first section, in which we are encouraged to match with Cleon, to see him as he sees himself and to find ourselves in him.[22] We here read in lyric fashion, and we do so primarily because we are not invited to do otherwise. But because the very blackness of Cleon's mood is potentially distancing, more active strategies also come into imaginative play. Length is one: the longer we are in a speaker's mind the greater our adherence to his vision. Making Cleon at once ideal and existentially tortured is another: because he is superior we will find judgment difficult; because he despairs, we will find empathy easy. Displaying Cleon's self-knowledge is yet another: were his knowing to seem inferior to ours, he would seem so as well. But this display is risky: the reader may interpret Cleon's self-knowledge as pride. So this strategy is supported by others, Cleon's self-knowledge being at once extensively justified by his accomplishments and intensively tempered by his own ironic discounting:

> And I have written three books on the soul,
> Proving absurd all written hitherto,
> And putting us to ignorance again.
> (ll. 57–59)

These seductive and defensive strategies invite and sustain our matching with Cleon. But perhaps the most basic invitation is what the mimetic model treats as the sole cause and end of the poem: the speaker's complexity. Granted: it is pleasing and interesting to dwell in complex minds. We enter into them with eagerness and depart with reluctance. Such complexity accordingly proves an invaluable poetic strategy. But because the dramatic monologue, as it is here and traditionally defined, also requires our distance from the speaker, this strategy threatens the very effect it serves. Browning's monologues in large part distinguish themselves from their facile and sensationalist congeners by encouraging and yet managing this treat, by inviting the reader to dwell in the speaker's problem while simultaneously denying his solution. Hence their power—and their explanatory elusiveness.

In "Cleon" the epistolary form is itself instrumental to this power. Unlike the spontaneous and face-to-face encounters that typify most monologues, the epistolary encounter tolerates and even encourages the self-distanced involutions of Cleon's intellection. Thus the "writtenness" of his language and the studied precision of his argument not only give us his character, they are intellectually yet powerfully seductive. But as always in the monologue, powerful effects are double-edged. The extensive and careful self-presentation so encouraged by the epistolary form threatens to seem cooly premeditated, not something to experience but something to consider, perhaps to suspect. The risk is that the speaker's "life" will be dimmed and our judgment pat. In "Cleon," however, this risk is particularly well run. The poem reminds us that, most immediately, it is a letter, and these reminders, however paradoxically, rescue the effect from the preponderance of its own design. Because even real-life letters are more formal than spoken utterance, because they typically parade their beginnings, middles, and ends, their conventional phrasing and set topics, an epistolary monologue can display far greater evidence of design and even premeditation without risking either the speaker's verisimilitude or his ethos. Thus does Cleon's controlled self-reflection come to seem a "natural" consequence of his "real-life" act, and thus does the epistolary form doubly further our lyric alliance, simultaneously securing the advantages of both art and its seeming absence.

I have been talking as if Cleon were writing to the reader, but this is so only indirectly. Cleon writes to Protus, who, like most epistolary audiences, "speaks" only at Cleon's bidding. His generic virtue is passive receptivity. But, considered closely, his passivity as a "person" is revealed to be actively strategic in the poem, his shadowy presence a catalyst for not only Cleon's response but ours. Consider how finely Protus has been fashioned to serve the specific rhetorical needs of the monologoue: 1) the audience must be a peer lest Cleon's discourse seem condescending or self-serving; 2) he must be physically absent—although imaginatively present—to allow Cleon's lyric unfolding to proceed uninterrupted and unchallenged; 3) he must protect the lyric alliance from Cleon's seeming arrogance while simultaneously establishing Cleon's stature. Further, like all narratees in dramatic monologues, Protus is our dramatized stand-in: we recognize his otherness, but we also read the epistle as if it were written to us, as if we were Protus.[23] Thus when Cleon flatters his audience—"Nay, thou art worthy of hearing my whole mind" (l. 181)—we are by empathetic extension flattered. And when Cleon repeats Protus' praise,

> It is as thou hast heard: in one short life
> I, Cleon, have effected all those things
> Thou wonderingly dost enumerate.
>   (ll. 44–46)

he praises himself with impunity. Just as the point and counterpoint of Cleon's argument build its seductive logos, so do such praise and counterpraise build his seductive ethos. The two constructions are powerfully convergent precisely because Protus provides the occasion for one and the means for the other.

Having shared intimately and at such length the revelations of this complex and private man, we are loath to break the bond even when his revelations grow disturbing. We accordingly accept his emotions as just, which is to say as ours, even when the emotion is envy:

> Indeed, to know is something, and to prove
> How all this beauty might be enjoyed, is more:
> But, knowing nought, to enjoy is something too.
> Yon rower, with the moulded muscles there,
> Lowering the sail, is nearer it than I.
> I can write love-odes: thy fair slave's an ode.
> I get to sing of love, when grown too gray
> For being beloved: she turns to that young man,
> The muscles all a-ripple on his back.
> I know the joy of kingship: well, thou art king!
>   (ll. 291–300)

Even when, as here, the envy deepens into despair, then into horror:

> Say rather that my fate is deadlier still,
> In this, that every day my sense of joy
> Grows more acute, my soul (intensified
> By power and insight) more enlarged, more keen;
> While every day my hairs fall more and more,
> My hand shakes, and the heavy years increase—
> The horror quickening still from year to year,
> The consummation coming past escape
> When I shall know most, and yet least enjoy—
>   (ll. 309–17)

The first section of the poem ends with Cleon's vision of himself as dead, as longing for his soul's release but rejecting even the possibility:

> I, I the feeling, thinking, acting man,
> The man who loved his life so over-much,
> Sleep in my urn. It is so horrible,

> I dare at times imagine to my need
> Some future state revealed to us by Zeus,
> Unlimited in capability
> For joy, as this is in desire for joy,
> —To seek which, the joy-hunger forces us:
> That, stung by straitness of our life, made strait
> On purpose to make prized the life at large—
> Freed by the throbbing impulse we call death,
> We burst there as the worm into the fly,
> Who, while a worm still, wants his wings. But no!
> Zeus has not yet revealed it; and alas,
> He must have done so, were it possible!
>
> (ll. 321–35)

The poem now pauses, its speaker's despair exhausted by its wording, its reader's expectations modulated to closure by Cleon's unconditional rejection of all hope. That this rejection and its attendant gloom is contained within the lyric alliance testifies to the strategic finesse of Browning's art. But the final stanza, whose job is to shatter this very alliance, is a yet more striking testimony:

> Live long and happy, and in that thought die:
> Glad for what was! Farewell. And for the rest,
> I cannot tell thy messenger aright
> Where to deliver what he bears of thine
> To one called Paulus; we have heard his fame
> Indeed, if Christus be not one with him—
> I know not, nor am troubled much to know.
> Thou canst not think a mere barbarian Jew,
> As Paulus proves to be, one circumcised,
> Hath access to a secret shut from us?
> Thou wrongest our philosophy, O king,
> In stopping to inquire of such an one,
> As if his answer could impose at all!
> He writeth, doth he? well, and he may write.
> Oh, the Jew findeth scholars! certain slaves
> Who touched on this same isle, preached him and Christ;
> And (as I gathered from a bystander)
> Their doctrine could be held by no sane man.
>
> (ll. 336–53)

The lyric alliance shatters not only because Cleon here rejects the very salvation sought but also because he rejects it for reasons that must strike us, no matter what the state of our belief, as inadequate and incriminating. His suddenly revealed prejudice, both racial and intellectual, his perverse failure to submit Paul's "secret" to his habitual intellection, his facile acceptance of the bystander's opinion—all overwhelm and cancel the ethos, logos, and pathos of the first part. The stunning impact of the final line measures our distance from Cleon and the self the poem has shaped and, therefore, shown us to be. We stand, as it were, surprised in belief.

For the poem's reader, this surprise transforms Cleon from the paragon of Hellenism to the paradigm of its hubris. But we must remind ourselves here that there is no actual transformation, that Cleon, like all monologic speakers, never changes. What changes is our reading of him and, potentially, our reading of ourselves *as* readers. How Browning manages this seeming change is nevertheless a central question, whose answer articulates his polemical point. We have seen how the monologue converts our interpretive time and energy into a lyric alliance with Cleon and then destroys this alliance with a conspicuously brief conclusion, a brevity that in itself contributes to our surprise. But the seductive pathos of Cleon's metaphysical plight is such that an overwhelming reversal is necessary to turn us from his side, and brevity alone can not manage this turn.

Of course, its very position gives Cleon's rejection the force of all closure. But this ending also and primarily gathers its force from the reader's increased interpretive activity, an activity that can be variously phrased. Gombrich would say that enlarging the beholder's share intensifies meaning, making it, quite literally, more ours. Fish would say that this activity is essentially revisionary, that we have been invited to revise our assumptions, regret our judgments, abandon our conclusions, and withdraw our approval. And Booth would say that the reader of poems like "Cleon" finally rejects the speaker's meaning for that of the implied poet. These three critical languages are complementary ways of unfolding and praising Browning's conclusion, of variously saying how the reader's completing and correcting activity creates his emotional, ethical, and historical superiority.

In other words, each of the three languages enables us to say why the poem is polemically effective regardless of the reader's actual belief or lack thereof. True, his superiority depends upon his knowledge of Paul, Jesus, and the historical consequences of their existence. But the suasive force of that superiority depends upon his constructing the position of belief for himself. If the poem overtly asserted belief or overtly condemned Cleon for his disbelief, our discounting of either assertion would come too readily, thereby leaving us as we were when we began to read. As it is, the disbeliever "discovers" belief and the believer conviction precisely because each has made the interpretive effort of correcting Cleon's delimited vision.

Santayana wrote that even Browning's "short poems have no completeness, no limpidity. They are little torsos made broken so as to stimulate the reader to the restoration of their missing legs and arms."[24] Just so: throughout "Cleon" we infer the writer behind the letter, attempting to match, to erase the traces of our selves, to think and feel as if we were he. But the conclusion redoubles this activity and in what Hofstadter has called "strange loop" fashion turns the poem back on itself, foregrounding its incompletion as an epistle and, as it does so, suggesting its completion as a poem. "Cleon" thus perfectly exemplifies Browning's own vision of poetry as "putting the infinite within the finite."[25] The discrepancy we "discover" between Cleon's lucid explication of the problem and his prejudiced rejection of Paul's solution has led us to complete and correct the immediately present writer (Cleon) and genre (the epistle) by constructing another and less present writer (the implied poet) as well as another and less present genre (the poem). And it is precisely our ironizing contribution to this construction that turns or tropes these shadowy presences into substance.

Because such completing and correcting activity is so pronounced in dramatic monologues, their radical difference from other poems seems to admit no similarity. But even brief scrutiny reveals multiple authors and readers in all literary texts. In life we normally assume and discover one speaker for every utterance and believe what someone says unless we have reason to believe otherwise. This routine belief, what H. P. Grice has termed the "Cooperative Principle," is the conventional contract that enables social intercourse.[26] But a literary text normally has at least two speakers. Every lyric poem, to take the case that is at once most familiar and least obvious, has a real but submerged speaker, the poet who made the poem, and an immediate but fictive speaker, the poet who speaks the poem. These two speakers may be virtually conflated, as in "Tintern Abbey," but even there our response depends upon our treating the making of the poem and the saying of the poem as two different activities that, moreover, happen in two different time frames. The tenses used to speak about the poem are telling: Wordsworth, we say, *wrote* "Tintern Abbey" in 1798, but in that poem he *says* "That in this moment there is life and food/For future years." He wrote the poem once but is forever saying it in an eternal present. The success of the illusion is such that the two activities and the two speakers seem to be one, but we have only to ignore the submerged real poet and regard the poem as the transcription of a real utterance to realize how deeply our response is conditioned by his presence. We would then marvel at the phenomenon of a real man meditating poetically rather than at the more marvelous phenomenon of a poem whose seeming naturalness and spontaneity has seduced us into mistaking it for meditation itself. Insofar, then, as the immediate and covert speakers are conflated, we seem to be hearing the poet speak, whereas in actuality he whom we hear speaking is himself part of what is being spoken.

The relationship between the speakers of a literary text admits of infinite gradations in distance and slant. The distance may be moral, intellectual, historical, or, as in Wordsworth's *The Prelude* or Eliot's *Four Quartets*, there may seem to be no distance at all—a situation as rhetorically if differently potent as that of "Cleon." Curiously, distance is not necessarily, if ever, a function of strangeness: the narrator of Bellow's *Henderson the Rain King* is accepted at his own valuation whereas the "normal" narrator of Ford's *The Good Soldier* prompts subtle and complex discounting. This is so because we try to match whenever we can and with whichever speaker is most immediately present, and only when such matching fails to make a "good" sense of the text do we seek a less present speaker and construct a new meaning in terms of that speaker. Thus in the lyric we treat the speaker's meaning as if it were the poem's because the poem does not invite us to do otherwise or, to be precise, the poem's value is best served by our not doing otherwise. In life we assume that someone means what he says unless we have reason to think otherwise, but in reading we assume not only that the speaker or most immediately present writer means what he says but also that this meaning coincides with the text's meaning. Unless, that is, we have reason to think otherwise.

But what happens when we do have reason to think otherwise? As Mary Pratt has persuasively argued, our response varies with the ontological status of our situation.[27] Whereas in life we look for causes within the present speaker— "discovering," for example, his ignorance or perfidy—in literature we also look for another speaker, who is at once less present and more powerfully determining. When the speaker of a literary text lies, violates the generic conventions of his discourse, or knows less than we do, we typically assume that his failure is part of a larger design and set about "discovering" a speaker and genre that subsume and thereby explain those more immediately present. But the impetus for this interpretive activity is invariably not emotional but conceptual. Our empathetic tolerance is strained not by the extremity to which our imaginations are stretched but by our sense that we know more than the speaker, that we "see" more clearly. Thus the strangeness of a lyric speaker is not only not a sufficient reason for the reader to pull back, it may be and, indeed, typically is the main reason he enjoys reading as if he were the speaker. Many reading experiences traditionally termed "lyric"—that of "Tithonus" is one example— turn or trope this "as if" leap into their distinguishing intensity. As do many modern novels: Nabokov's *Lolita* and Gide's *The Immoralist* are two. Our strained yet unbroken alliance with such conspicuously strange speakers results only incidentally from emotional consanguinity and always from rhetorical technique, from the way in which the tropological density of the speaker's discourse attracts us to his vision even as his awareness anticipates and thereby deflects our judgment. Analogously, in dramatic monologues our broken alliance results only incidentally from the lack of emotional consanguinity and always from the speaker's not knowing his tropological activity as such: we and the poet are aware of his tropes as he is not. Hence our ironic vision of Cleon.

But with repetition tropes seem to die into the thing itself, to become transparent windows to their tenors or texts. Although we and the implied poet "see" Cleon ironically, in a way other than he sees himself, when the poem is read in isolation the opacities of our vision tend to seem inherent in what is seen, namely, in Cleon himself. When a poem is read intertextually, however, in active collation with other poems, the trope reawakens and the poet's rhetorical technique becomes "visible." The poem that best performs this service for "Cleon" is Browning's other epistolary monologue, "An Epistle Containing the Strange Medical Experience of Karshish, the Arab Physician." Linked not only by their epistolary form but also by their overt didacticism, in each the partiality of the speaker's vision is made manifest by our superior historical knowledge, and in each our attempt to correct this vision manuevers us into a position of Christian belief. But the ways of manuevering are different, and this difference is no less instrumental in defining the art of these generic twins than their similitude.

Let us begin as critics of "Karshish" usually begin, with the character of the speaker and the nature of his experience.[28] Karshish is an Arab physician who, in his travels through Judea, encounters the risen Lazarus. The encounter disturbs his objectivist equilibrium, a disturbance that prompts and pervades his letter to his mentor. Like Cleon, Karshish is a first-century pagan confronting an experience that his intellectual training and cultural background cannot countenance, and both poems accordingly pique and satisfy our curiosity about what it was like to be alive at the dawn of the Christian era. But this "slice of life" reading of Karshish and his epistolary discourse is ultimately no more satisfying than it was for "Cleon." A language that explains "Karshish" as the display of an interesting man in an interesting situation leaves too many questions unanswered and, what is the same, leaves the poem's aesthetic and ethical value unfolded. Such a language cannot explain why Browning chose the epistolary form or Abib as the immediate audience, why Karshish's character is as it is and not otherwise, why the poem has the order and proportion that it does.

The monologue's interpretive history has typically left such questions not only unanswered but unasked, and this muteness, once again, reveals the fundamentally mimetic grammar of the conversation. But the rhetoricity of "Cleon" and "Karshish" is so conspicuous that it seems, as it were, to speak itself:

> Take as an example Browning's dramatic monologues in defence of Christianity. Although the poet has undoubtedly an axe to grind, he maintains a distinction between the undeniable fact of the speaker's response to the conditions of the poem and the general Christian formulation which the reader may or may not draw for himself. (P. 98)

Faced with poems whose palpable designs on the reader cannot be ignored, Langbaum concedes that Browning has "an axe to grind." But because he is not using a rhetorical language, Langbaum cannot elaborate this insight. He must speak as if the poem were teleologically indistinct from life, as if the speaker were the sufficient cause of his own words. The explanatory difficulties thus created soon become clear:

> The speaker starts with a blank slate as regards Christianity, and is brought by the conditions of the poem to a perception of need for the kind of answer provided by Christianity. Nevertheless, the perception is not expressed in the vocabulary of Christian dogma and the speaker does not himself arrive at a Christian formulation. (P. 98)

Well, we might ask, why doesn't the speaker use the vocabulary of Christian dogma, and why doesn't he arrive at belief? Because Langbaum's language cannot ask these questions, it cannot answer them.

Critics agree that in "Karshish," as in "Cleon," Browning intended to sway the reader to belief. If this is so, and let us provisionally proceed as if it were, we also do well to proceed as if some means to this end were better than others and as if these were the ones that Browning used. Such procedural assumptions, so customary they customarily remain unstated, are the most fruitful starting place of explanation and are properly made explicit. What then, we ask, was Browning's primary or generic choice in writing "Karshish?" As often happens, the question is best answered indirectly, by considering what he did not choose: to write a lyric. In most ways it seems the obvious choice. Consider how the sheer sensuous immediacy of an eyewitness lyric utterance—Pound's "Ballad of the Goodly Fere," discussed in the next chapter, is one example—can sway us, however momentarily, to belief: seeing with the speaker's eyes, we seem to see what he sees. Thus, given Browning's posited aim, he could have written his monologue from the point of view of Lazarus. Knowing as Lazarus knows, we would directly participate in the intensity and unmediated presence of this archetypal awakening. Yet in the poem we have, this awakening is obscured by time, the inarticulateness of Lazarus, and the misreadings of Karshish. In short, Browning chose to conceal the very experience that is to move us to belief. It behooves us to ask why.

By way of answer let us consider more closely the working of his lyric alternative, exemplified by a poem that also has designs on the reader's belief. In Hopkins' "The Windhover" we are invited to match with the speaker as he in turn matches with the bird and then matches the bird to Christ. The poem, that is, invites us to perform a series of imaginative or "as if" suppositions, the last of which is explicity such: we read as if we were the speaker; the speaker reads his world as if he were at once the bird and its prey ("My heart in hiding/stirred for a bird,—the achieve of, the mastery of the thing!"); the speaker rereads his initial reading as if the bird were not a bird but something different. It is like the "plod" that "makes plough down sillion shine." It is like "blue-bleak

embers" that "fall, gall themselves, and gash gold-vermilion." Most of all it
is like Christ. But this last metaphor is unlike the others: made explicit only in
the epigraph ("To Christ Our Lord"), it is dramatized by the poem itself, in
particular by the poet-speaker's implicit act of poetic composition. In the octet
the poet-speaker represents himself as seeing literally and then, in the sestet, as
making a metaphor for that seeing, a metaphor that not only discovers a religious
significance in the windhover's hovering and stooping but also discovers the
poem to the poet. Indeed, the represented discovery of the metaphor *is* the poem
he has made for us to read, and the epigraph, an *hors du texte* that invades the
text, comments on that making. Once again, a strange loop.

But how, we began by asking, does "The Windhover" sway us to belief?
Precisely by the studied implicitness of its enabling metaphor. By keeping the
limitless implications of his discovery carefully implicit, the poet-speaker protects them from our discounting activity. He claims only that for him this bird
at this moment is like Christ. But because the epigraph has predicted these implications, our reading strives to fulfill this prediction by seeing more than is
"really" there, by seeing the very significance seen by the poet-speaker. We
thus quite literally realize the implication of the bird-Christ metaphor and, in so
doing, make it ours.

But because Browning would more forcefully intrude upon his reader's belief, he needs a strategy that more forcefully commits us to the meaning we
make. In part this strategic need is filled by locating the speaker historically:
what he sees, hears, or even rehears will then seem bonded to actual rather than
imaginative fact. But such bonding also raises a problem: the speaker cannot
now *assert* his belief without opening his assertion to the discounting vicissitudes
of the reader's actual belief or lack thereof. Whether we take his word would
depend less on our reading experience than on the state of our belief as we come
to the poem. Powerless to *change* our minds, a strictly historical "Karshish,"
like a purely lyrical "Karshish," could only confirm an already existent belief
or leave the disbelieving reader unmoved.

Browning's solution was to write the poem as a denial of belief and then
prompt the reader to correct this denial, a correction that, however inadver-
tently, places him in the position of belief. Browning thus has the best of both
worlds, as the ironist always does: he protects his suasive point by its surface
contradiction whereas our contradiction of this contradiction in fact secures it.
But with "Karshish" as with "Cleon," our correcting activity must have a sec-
ular basis or it won't happen—particularly for the unbeliever. Recall that we correct Cleon's denial not for its rejection of Christianity but because his reasoning
is itself unacceptable to believer and unbeliever alike. In "Karshish" the
speaker's ignorance of the historical significance of his encounter puts him at
a similar if less devastating disadvantage vis-à-vis the reader, a disadvantage
that, once again, is the cutting edge of Browning's strategy. Since the Lazarus

story is virtually mythic, Karshish's ignorance manuevers even the unbelieving reader into a position at once superior to the unbeliever and congruent with that of belief.

I have been reading "Cleon" and "Karshish" in terms of their similarities. Indeed, the closeness of their suasive and structural design is such that we follow the hermeneutic grooves of "Karshish" with added agility for having read "Cleon." This is one goal of generic explanation: by remarking similarity we make synecdoches for our criticism. But thinking generically, like all syllogistic and metaphoric thinking, is also thinking of difference, and to value texts as alike as "Cleon" and "Karshish" requires particular attention to their difference. In the preceding chapter I argued that a text's uniqueness is fruitfully if paradoxically laid out in terms of likeness, that to say how a literary text differs from other literary texts we need first to say how it is like these others or, what is the same, to define its genre. In "Cleon" we found that the speaker's lyrically phrased longing for immortality and his prejudiced rejection of that very immortality invite the reader's generically typical act of reconstruction. But in "Karshish," where emphasis is placed not on the speaker's sudden and concluding rejection but rather on his hesitations, his repeated turnings toward and away from belief, our reconstruction is more comlex, more closely woven of lyric and ironic threads. Whereas Cleon forecloses belief despite his desperate need, Karshish is intrigued by the possibility. Whereas the drama of "Cleon" resides in the sudden violence of this foreclosure, the drama of "Karshish" resides in the dialectical struggle of extraordinary with ordinary, of unknown with known, of unique with common, of irreducible and unmediated experience with the thought that reduces it to order and the words that figure its life.

In the opening formalities of the epistle, Karshish characterizes himself and his correspondent. Writing "now the twenty-second time," he establishes the quotidian base against which we will gauge the miracle of Lazarus. He shows himself a careful and curious observer:

> there's a spider here
> Weaves no web, watches on the ledge of tombs,
> Sprinkled with mottles on an ash-grey back;
> (ll. 45–47)

He is a man given to ordering his observations:

> I reach Jerusalem at morn,
> There set in order my experiences,
> Gather what most deserves, and give thee all—
> (ll. 52–54)

He is a man of sufficient modesty to admit he is stumped:

> Scalp-disease
> Confounds me, crossing so with leprosy—
>
> (ll. 57-58)

As in "Cleon" the speaker's character proves strategically central: he must be a careful observer lest we doubt his reporting of events; we must take him seriously, lest we discount his movements toward belief; we must recognize his humility lest we attribute his hesitations to a Cleon-like arrogance rather than to the enormity of the event. Once again, the speaker's character proves the tool of the poem's suasive design, and, once again, he proves complex and seemingly real. As in "Cleon," this complexity seduces, and, again as in "Cleon," its display is inspired by a silent audience, a listener who functions as the speaker's double and thus makes possible his dramatized dialogue with himself.

The text is woven of Karshish's detailed observations of Lazarus, which we accept as accurate, and his interpretations of those observations, which we question. We accept, for instance, Lazarus' own interpretation of his experience, as reported by Karshish, because it meshes with the story Browning assumes we know:

> the man's own firm conviction rests
> That he was dead (in fact they buried him)
> —That he was dead and then restored to life
> By a Nazarene physician of his tribe:
>
> (ll. 97-100)

But we question Karshish's interpretation because it does not mesh and, perhaps more significantly, is conspicuously reductive:

> 'Tis but a case of mania—subinduced
> By epilepsy, at the turning point
> Of trance prolonged unduly some three days:
>
> (ll. 79-81)

The pseudo-scientific jargon prompts our discounting of his interpretation, as does the poem's allusive figuration:

> Contrariwise, he loves both old and young,
> Able and weak, affects the very brutes
> And birds—how say I? flowers of the field—
> As a wise workman recognizes tools
> In a master's workshop, loving what they make.
>
> (ll. 227-31)

Because the gospels are yet unwritten, Karshish here speaks a language whose Biblical resonance is necessarily unkown to him. We, however, do recognize this resonance. As a result, we posit another writer, one more knowing than Karshish, and another genre, one whose formal design includes this resonance and whose suasive design includes this recognition. We posit, that is, a poet and a poem.

Nevertheless, our victory over Karshish is neither as easy nor as certain as was our victory over Cleon. For we are moved to accept Lazarus' version of the miracle not only because it is familiar, an acceptance that casts Karshish's reading in the wrong, but also because Karshish himself, despite his skepticism and empiricism, is transported by the encounter:

> This man so cured regards the curer, then,
> As—God forgive me! who but God himself,
> Creator and sustainer of the world,
> That came and dwelt in flesh on it awhile!
> —'Sayeth that such an one was born and lived,
> Taught, healed the sick, broke bread at his own house,
> Then died, with Lazarus by, for aught I know,
> And yet was . . . what I said nor choose repeat,
> And must have so avouched himself, in fact,
> In hearing of this very Lazarus
> Who saith—but why all this of what he saith?
> Why write of trivial maters, things of price
> Calling at every moment for remark?
> I noticed on the margin of a pool
> Blue-flowering borage, the Aleppo sort,
> Aboundeth, very nitrous. It is strange!
>
> (ll. 267–82)

Such hesitations and retreats dramatize the psychological force of the experience and, however illogically, testify to its actuality. Karshish's attempt to reduce this experience to a "trivial" matter thus makes us doubt not his vision but his reductive reading of that vision. The compound strategy proves irresistible: the more Karshish denies, the more we discount his denial and thereby support what he denies, but these very denials simultaneously lend credence and power to his intermittent surrenders to belief, thereby leading us by yet another route to take the stance of belief. Thus does the poem dynamically tutor us in its reading, a lesson finished when the speaker's final outburst of faith and denial leaves us only one place to stand:

> The very God! think, Abib; dost thou think?
> So, the All-Great, were the All-Loving too—
> So, through the thunder comes a human voice
> Saying, "O heart I made, a heart beats here!

Face, my hands fashioned, see it in myself!
Thou hast no power nor may'st conceive of mine,
But love I gave thee, with myself to love,
And thou must love me who have died for thee!"
The madman saith He said so: it is strange.

(ll. 304-12)

All but the last line reads as if emanating from the poet as well as from Karshish, a lyric reading that makes the thought seem as much ours as theirs. But Karshish ends by performing a final reversal, by dismissing Lazarus as a "madman," the experience as a quirk: "it is strange." These words gather force from their echo of the "blue-flowering borage" passage, from their closural position, and from the completing and correcting activity they prompt in the reader. Using the same technique as in "Cleon," Browning once again asks his reader to question the speaker's answer, once again insists that his reader stand in the stance of belief.

But not in quite the same position, nor with quite the same confidence. Because in "Karshish" the poet is making a larger claim ("So, the All-Great, were the All-Loving too"), he needs his speaker to help him make it. Karshish thus provides not only the "error" that we "correct" but also the model for our correction; he offers us glimpses of the "truth" even as their brevity prompts our revisionary rereading. The resulting dialectical tension once again confirms the poem's generic kinship with "Cleon," but the greater complexity of this tension—the swings between belief and disbelief are at once more frequent and more subtle—distinguishes the poem from its equally polemical twin, thereby defining its uniqueness. We do commit ourselves to the poet's vision and thus to belief, but our commitment, like Karshish's disbelief, is a thing of subtlety.

I began this inquiry into the dramatic monologue with "Cleon" and "Karshish" because their obvious designs on the reader so boldly display the genre's suasive power. But because these poems are also the most literally "written" of Browning's monologues, they simultaneously display its less obvious but no less potent power: the power of words to move us *as* words. Indeed, their rhetoric is as manifestly tropological as it is suasive.[29] As observed above, these monologues can display the conspicuous formality characteristic of poetry without harm to their *vraisemblance* precisely because they mask as epistles. It is when this epistolary mask collapses into the poem that the verisimilar fabric wrinkles or turns back on itself, creating the imaginative or "aesthetic" opacity of conscious illusion.[30] The opening lines of "Cleon" exemplify this turning:

"As certain also of your own poets have said"—

Cleon the poet (from the sprinkled isles,

> Lily on lily, that o'erlace the sea,
> And laugh their pride when the light wave lisps, "Greece")—
> To Protus in his Tyranny: much health!
>   They give thy letter to me, even now;
>   I read and seem as if I heard thee speak;
>
> (ll. 1–6)

Following the practice of the poem's interpretive history, I have treated the line—"As certain also of your own poets have said"—as functioning like "To Christ Our Lord" in "The Windhover." But even for an epigraph the line hovers in a liminal space of unusual ambivalence: it is a guide to interpretation that itself conspicuously demands interpretation, asking us to read it both as the poet's and as Cleon's, asking us to decide who says or, to be precise, who writes it. But the question is unanswerable not only because it seeks to locate the origin and, what is much the same, the textual boundary, but also because this poem particularly delights in thwarting such traditional searches, in displaying, even flaunting its simultaneous and thus paradoxical allegiance to *verba* and to *res*.

Such display occurs throughout, but in the lines just quoted it is most conspicuous in the word "Greece," presented simultaneously as *res*, representing the origin of the epistle, the "sprinkled isles" from which Cleon writes, and as *verba*, a word set forth *as* word, as the sound "the light wave lisps." The dual allegiance also becomes conspicuous as Cleon announces the ever-presentness of his and, by implication, the reader's interpretive activity: "I read and seem as if I hear thee speak." Of course, Cleon's "reading" is in literal fact a writing, as is all critical or intertextual reading, and Protus' "speaking" is in literal fact also a writing, as is all textualized speech. But the power of this and of all dramatic monologues is in large part a power to engender just this seeming: more than any other literary genre, the monologue challenges its maker's power to join the speaking voice to the written word, to invite and reward its reader's act of "as if." When the challenge is successfully met, poet and reader perform this act simultaneously, at once making an illusion and watching the illusion made. In the particular case of "Cleon," the poem convincingly simulates a letter and the poet another poet (for Cleon *is* a poet), yet in the midst of our conviction we are continually reminded that this simulation is just that.

But "Cleon," like many dramatic monologues, not only dramatizes but comments upon the issues that increasingly focus contemporary literary theory: the diseases of representation and the uses of tradition. In *Browning's Beginnings*, Herbert F. Tucker, Jr., has in masterful fashion laid out Cleon's "strict will to interpretive closure" (p. 212), a will that leads him to read his life as itself complete *and* as completing a tradition.[31] According to Tucker, this self-reading in turn leads him to judge himself and "his multifarious accomplishments in poetry, sculpture, painting, and music" as "worthy because of their climactic position" (p. 210). Cleon's judgment, in sum, is "proto-Arnoldian": like all representationalists, he defines value in terms of completion and closure.

As he tells us, Tucker is reading in Derridean fashion, yet in an important sense he reads "Cleon" in the way critics have traditionally read all monologues: as if spoken or written by the characterized "I" and as if the value and interest of the monologue lay in the content of that speaking or writing. In part it surely does. But my continuing argument here is that we can make fuller explanations by discussing such speaking or writing in strategic terms, as but part of a larger design, and by pondering not only what the speaker says but also how we make sense of what is said by the multiple speakers implied by his speech. The point is not that Tucker is not perfectly well aware that Cleon did not write "Cleon," but rather that his explanation turns on this fact no more than did those of earlier critics.

His reading, it is true, unfolds a magnificent Cleon and a profound content:

Cleon is less grotesque than he is horribly great, because he understands the logic of self-possession and pursues that logic to its irresistible conclusion in the vision of his own ashes asleep in their enclosing urn. This vision, the ultimate reduction of human potential, puts "the infinite within the finite" in a sense precisely antithetical to Browning's art. It represents all that his philosophy of the imperfect, and the violent and subtle ploys of his corresponding poetics, endeavor to contest. (P. 218)

But a rhetorical critic would put further questions. Why did Browning choose to "represent" a philosophy "precisely antithetical" to his own? How does the reader read this representation, if that is what it is? Are Cleon's hermeneutic and religious stances only coincidentally related? By way of answer, we might posit a reader who understands not only that Cleon's reach has not exceeded his grasp but also that this lack of excess is to be bitterly mourned, not repeatedly praised. This reader's understanding in part mirrors Cleon's, who himself seems to recognize both the pathos that would attend fulfilled representational desire—"Was the thing done?—then what's to do again?" (1.81)—and its ironic invulnerability: "How shall a certain part, pronounced complete,/Endure effacement by another part?" (ll. 79–80). But this reader's understanding is more than a mirroring. It is active and devastatingly so: his correcting and completing of Cleon's self-reading makes a mockery of such avowed self-sufficiency, thereby redoubling the poem's irony. In this way the reader learns that Cleon's self-ironic stance is but another of his self-aggrandizing maneuvers, that the poem's irony is not undone by Cleon's proleptic proficiency but, rather, is compounded. In the same way, then, that Cleon's reader proved more historically knowing than Cleon, this same reader ends as more hermeneutically knowing: whereas Cleon reads himself, his reader also reads a poem.

That the hermeneutic argument of "Cleon" persuades us in the same manner as the historical suggests that these arguments are finally the same: that once perfection is defined as completion it necessarily abhors even the possibility of new and endless beginnings, whether they be human or hermeneutic. Like Karshish, Cleon is a writer who is self-consciously writing himself even as he is written by another writer, the poet who writes the poem. But his self-consciousness proves at once too developed for ready belief and too naive for self-salvation: he fails to realize that his will to interpretive closure closes off the very possibility of an afterlife, both spiritually and intertextually. He also seems not to realize that he is closing off the redemptive possibility latent in his correspondence with Protus. For Cleon's letter seems not only to end but, in ending, to be an end: "Live long and happy, and in that thought die;/Glad for what was! Farewell." It terminates the correspondence both in the literal sense, in that it is difficult to imagine Protus' ever writing back, and in Gombrich's sense, in that Cleon here abandons the attempt to bring about the meeting of minds, the correspondence or, as Gombrich would say, the matching that is the goal of all suasion.

The emergent lesson is that of Eliot's "Tradition and the Individual Talent": that "no poet, no artist has his complete meaning alone," that the writer's self or text is not only open-ended, it is Janus-faced.[32] Closely scrutinized, completion reveals itself to be not only a perfection but also an ending, a silence, and a death. By no accident is Cleon's greatest horror felt as he imagines himself asleep in his urn or, as Donne and Keats have taught their own interpretive tradition to say, his well-wrought words. By inscribing himself without leaving open the possibility of future rewriting, whether by himself or by others, he would immortalize himself, but the end of such an immortality is undone by its means: it necessarily proves a cold and silent canonization, one from which not "a soul to tell" the story of his desolation "can e'er return."[33] Of course, the reader of Browning's poem does return, tutored, as by many of Browning's poems, in the intolerable wages of literalized representational striving. But the lesson of "Cleon" is the most explicitly mortuary, teaching that the intertwined closures for which its speaker strives—temporal and traditional, human and divine, hermeneutic and self-inscriptional—are not only not salvational, they relentlessly delimit and, in fine, embalm the self.

"Cleon" thus pushes the logic of our self-immortalizing desire to its bizarre conclusion, exposing the Thanatotic consequence of the very logic traditionally employed in attempting to evade our end. But does not this exposure contradict the Christian solution so heavily implicit in this monologue? Only if negation is confused with loss. For it is the traditional Christian distinction between the two that creates the possibility and significance of sacrifice, including the sacrifice of previous selves necessary to the writing of a present self. Yet another way of phrasing Cleon's error, then, is to say that he fails to recognize this necessity: that self-writing requires self-erasure, that the presence of the present self is composed of the negation of previous selves, of the textualized vestiges from which their replacement is woven or written. Cleon, moreover, compounds his error by displacing the seemingly "natural" mourning of his past self into the future, mourning in advance a self who sleeps in his urn. The wonderful illogic of both mournings, of course, is that their enactment precisely defies their content: they give words, substance, and hence life to the self who presently writes. But the monologic speaker is blind to this illogic. It and his blindness are visible to his reader alone.

Like "Cleon" and "Karshish," Browning's other great monologues—one thinks particularly of "The Bishop Orders His Tomb," "Andrea del Sarto," and "Fra Lippo Lippi"—also have designs on their readers. But because their polemical energy is subdued and their speakers less boldly drawn, their affective designs are more difficult to define. In the preceding pages I imply that "Karshish" is a more complex if not a more powerful poem than "Cleon" because both reader and speaker perform not one reconstruction but many. The multiplicity of these self-revisionary acts perplex not only the speaker but our reading experience. The design of "Karshish" on its reader is thus more elusive, an elusiveness that may be generalized as follows: the more conspicuous a monologue's poetic patterning and the more introspective its speaker, the more difficult the definition of its suasive design. The following readings would justify this generalization and, thereby, our developing generic model. But they would also argue against another generalization, more easily and commonly made: that a "poetic" poem and a complex speaker signal the absence of suasive design. As I am arguing throughout, a conspicuously "poetic" design is not less designing than one that is conspicuously polemical. It is simply—or not so simply— more devious.

Defending against Death: "The Bishop Orders His Tomb"

The interpretive histories of dramatic monologues repeatedly testify to the lure of realism. To discuss speakers such as the Bishop, Andrea, and Fra Lippo as if they were found and gratuitous, as independent of the poet's making and irrelevant to the poem's suasive design, is an apparently irresistible temptation. But we can learn much by provisionally succumbing to this temptation and asking, for example, why the Bishop speaks and why he speaks as he does. Langbaum gives this answer:

> We find that the motive for speaking is inadequate to the utterance, that
> the utterance is in other words largely gratuitous—it need never have

occurred. The result is that the dramatic situation . . . serves an ultimately self-expressive or lyrical purpose.

. . .

Even where the speaker's motives come closer to the business at
hand—as where the Bishop wants to convince his sons to give him the
magnificent tomb he plans, or Andrea del Sarto wants to convince
Lucrezia to spend the evening home with him—there remains a superabundance of expression, more words, ingenuity and argument than seem necessary for the purpose. (P. 182)

This treatment of the speaker's character as something real, as a content that the
monologue bodies forth, dominates the interpretive history, although Langbaum
alone exposes its devaluing logic: when the motive for speaking seems inadequate to the utterance, then that utterance becomes largely gratuitous.

But mimesis is not the only critical language that concludes thus. Even the
most expressly nonmimetic of critical languages similarly equates character with
person, person with poem. Roma A. King's *The Bow and the Lyre*, our finest
formalist study of Browning's monologues, is a case in point. Like most readers
of "The Bishop Orders His Tomb," King finds that its irony issues from the
juxtaposition of two ways of seeing or valuing, and like many readers he concludes that the poem is nevertheless "not a persuasive for any point of view or
code of behaviour, that is, the discrepancies do not exist between Browning's
obviously 'right' world and the Bishop's obviously 'wrong' one."[34] This lack
of suasive design is considered a "poetic" virtue. But King, unlike these
readers, concludes that the poem's oft-remarked tropological elaborateness, the
tendency of its words to call attention to themselves *as* words, issues from and
thereby characterizes the speaker himself: "The decorative elements of his
style, then perform a double function. They mark him as a man of learning and
culture, but at the same time, because of their tenuous relationship to the thought
of the poem, suggest his lack of intellectual and moral depth" (p. 60).

King's formalist language enables him to discuss rather than dismiss the
verbal artifice of the monologue, but his mimetic conception of character nevertheless leads him to speak against his language by locating the source of the
poem's art in the speaker rather than in the poet implied by this "speech." Thus
do both Langbaum, whose critical language has only negative words for verbal
artifice, and King, whose critical language has words for little else, remain similarly silent on the strategic design of Browning's art. Both muster sophisticated
arguments: Langbaum decides that these poems are ultimately lyrics, but this
decision commits him to treating them as if they were the *speaker*'s lyrics; King
welcomes the irony, but because his language lacks a conceptual grammar for
discussing the reader's experience of the monologue, he finds that irony difficult

to justify. In each of these otherwise radically different readings, readings that synecdochically map the boundaries of the monologue's interpretive history and plot its primary conflict, the poem is read essentially in terms of its speaker, only incidentally in terms of its poet and its reader.

However variously, then, the interpretive history of "The Bishop Orders His Tomb" explains the poem's irony as a discrepancy between the Bishop's view of himself and another perspective somehow implied by the poem. But many poems could be explained in these terms and, indeed, most monologues are, a point that suggests that the traditional readings are less "wrong" than too general: they effectively articulate a generic intuition but remain mute to this particular poem's unique power. Both Langbaum and King recognize the inadequacy of the generic explanation, but their attempts to remedy this inadequacy are doubly blocked: by the speaker's conspicuous verisimilitude and by the mimetic model of character that his verisimilitude seems to confirm.

Let us take a different tack and attempt to lay out the strategic choices that plausibly went into the poem's making. John Ruskin's reading is a good starting place, in large part because virtually every subsequent critic has used it to supplement his own:

> I know of no other piece of modern English, prose or poetry, in which there is so much told, as in these lines, of the Renaissance spirit,—its worldliness, inconsistency, pride, hypocrisy, ignorance of itself, love of art, of luxury, and of good Latin. It is nearly all that I have said of the central Renaissance in thirty pages of the *Stones of Venice*, put into as many lines, Browning's also being the antecedent work.[35]

The interpretive history repeatedly affirms the explanatory value of Ruskin's insight. It no less repeatedly affirms that the poem is a dramatic monologue. Taken together, these two affirmations suggest a beginning premise: "The Bishop Orders His Tomb" captures the spirit of the Italian Renaissance by leading its reader to make the corrective and completing maneuvers here defined as characteristic of the dramatic monologue, maneuvers that finally sever the speaker's meaning from the poem's. This particularized premise or definition is initially justified by its typicality: "Andrea del Sarto," "Fra Lippo Lippi," "My Last Duchess," and many monologues in *The Ring and the Book* share a similar goal and technique. But this very typicality immediately raises another question: What sets this monologue apart? Ruskin's comment itself suggests an answer by defining the monologue's "Renaissance spirit" in terms of "worldliness, inconsistency, pride, hypocrisy, ignorance of itself, love of art, of luxury, and of good Latin." But lest this definition be itself seen as necessary, we need only remark the cheery robustness of Fra Lippo's "Renaissance spirit" or the dispassionate intellection of the Pope's in *The Ring and the Book* to realize that the *Zeitgeist* of this monologue is no less chosen and specific than is the speaker himself.

Let us then speculate about the composition of a poem that would make us realize, in the full sense of that word, this Renaissance spirit—not only its power but also its price. To begin with the generic choice, the dramatic monologue is apt: its reader will seem to discover for himself the tarnish on the Bishop's brightness. Because the overtness of a position opens it to rejection, the speaker should speak forcefully on his own behalf. And the stronger his case, the greater the irony generated by its failure. He should be a man of sensuality, learning, and aesthetic sensitivity: hence the love of luxury, good Latin, and art. And since these "loves" reached a combined and conspicuous height in the Italian Renaissance, he should be of that time. Even better, let him be a churchman, particularly of high rank, a choice that will generate expectations whose frustration will further heighten the irony. This last choice also settles the speaker's sex. A deathbed setting is perfect: it wonderfully concentrates a man's mind on the errors of his ways. But unlike Ivan Ilych the Bishop should not realize his error, lest our ironic pleasure and edification be lessened. Still, he must be seductive: his dilemma will otherwise be too easily dismissed, the reader's superiority too easily achieved. So we will give him a rich imagination and verbal virtuosity. He will be a poet or poet-like. And to whom should he speak his "poetry"? Only sons will by their very existence amplify the ironic counterpoint of what is and what should be. What should he speak about? Life and death to be sure, but we will dramatically particularize this well-worn topic by presenting the Bishop in the act of ordering his tomb. Browning himself apparently intended to emphasize the Bishop's "ordering," rejecting as possible titles "The Bishop" and "The Tomb at St. Praxed's" for "The Bishop Orders His Tomb at Saint Praxed's Church." This choice precisely locates the Bishop's worldly pride: it resides in his power to order a grandiose self-monument. But for added drama and ironic point, he will not have the power to *build* that tomb. Rather he must plead with others to build it for him: hence the pathos and the agon. Of course his pleas will be denied, widening further the discrepancy between how he sees himself and how he is seen. But the irony should be complex as well as bold, so of course it should be his own sons who deny him.

Browning may or may not have made the choices this elaborated definition suggests. Such a definition does not claim correspondent verity but, rather, pragmatic power: it is designed for the express explanatory purpose of unfolding and justifying the poem's aesthetic richness and ethical point. Emphasizing the strategic nature of the speaker and his situation as well as the paradoxical nature of the reading experience, it shows how we immerse ourselves in the Bishop's perspective in order to experience the full force of its seductiveness and yet retreat from that perspective in order to experience the full force of its irony.

It shows, in other words, how we perform an act of conscious illusion: deeply immersed, we yet know our immersion for the illusion it is.

The capacity to engender and reward such conscious illusion defines the distinctive power of the genre. While many poems are made to sound like speech, dramatic monologues are uniquely adept at creating the illusion of someone speaking *and* at making us aware of that illusion. Their characteristically dense and explicit figuration joins with their speaker's implicit error to opacify the verisimilar surface, repeatedly turning the poem and our attention back on themselves. But this generic capacity to engender and reward conscious illusion can and should be made specific as well: the Bishop must seem to be real, to be really speaking, and to be in a real predicament; he must also seem to be himself spoken and his seeming reality to serve a larger design. Our imaginative belief and emotional immersion require the success of the illusion even as our ironic pleasure and edification require that we see the illusion as just that. Attending to this paradox is, I would argue, the single most important factor in making satisfying explanations of these problematic and powerful poems. Without such attention we "see" only the more visible half of the reader's paradoxical experience: his recognition of the speaker's seeming reality and the speech's seeming literality or "naturalness."

This paradox must challenge the making of the poem much as it does the explaining. The Bishop is on his deathbed, rapidly alternating and at times conflating the real and imagined worlds. It would seem that his "naturalistic" discourse could tolerate little evidence of a designing presence. But the seemingly incompatible demands of verisimilitude and artifice are once again met as each is made to answer the other's end as well as its own. On the one hand, "The Bishop Orders His Tomb" displays its "poetry": it has a marked beginning, middle, and end; the dominant meter is noticeably iambic; most lines have ten syllables; its tropological richness marks its difference from ordinary discourse. On the other hand, it seems to happen "naturally": its beginning and ending coincide with the sons' arrival and departure as well as with the Bishop's invocation and concluding blessing; it is replete with stops and starts, with the broken syntax of half-formed thought; its erotic figuration seems to mirror a mind as sensual as it is wandering.

In other words, art and artlessness coexist, not only here and there but throughout:

> Draw close: that conflagration of my church
> —What then? So much was saved if aught were missed!
> My sons, ye would not be my death? Go dig
> The white-grape vineyard where the oil-press stood,
> Drop water gently till the surface sink,

> And if ye find . . . Ah, God, I know not, I! . . .
> Bedded in store of rotten fig-leaves soft,
> And corded up in a tight olive-frail,
> Some lump, ah God, of *lapis lazuli*,
> Big as a Jew's head cut off at the nape,
> Blue as a vein o'er the Madonna's breast . . .
>
> (ll. 34–44)

This art seems real because its "strangeness" is "natural" for both its immediate and covert speakers, for both the "poetic" Bishop and the poet who made him. It also seems real because the overt and covert genres coincide, because, for example, the Bishop's beginning and the poet's beginning seem one:

> Vanity, saith the preacher, vanity!
> Draw round my bed: is Anselm keeping back?
>
> (ll. 1–2)

The Bishop is presumably thinking, as we are meant to think, of the lines from Ecclesiastes 1:2: "Vanity of vanities, saith the preacher; all is vanity." A bishop on his deathbed fittingly alludes to such a text, and a poem that preaches the ironies that plague earthly glory fittingly opens with the text it thematizes.[36] The dramatic occasion likewise wears the air of reality: the sons draw near the bed; the Bishop orders and then pleas for his tomb; the sons deny him and depart. A few verbal stumbles, an occasional incompleteness of thought and syntax are all that is needed to make poetry seem speech.

But this "men in action" plot cannot explain away the felt excesses and digressiveness of the Bishop's discourse, nor can the signs of verbal naturalness lessen the attention-getting opacity of the verbal medium.[37] In the midst of hearing his speech we are continually reminded that we are reading a poem. Indeed, the Bishop's seeming realness is itself a matter of paradoxical design. Endowed with what Langbaum terms "superabundance of expression, more words, ingenuity and argument than seem necessary for the purpose," the Bishop exceeds our understanding and seems to live independently of the poet's creating presence, at once the source and end of his own being. As Kenneth Burke has argued, it is precisely such superabundance that fulfills Pygmalion's desire:

> In order to make a given character seem "real," the author must endow him with more traits than those most directly needed to account for his actions strictly in terms of his role, as determined by the particular needs of the plot. For the ends of verisimilitude may be shown to require that a character should not be too perfectly adapted to his specific function in furthering the plot just as one could not design even so simple a tool as a carpenter's hammer that could be used only for the purpose of driving nails.[38]

Thus are we persuaded that the Bishop is real, but this suasion ought not dissuade us from recognizing that he and all his gratuitous excess are designed *in order* to draw us into his perspective and convince us of its glory. Moreover, the way we know him is itself designed to deepen our sense of his realness and thus our imaginative immersion. We seem to see him from within and without simultaneously, a double vision that gives the Bishop a tactile roundness lacking in a lyric speaker, seen only from within.

When reading in terms of a mimetic language, the achievement of such a character's "realness" signals the absence of art. When read strategically, however, such achieved artlessness becomes itself an art. But King's objection—that the images have "a tenuous relationship to the thought of the poem" and thus imply the Bishop's "lack of intellectual and moral depth"—yet remains unanswered, and the purpose of the poem's energizing paradox—the suasive rationale behind the simultaneity of its artlessness and artifice—remains obscure. Why, we need to know, is the poetic elaborateness of the Bishop's discourse so emphatic? And why are we continually reminded that we are reading "as if"? The Bishop's attempt to persuade his sons to build the tomb so little requires that he speak a poem that for this immediate purpose his "poetry" is not only superfluous but also counterproductive. He himself seems to realize its futility, and yet he continues.

The interpretive history of the poem shows that these questions cannot be answered in terms of the speaker without "discovering" flaws in the poem. Hence King's objection. But does not the repeatedly remarked gratuitousness of both the poem's "poetry" and its speaker's motive suggest the direction an answer might take? Does it not suggest that the poem's densely tropological verbal surface and the Bishop's suasive persistence in the face of obvious defeat are intimately, even reflexively, related? A critical language of rhetoric, particularly a rhetoric that refuses its traditional separation into tropology and suasion, would answer "yes" to these questions. Such a language would give us a way of saying that the act "literally" represented by the poem, the Bishop's ordering of his tomb, masks another activity for which this first is both ironic emblem and deceptive tool. The Bishop, in other words, is fencing with death, and his strategic foil is the very imaginative sensuality that proves his doom. He never recognizes this double edge, but because we read not only his self but the poem, we dwell knowingly in his "as if"—ness, learning as he does not that lapis and peachstone are fragile and devious foils.

Elder Olson has argued that poetic images "should suggest a color clearer or brighter than would apply to the real perception, since mental images are necessarily fainter than real perceptions."[39] If this is so, then the Bishop is the master imagist, his tropes displaying no less than a Keatsian grasp of multisensory sensuousness:

> And then how I shall lie through centuries,
> And hear the blessed mutter of the mass,
> And see God made and eaten all day long,
> And feel the steady candle-flame, and taste
> Good strong thick stupefying incense-smoke!
> For as I lie here, hours of the dead night,
> Dying in state and by such slow degrees,
> I fold my arms as if they clasped a crook
> And stretch my feet forth straight as stone can point,
> And let the bedclothes, for a mortcloth, drop
> Into great laps and folds of sculptor's-work:
> And as yon tapers dwindle, and strange thoughts
> Grow, with a certain humming in my ears,
> About the life before I lived this life,
> And this life too . . .
>
> (ll. 80–94)

As in Keats's odes the tropological density of these lines attracts us to the speaker's vision, persuading us, however provisionally, to see, think, and feel as if we were he. But in finding the Bishop to be the source of his own poetry I come close to finding him to be the source of his own poem—the position I began by arguing against. The discrimination is this: reading Keats's odes we treat the speaker as if he were the poet in part because of his tropological activity, and for the same reason we treat the Bishop as if he were *like* a poet. This "like" is of the essence here, for it registers the double "as if" character of our imaginative activity as we read this poem and, indeed, all monologues. That is, our lyric or "as if" empathy for the Bishop is contained within and finally undone by our ironic or doubly "as if" awareness.

I am arguing, then, that the "poetry" of the Bishop is neither gratuitious to his thought, as King suggests, nor to the poem, as Langbaum suggests. Quite the contrary. The Bishop's troping is the *means* by which he thinks about and would defend against death. It is also the means by which the poem reveals itself to us *as a poem*. The critical language I am here using resembles Harold Bloom's in *A Map of Misreading*, which analogizes a Freudian theory of defense mechanisms and a rhetorical theory of tropes.[40] Bloom deftly alternates the two, arguing each in terms of the other: hence an "antithetical" criticism. And what is defended against? The answer is simple: death. For Bloom, then, writing is infused with purpose: "a poem is written to escape dying" (p. 19). And how is this purpose achieved? By using tropes, trope being defined as "a willing error" (p. 93). And why do tropes work? Because they enable our escape from literal meaning, which Bloom analogizes as death. The argument strongly echoes Vaihinger's in its emphasis on the utility of conscious and conspicuous

error, but it also echoes the argument of "Cleon" in its analogizing of representational desire—the longing for the literal, the complete, the closed, and the
silent—with the death wish. Bloom captures both echoes in the following "antithetical formula":

> Death is therefore a kind of literal meaning, or from the standpoint of
> poetry, *literal meaning is a kind of death. Defenses can be said to trope
> against death, rather in the same sense that tropes can be said to defend
> against literal meaning.* (P. 91)

As it is stated, the analogy is usefully appropriated by a rhetorical language,
but when modified it becomes yet more so. Whereas Bloom analogizes the relationship of trope to literal meaning as *like* the relationship or psychic defense
to death, so that "*Defenses can be said to trope against death*" in the same way
that "*tropes can be said to defend against literal meaning*," a rhetorical language would collapse the analogy into paradox, asserting that tropes do defend
against literal meaning and that defenses do trope against death. Thus modifying
Bloom's analogical grammar to a paradoxical or Vaihingerian grammar enables
us to say that this imaginative contradiction or troping *is* the force that "drives"
thought or, as it is here particularized, that the Bishop's troping *is* his defense
against death. And this modified conceptual grammar enables us to argue that
not only is the Bishop's troping not merely ornamental to his thought, it is the
very warp of its fabric and, thereby, the source of the poem's power. For
although the Bishop does not expressly choose and hold in conscious awareness
his troping, the reader does just that: whereas the Bishop creates an illusion, we
are conscious both of his illusion and, finally, of our own. The dooming irony,
then, inheres not in the failure of the Bishop's troping against death, since fail
we all ultimately must, but in his failure to know his own tropologically engendered illusions as such.

We veer very close to the speaker in this monologue, and its power in large
part issues from the closeness of this approach, from the way in which our
aesthetic and dramatic fascination with the Bishop's troping draws us into his
agon despite our growing awareness of its futility. Nevertheless, the irony
defined as the distinctive effect of the form requires the ultimate triumph of our
awareness over his. The creative problem, then, we may posit as having been
this: heighten our empathy and the poem approaches a lyric form and effect;
heighten our superiority and the poem approaches comedy. The solution, which
justifies both the poem's distinctive power and its distinctive explanatory difficulty, was to heighten both until the last possible moment—at which point the
Bishop slips into the tomb his poetry has made.

As the poem concludes, then, the pathos intensifies, and the tropological
threatens to unite with the literal. This union would be equivalent to the Bishop's
becoming conscious of his self-engendered illusion.

                                            Stone—
        Gritstone, a-crumble! Clammy squares which sweat
        As if the corpse they keep were oozing through—
        And no more *lapis* to delight the world!
        Well go! I bless ye. Fewer tapers there,
        But in a row: and, going, turn your backs
        —Ay, like departing altar-ministrants,
        And leave me in my church, the church for peace . . .
                                    (ll. 115–122)

If the poem were to end here, the failure of the Bishop's tropological battle with
death and his sons would be clear. But the superiority of our vision would be
threatened by his apparently deepening awareness, by the religious dignity of the
closing tableau (the Bishop as master imagist once more), by the pathos of "no
more *lapis* to delight the world!" Most of all it would be threatened by the increasing self-consciousness of his illusion: "Clammy squares which sweat *as if*
the corpse they keep were oozing through."

    But the last three lines release us from the Bishop's imaginative hold and hand
us over to the poet's:

        That I may watch at leisure if he leers—
        Old Gandolf, at me, from his onion-stone,
        As still he envied me, so fair she was!
                                    (ll. 123–25)

From the poem's beginning the Bishop's ancient sexual rivalry with Gandolf has
kept the tragic in check. In conclusion, just as our pity and fear rise to their full
strength, Gandolf reappears and, with him, the poem's comedy. The revival of
the Bishop's sexual vanity, inappropriate not only because he is a Bishop, not
only because he is dying, but also because his rival no longer exists, joins us
firmly to the poet's ironic vision.

    But we also abandon the Bishop because, like Cleon, he has literally en-
tombed himself or, what both poems teach is the same, because he has refused
to know the salvational power of his own imagining. He has chosen the literal
over the figurative, opted for the death that is born of perfectly fulfilled representational desire. There is, of course, a difference: whereas Cleon imagines
himself asleep in his urn, the Bishop imagines himself watching "at leisure,"
eternally frozen in an unfulfillable desire congeneric with that of the lovers on
Keats's urn. But this difference pales before their common fate: Cleon and the
Bishop end similarly embalmed, equally closed to future possibility and life.
Their reader, however, is saved. By the grace of his correcting and completing
reading, he opens the poem and himself to just such possibility and life, his
reconstructive act once again turning the poem and its reading back on them-

selves in strange loop fashion, once again "putting the infinite within the finite."

The Fault of Faultless Fancy: "Andrea del Sarto"

"The Bishop Orders His Tomb" plays our desire for separateness against our desire for union, the intellect against sensation, irony against empathy, our immersion in illusion against our awareness of that illusion as such. The paradoxical tension engendered by the attempt to sustain these contraries heightens toward a concluding release: separateness, intellect, irony, and conscious illusion suddenly triumph—and the poem just as suddenly ends. Yet this victory would be hollow rather than heuristic were it not difficult. If the agon between speaker and reader were missing or even diminished, the poem's power would be passive, purely "aesthetic." We shall find that the contraries of "Andrea del Sarto" are similarly but yet more strongly stressed, and for this reason alone it is perhaps Browning's finest and most powerful monologue—a valuation with which he himself agreed. Led to understand Andrea's search for self-knowledge as an exercise in self-deception, we are allowed our understanding only after reenacting both search and deceit.

Andrea purportedly speaks to persuade his wife Lucrezia to spend the evening with him rather than her "cousin," who, as both reader and speaker know, is not her cousin but her lover. Yet once again the speaker's emotional and verbal extravagance is in conspicuous excess of the facts as he himself presents them, an excess that once again has defied explanation in mimetic terms. We can make better sense of the monologue by arguing that it showcases Andrea's suasive failure not simply in order to represent an interesting drama but in order to achieve the poet's suasive end: to convince us of the error and consequences of choosing limited perfection over the richly imperfect, of choosing the "toned down" art over that whose reach deliberately exceeds its grasp.

Andrea makes this choice in the present of the poem. We seem to assist at the event. This temporal immediacy is necessary to our emotional response—a *fait accompli* would engage us only intellectually—but we must be made to see its significance as well as feel its vividness, to see that this particular choice patterns his earthly life and, as we in conclusion learn, his afterlife as well. Hence the fabric of retrospection and anticipation. To focus discussion on Andrea's present-tense attempt to persuade Lucrezia is to find his speech and Browning's poem primarily "lyrical" and inexplicably motivated. But to posit a poet and a poem as well as a speaker and a speech is to posit a reader who learns from both his attempts to match and his attempts to judge. The result is a poem of aesthetic *and* ethical design, one whose overwrought surface and seemingly real speaker are equally essential to its heuristic power. Like all monologues, then,

"Andrea del Sarto" is a strategic maze. It would simultaneously engender an illusion and make it conscious, encourage our sympathy as well as our judgment, invite our matching but thwart its success. "Andrea," however, is even more deliberate and devious than the monologues just read, for it would additionally tutor us in the perfidies of the expressly conscious illusion, in the fault of the deliberately faultless fancy.

Once again, the speaker is sensitive, cultured, and articulate. Like Cleon and the Bishop, Andrea is designed to seduce, and the fact that we are alone with his mind increases its seductiveness. Once again, our search for a covert speaker and a full meaning vies with this double seduction. To know where Andrea goes wrong we need to feel as he feels and see as he sees, but this privileged access tempts us to acquiescence, to a knowing that resists the knowledge we finally gain. In this affective contradiction lies the generic thrust of all dramatic monologues, but the best monologues are good precisely because they intensify this struggle, making the contradictory dynamics of our reading conscious. Thus in "Andrea del Sarto" the reminiscences and fantasies from which Andrea weaves the text of his self create our lyric alliance, but their damning content and tropological skewing simultaneously awaken that alliance, straining it to rupture.

In Browning's bolder monologues the disjunction between reader and speaker issues as much from the speaker's moral fault as from his faulty vision. In "Porphyria's Lover" and "My Last Duchess" the innocence of the murdered beloved shines through the morally and, it would seem, optically clouded eyes of the speaker. But "Andrea del Sarto" offers neither an unfallen Porphyria nor a victimized Duchess to simplify our response and make it bold. Indeed, Lucrezia's turpitude shows unambiguously black against the twilight grayness of her husband's, and this contrast hinders our moral judgment of Andrea, clearing space for sympathy. We want to believe what Andrea believes, to believe that were it not for Lucrezia he would have been a Leonardo or a Raphael:

> But all the play, the insight and the stretch—
> Out of me, out of me! And wherefore out?
> Had you enjoined them on me, given me soul,
> We might have risen to Rafael, I and you!
> Nay, Love, you did give all I asked, I think—
> More than I merit, yes, by many times.
> But had you—oh, with the same perfect brow,
> And perfect eyes, and more than perfect mouth,
> And the low voice my soul hears, as a bird
> The fowler's pipe, and follows to the snare—
> Had you, with these the same, but brought a mind!
> Some women do so. Had the mouth there urged,
> "God and the glory! never care for gain,

> The present by the future, what is that?
> Live for fame, side by side with Agnolo!
> Rafael is waiting: up to God, all three!''
> I might have done it for you.
>
> (ll. 116–132)

This passage typifies the affective riskiness of the entire monologue. Andrea paints himself as a man seduced by the "low voice" that his "soul hears, as a bird/The fowler's pipe, and follows to the snare.'' To see the comparison is in large part to see its justice: the greater our beholder's share, the more the meaning seems ours and the more the metaphor of its making dies into the thing itself. Our interpretation, in other words, comes to seem less interpretation than fact, and insofar as it does we are effectively seduced.

But our assenting vision would prove as ephemeral as Andrea's self-respect did he himself not imediately revise this too convenient indictment of his wife and assume the burden of his failure:

> So it seems:
> Perhaps not. All is as God overrules.
> Beside, incentives come from the soul's self;
> The rest avail not. Why do I need you?
> What wife had Rafael, or has Agnolo?
> In this world, who can do a thing, will not;
> And who would do it, cannot, I perceive:
> Yet the will's somewhat—somewhat, too, the power—
> And thus we half-men struggle.
>
> (ll. 132–40)

Here as throughout Andrea proves a superb dialectician. He defends himself by anticipating and thus finessing the objections of an audience that, like those of "Cleon'' and "Karshish,'' is not only the speaker's self but also the poem's reader. But Andrea is additionally devious, greedily acquisitive of proleptic power. Unlike the self-writings of Cleon and Karshish, his prefigures its reading throughout, just as that reading in turn prefigures its own rereading. In other words, Andrea's revisions always precede ours, and so we are doubly lured into a naive dependency on his dazzling hermeneutics. The precedence of his self-correction not only teaches us to value a self-aware "half-man'' over one whose integrity is held unawares, it also blocks attempts to move beyond that valuation. He is our tutor, and his errors ours to repeat.

But we have defined the dramatic monologue in agonistic terms. However intense our sympathy for Andrea as a "person,'' however enthralled our imagination, however confuted, tempered, and retarded our judgment—the generic effect nevertheless demands that judgment. We may posit, then, that the creative challenge was to build judgment into our sympathy, a challenge ingeniously met by making our every move toward Andrea a move away and vice versa. The ironic and predictive force of the epigraph, "Called 'The Faultless Painter,' " is thus both confuted by Andrea's conspicuous awareness of the fault inherent in his "faultlessness" and confirmed by his ethically faulty use of this very self-awareness. And whenever Andrea argues most seductively he simultaneously displays the fault of a facile faultlessness—the too easy acquiescence, the too convenient philosophy, the virtually blasphemous placement of blame:

> Love, we are in God's hand.
> How strange now, looks the life he makes us lead;
> So free we seem, so fettered fast we are!
> I feel he laid the fetter: let it lie!
>
> (ll. 49–52)

True, Andrea's placid acceptance of his pandering and stealing lulls our condemnation, but this exaggerated placidity itself finally makes us suspicious:

> I am grown peaceful as old age to-night,
> I regret little, I would change still less.
> Since there my past life lies, why alter it?
>
> (ll. 244–46)

Similarly, Andrea's display of Lucrezia's indifference and perfidy damns her, deflecting blame from himself, but it in turn damns him as well:

> Must you go?
> That Cousin here again? he waits outside?
> Must see you—you, and not with me? Those loans?
> More gaming debts to pay? you smiled for that?
> Well, let smiles buy me! have you more to spend?
> While hand and eye and something of a heart
> Are left me, work's my ware, and what's it worth?
> I'll pay my fancy.
>
> (ll. 219–25)

"Loans," "debts," "buy," "spend," "ware," "worth," "pay": for Andrea this economics is the language of love. His art transfigures to coin and his soul to barter. Once again, Andrea is not unaware of the moral humiliation inherent in this transfiguration—such unawareness would diminish both his stature and our response—but the habit and dissonance of his figurative language make it conspicuous, turning our attention at once to the textual surface and to its ultimate maker.

The poem's interpretive history has dwelt upon this tropological density, but, as with "The Bishop Orders His Tomb," even formalist critics have found its justification difficult. Read as purely ornamental to the speaker's or poet's thought, as a cloth that cloaks even as it adorns, it becomes a purely "aesthetic" beauty, a passive virtue strategically irrelevant to the poem's emotional and heuristic power. Only a rhetorical language can articulate how the monologue's tropological rhetoric drives its suasive rhetoric and vice versa. Thus Andrea's self-figuration as a bird snared by Lucrezia and fettered by God enables him both to displace his failure and to make this displacement so conspicuous it becomes suspect—even to himself: "So it seems;/Perhaps not." Like the extended figuration of coin, the avian metaphor gives him a way of turning or troping guilt to his self-declared end of self-justification, but, once again, this turning returns to haunt him. Like the Bishop, then, Andrea wields tropes as a defense. But there are two critical differences: whereas the Bishop defends against death Andrea defends against himself, in particular, against the threat of self-judgment; whereas the Bishop fails to know his tropes as such, Andrea's use is self-conscious, purposeful, even cannily poetic. His defense, in short, is just that. It is a "strange loop," a daring attempt to use strange or "poetic" language to confuse and confute his—and our—every attempt to judge.

This confusion, moreover, is strategically compounded throughout by the "content" of the tropes. Like many of Browning's monologues, "Andrea del Sarto" is a painterly poem, and so its tropes, which are predominantly visual, are more than usually deceptive in their painting of the psychic drama. The vehicle is deceptively at one with the tenor, the figurative cloth with the literal body:

> A common greyness silvers everything,—
> All in a twilight, you and I alike
> —You, at the point of your first pride in me
> (That's gone you know),—but I, at every point;
> My youth, my hope, my art, being all toned down
> To yonder sober pleasant Fiesole.
>
> (ll.35–40)

Once again the metaphor Andrea makes is fully within his awareness, the temptations of shared awareness and tropological mastery too great for us to resist. Or so it seems. For Andrea himself tutors us in the maneuvers of objection, and, as we learn to anticipate his self-reading, we also learn that the tropological convergence of atmospheric and moral monotones is too practiced to work, the quiet of the tableau too studied not to become itself disquieting. Our reading, in short, grows careful, even cagey.

Yet even this readerly lesson is made difficult, continually perplexed by another: the spectacular, even garish contradiction provided by the gold that is at once the cause and counterpoint of the poem's neutral tones. Just as silver tarnishes when made to serve Andrea's ends, so gold also acquires a talent for self-irony. The longer and more closely we read, the more the gold of Lucrezia's hair, of Francis' money, and of the very walls built from that money seem to shine with a brightness that is unnatural and, as Andrea himself says, "fierce":

> God is just.
> King Francis may forgive me; oft at nights
> When I look up from painting, eyes tired out,
> The walls become illumined, brick from brick
> Distinct, instead of mortar, fierce bright gold,
> That gold of his I did cement them with!
> Let us but love each other.
>
> (ll. 213-19)

Couched to invite our objection, Andrea's vision here collapses into the poet's subsuming vision. It is the rasping juxtaposition of God and gold that warps this deceptively smooth text, that teaches us to condemn Andrea for the tactlessness of his tactics, for using God to justify gold. His concluding plea to Lucrezia similarly contradicts its prelude of stolen gold, a speaking against or warping that further opacifies Andrea's vision and shows us the poet's.

But if similarity implies difference, so too does difference imply similarity. If Andrea's vision is opaque, it also has its points of lyric transparence, where untainted gold and his love for Lucrezia shine through, where we do, if only provisionally, see as he sees. At such points our understanding and empathy implicate us in the speaker's fate, as they do in lyrics, and because we are implicated our developing judgment of Andrea becomes a developing self-judgment as well. The very richness of the poem's tropological rhetoric both teaches us to judge and turns that judgment back on ourselves. Thus does this "gratuitous" adornment, so blandly if repeatedly admired in the interpretive history, prove the doubly devious agent of the poem's heuristic power.

We fault Andrea, then, not as we fault the Bishop, for failing to know his tropological strategy as such, but for the faulty use he makes of his knowingly wielded tropes: not to open but to close meaning, not to create possibilities but to preclude even their foreshadowing. "Andrea del Sarto," of course, not only dramatizes but thematizes Browning's doctrine of imperfection, a doctrine that finds "fault" in "faultlessness." Nevertheless, the poem's interpretive history has left its recognition of the poem's "imperfection" unconnected to its recognition of the poem's tropological density. And it is this repeated proximity that suggests that these recognitions are finally inseparable, that Andrea's moral fault, his failure to make his reach exceed his grasp, *is* his tropological fault: he works his tropes "unnaturally," using them to confirm a deadly perfection rather than create a living imperfection.

Tucker faults Andrea for letting "his technique dictate his creative intention" (p. 195), a point with which the interpretive history agrees. But if we recall

THE DRAMATIC MONOLOGUE   93

Gombrich on this same point—"Painting is an activity, and the artist will there-fore tend to see what he paints rather than paint what he sees" (p. 86)—we learn that such dictation is unavoidable and that Andrea is more properly faulted for not using his technique as fully and rigorously as he might, for failing to suggest the infinite that necessarily eludes all finite or literalized representation. Rather than "putting the infinite in the finite," he seeks to literalize his tropes, to make them transparent to the thing itself, to ignore the liberating play of medium in representation—including representation of the self. By no accident does his coin metaphor die: "I'll pay my fancy," he announces, and he does just that. Nor is it by accident that Andrea serves a Lockean "fancy" rather than a Cole-ridgean "imagination," that he prefers the "essentially fixed and dead" to the power that "dissolves, diffuses, dissipates, in order to recreate," that "strug-gles to idealize and to unify."[41] As in "Cleon" and "The Bishop Orders His Tomb," the wages of fancy prove too high: they end in a meaning so literalized and a self-writing so "faultless" that they amount to a self-embalmment. But because Andrea is the most hermeneutically sophisticated of Browning's self-writers and self-readers, he is for this very reason most at fault. Unlike the Bishop, he knows the aesthetic and ethical superiority of imperfection:

> Ah, but a man's reach should exceed his grasp,
> Or what's a heaven for? All is silver-grey
> Placid and perfect with my art: the worse!
>
> (ll. 97–99)

Yet despite this knowledge he knowingly uses his verbal tropes as he uses his visual art: to elevate the deadliness of fanciful perfection over the power of imagined imperfection.

Returning from the hermeneutic to the human drama, we find that it con-cludes similarly, suggesting that, as in "Cleon," the two dramas are finally one. Browning has throughout protected and nurtured our empathy for Andrea, bal-ancing his self-incrimination with his self-justification, but as the poem closes, Andrea introduces evidence against himself that cannot be justified without incurring the very incrimination such justification is designed to avoid:

> The very wrong to Francis!—it is true
> I took his coin, was tempted and complied,
> And built this house and sinned, and all is said.
> My father and my mother died of want.
> Well, had I riches of my own? You see
> How one gets rich! Let each one bear his lot.
> They were born poor, lived poor, and poor they died:
> And I have laboured somewhat in my time
> And not been paid profusely. Some good son

> Paint my two hundred pictures—let him try!
> No doubt, there's something strikes a balance.
>
> (ll. 247–257)

Compounding squandered gold and pandered art, Andrea's rationalized portrait of his parents dying of hunger turns us against him and our reading against itself. Had this passage come earlier, it would have precluded our empathy and made our judgment too easy, both aesthetically unsatisfying and heuristically impotent. Had it not come at all, our concluding vision would lack the self-contradiction necessary to irony and self-conscious illusion.

The poem could at this point achieve satisfying closure. But by extending Andrea's commitment to Lucrezia beyond this life, Browning invites us to judge Andrea not once but twice:

> What would one have?
> In heaven, perhaps, new chances, one more chance—
> Four great walls in the New Jerusalem,
> Meted on each side by the angel's reed,
> For Leonard, Rafael, Agnolo and me
> To cover—the three first without a wife,
> While I have mine! So—still they overcome
> Because there's still Lucrezia,—as I choose.
>
> Again the Cousin's whistle! Go, my Love.
>
> (ll. 259–67)

This, the last lyric outburst of the poem, is all the more remarkable given the immediately preceding account of Andrea's filial turpitude. One last time Andrea succeeds in tempting us to see as he sees. By now, however, we have been so thoroughly tutored in his ways that we are firmly of two minds at once, simultaneously tempted and beyond temptation. The panorama of heaven holds out one last hope, but we know that even this staggering price will be paid: "there's still Lucrezia—as I choose." Insofar as Andrea knows the magnitude of his fault, we share his knowing. But because he knowingly commits his fault, we also fault him for choosing the lesser good in full awareness of the greater. Only at the last moment do we finally sever Andrea's vision from ours. We see not a man of forgivable imperfection but a man who deliberately fits his grasp to his reach, a man whose self-definition in terms of the trope of the "common grayness" that "silvers everything" names *all* his faults, whether ethical, aesthetic, or tropological. The perfection that marks Lucrezia's beauty is one with the faultlessness that mars his art, a faultlessness that in turn is one with his knowingly devious and hence too facile use of tropes: all alike serve the dead-end fancy instead of what Coleridge called the "vital" imagination.[42]

It is fitting that Andrea should in conclusion prove too canny for even his self-advertised perfection. Acquiescent throughout in his fate, an acquiescence increasingly and finally fully suspect, in conclusion he suddenly affects control. He tells Lucrezia to go when her going is already a foregone conclusion, for him as much as for her, and he names her "my love" when both know her love to be no less foregone. He doubtless "sees" the local irony as well as we do, but to the prodigious shadows cast by this misused trope the speaker seems suddenly to have gone blind. His blindness, however, is precisely what lets us see or, more precisely, is what we see. It is only as we negotiate the sharp turning of this final and conspicuous trope that Andrea's speech irrevocably opacifies and the poet's design becomes fully visible.

Once again, then, the monologic speaker gives way to the poet who made him and to the reader who, by reading the speaker's self-writing, remakes him, correcting the errors and completing the incompleteness of his textualized self. Repetition of this interpretive pattern, which typifies our reading of these poems, suggests that the distinctness of these personalities is informed by a complex of strategic traits. Just as in our reading of dramatic monologues we continually "discover" not only difference within their generic similarity but also similarity within difference, so our reading of their speakers gradually reveals them to be as fundamentally alike as they are obviously different.

What, then, is the error that links the distinctive, even idiosyncratic self-writings of these speakers? Most importantly, the monologic speaker errs by conspicuously failing to know himself as we know him. This failure can be simple—as when the Duke fails to "see" himself as morally black—or it can be subtle—as when Andrea not only refuses the struggle that fuels a "vital" imperfection but is blind to the deadly consequences of dwelling in a "perfect" twilight. Whatever its complexity, however, the monologic speaker's quest for self-knowledge always fails, a failure that, in an ironic redoubling, he always fails to see. But even were he to see it—to see that his quest does not, indeed cannot conclude—he would nevertheless fail to see that this very inconclusiveness offers the life whose absence he alternately fears and mourns.

Haunted by a complex of linked fears—loneliness, death, temporality, self-erasure, entrapment—he strives in his self-writing to defend against them by penning the boundaries of his selfhood, even at the expense of the very life he is trying to preserve. He strives, that is, to finesse the dread consequences of unidirectional time by textualizing himself. And to a certain and sufficiently self-deceptive extent he succeeds: the spatializing tropes of self-announced metaphor and self-directed irony do transfigure his imagined being, giving it the "feel" of substance. Imagining his arms folded, "as if they clasped a crook," his feet stretched "straight as stone can point," his bedclothes, like a "mortcloth," dropping "into great laps and folds of sculptor's work," the Bishop succeeds in making himself—and us—"feel" him as if he were his own effigy.

But words run in time and so drag into their employment the very chronology he would have them defeat. Moreover, his wording of his present self is itself composed of gesturings forward and backward to selves no longer or not yet or never existent. He cannot write himself without using spatializing tropes whose use implicitly extends in and thereby implicates them in time: folding, stretching, and dropping are at once temporal actions and themselves ordered in time. Nor can he avoid more explicitly temporal tropes: the turning toward the past ("Old Gandolf cozened one, despite my care"), the turning toward the future ("And then how I shall lie through centuries/And hear the blessed mutter of the mass"), and, most twistingly, the turning toward those forever vacant spaces and selves that, whether past or future, we call conditional ("Had you enjoined them on me, given me soul,/We might have risen to Rafael, I and you!"). The monologic speaker typically uses these tropes with practiced facility and to immediate purpose: they are essential to his self-defense. But as with his other procedures of self-transfiguration, he fails to see them as such. They could serve to liberate him from the time and personality that confine his present self, but he uses them precisely otherwise: to fix those confines, thereby making them adamantine, his self its own effigy. He could purchase the freedom to move knowingly in imaginative time and space, but he chooses precisely otherwise: to enclose his self, making it *un*knowing, preserved in only the most literal and therefore the deadliest of senses.

Among its many lessons, the monologue thus teaches that the acts of remembering, of anticipating, and of supposing are all present-tense acts, which, moreover, themselves occur in time. Their "content," particularly when it is "past," only masks this presentness. How, then, can using these temporal tropes free the speaker from his present self? They can do so precisely because their enactment, both the acts of self-writing and of reading or rewriting that writing, happen in the eternal present of textualized time. This time, which is capable of infinite repetition, is the discourse time of the text. Thus when reading Eliot's wording of this very point, we repeat or echo his words into presence and the present:

> What might have been and what has been
> Point to one end, which is always present.
> Footfalls echo in the memory
> Down the passage which we did not take
> Towards the door we never opened
> Into the rose-garden. My words echo
> Thus, in your mind.
>
> *Burnt Norton*

Similarly, when reading the words of Andrea and the Bishop we repeat them into presence and the present tense. But because the monologic speaker cannot "see" either his temporal or his spatial transfigurations, he remains blind to their redemptive potential, to his power to write himself into a state of what Eliot called perpetual possibility and Kierkegaard, with disarming simplicity, called happiness: "Repetition and recollection are the same movement, only in opposite directions; for what is recollected has been, is repeated backwards, whereas repetition properly so called is recollected forwards. Therefore repetition, if it is possible, makes a man happy, whereas recollection makes him unhappy— provided he gives himself time to live and does not at once, in the very moment of birth, try to find a pretext for stealing out of life, alleging, for example, that he has forgotten something."[43]

Insofar as it is achieved, then, the stasis of the monologic speaker proves an entombment. Most frequently, this imaginative thesis remains implicit, a consequence of our interpretive work, but at times the poet makes it explicit: the Bishop is an effigy; Cleon is in his urn. Thus it happens that the speaker's struggle against death paradoxically guarantees that death. Always "thinking that he has forgotten something," he strives to resurrect his past selves, fearing the very self-erasure that makes self-writing possible. Put otherwise, he refuses to recognize the paradox that drives his doom, to learn that the boundaries that define his present and past selves, however natural these boundaries seem, are always a provisional product of a present-tense self-writing, the telling of the "story" of one's life. The lesson of the speaker's own narrative act is thus lost upon him: he never learns that these selves are always and desirably open to revision, to rereading and rewriting. Moreover, he persists in denying this openness, in trying to affirm the natural connection between an inner living origin and its textual "expression." The monologue's reader, however, learns that it is only by affirming the perpetual openness and arbitrariness of this connection that life is permanently secured, that only in this way can the self-writer empower himself to cast off potentially infinite selves, both by means of his own revision and, as well, by the completing and correcting act of his reader.

Thus does the poet invite his reader to rewrite the speaker's self-writing. But if we become the careful readers that these monologues tutor and expect, we will suspect the deviousness of this invitation. We are asked to judge the monologic speaker for the presumption of his authority, for claiming to have written the fixed and final word. Exposing and correcting his error, we repudiate his claim. But in so doing do we not thereby repeat his presumption? Although we break open his "completed" self in order to complete the poem, do we not thereby exercise the very authority we condemn? Yes and no. For if we are cagey as well as careful readers, we allow ourselves to fall into this trap—even attend to the dynamics of that fall—in order to learn the lesson that the speaker never learns: that *author*ity, whether exercised over the self or others, ought always to be exercised provisionally and by implication. But does not the poet now fall into his own trap? Does he not commit the very same sins condemned in his speaker? He justifiably answers that he has left his poems so conspicuously and unusually open to his reader's inferential completion—they are the "little torsos made broken so as to stimulate the reader to the restoration of their missing legs and arms"—that he has largely cleansed himself of the hubris of authorship, if not lightened its burden. By so thoroughly recessing himself from our view, he and his claims acquire a self-redeeming indirection. When we move to the mask lyric, we shall find that this deliberate indirection is the speaker's as well as the poet's, that both are dedicated to opening meaning rather than to its enclosure. We shall also find that those poems generate an interpretive history no less rich than the monologue's, a richness that, once again, testifies to the heuristic power and hermeneutic interest of the "broken torso."

Self-Painting and Self-Entrapment: "Fra Lippo Lippi"

The pleasure and power of "Andrea del Sarto" turn on the extreme threat posed by empathy to judgment. In "Fra Lippo Lippi" this threat all but breaks the generic bounds, our judgment of Lippo being so thoroughly beguiled by imaginative desire that the monologic strategy of affective complication verges on lyric simplicity. As David DeLaura observes, "we are not allowed to judge—indeed we readily *forgive*—the real shortcomings of a rogue *who remains a rogue* . . . . "[44] Yet we do finally sever our vision from Lippo's, but for reasons more conceptual and subtle than, as the circumstances of his speech would seem to imply, moral and bold. "Fra Lippo Lippi" is thus a critically important instance of the genre, its generic extremity pushing the genre as here defined to its explanatory limit.

From the start Lippo is clearly in the wrong by any conventional moral standard, and, far from denying this fact, the poem opens and turns on its emphasis. We accordingly find him in the most compromising and incriminating situation possible for a friar:

> I am poor brother Lippo, by your leave!
> You need not clap your torches to my face.
> Zooks, what's to blame? you think you see a monk!
> What, 'tis past midnight, and you go the rounds,
> And here you catch me at an alley's end
> Where sportive ladies leave their doors ajar?
>
> (ll. 1–6)

Yet Lippo baldly refuses to be compromised, and as we read we learn that the poet who made him presents this sin as not merely unavoidable and forgivable but as virtue in disguise. We posit, then, that the initial creative challenge was to rescue Lippo from our moral condemnation and the "alley's end." It is a challenge met with generic strategies by now familiar. Once again, the extenuating cause of the speaker's predicament is made compelling and its inherent pathos intensified by extension in textual time:

> But, mind you, when a boy starves in the streets
> Eight years together, as my fortune was,
> Watching folk's faces to know who will fling
> The bit of half-stripped grape-bunch he desires,
> And who will curse or kick him for his pains,—
> Which gentleman processional and fine,
> Holding a candle to the Sacrament,
> Will wink and let him lift a plate and catch
> The droppings of the wax to sell again,
> Or holla for the Eight and have him whipped,—
> How say I?—nay, which dog bites, which lets drop
> His bone from the heap of offal in the street,—
> Why, soul and sense of him grow sharp alike,
> He learns the look of things, and none the less
> For admonition from the hunger-pinch.
>
> (ll. 112–26)

That at age eight Lippo was forced by hunger to renounce worldly joys tempers our judgment of his adult transgression—as does the unembittered verve of his survival. We eagerly take Lippo's side against a straightlaced world, an allegiance rationalized by his impeccable reasoning:

> You should not take a fellow eight years old
> And make him swear to never kiss the girls.
>
> (ll. 224–25)

Yet he undeniably "remains a rogue," and our judgment undeniably remains threatening. The poet accordingly provides Lippo with an adversary who voices the reader's objections and whose defeat effectively rebuts those objections. Hence the strategic foolishness of the prior:

> "Your business is not to catch men with show,
> With homage to the perishable clay,
> But lift them over it, ignore it all,
> Make them forget there's such a thing as flesh.
> Your business is to paint the souls of men—
> Man's soul, and it's a fire, smoke . . . no, it's not . . .
> It's vapor done up like a new-born babe—
> (In that shape when you die it leaves your mouth)
> It's . . . well, what matters talking, it's the soul!
> Give us no more of body than shows soul!"
>
> (ll. 179–88)

We are also led to suspect that the prior has a mistress: " 'Oh, that white smallish female with the breasts,/She's just my niece' " (ll. 195–96). His attempt at concealment only confirms our suspicion, which is additionally fueled by repetition of the phrase, "the prior's niece." And this repetition, in turn, emphasizes Lippo's comparative lack of hypocrisy, his superior if unconventional virtue. Such continued blocking of our every attempt to judge Lippo makes lyric reading seem the only "right" explanation. Not surprisingly, then, Langbaum ignores the poem. His language of judgment readily explains the criminal, insane, and hypocritical speakers common to the commonplace instances of the genre, but it falls mute before the disturbing anomaly of a monologic speaker who knows himself this thoroughly and a monologue that exhibits his knowledge to such advantage. More than any of the great monologues, "Fra Lippo Lippi" thus exhibits the inadequacy of judgment as a definitive generic response, leading us to conclude that all poems whose speakers we judge may indeed be well explained as dramatic monologues, but not all dramatic monologues have speakers that we judge to be morally or mentally deficient. We have already discovered that the moral difference between speaker and reader may be negligible as in "Karshish," virtually beside the suasive point as in "The Bishop Orders His Tomb," or added ballast as in "Andrea del Sarto." And this discovery enables another: that the characteristic irony of dramatic monologues is more fruitfully discussed in terms of the speaker's *imaginative* failure, his failure to know the tropes with which he textualizes his present self.

Its interpretive history repeatedly reads "Fra Lippo Lippi" not as a lyric but as congeneric with "Andrea del Sarto" and Browning's other major monologues, and I would agree that our vision of Lippo is finally cast in irony. But I would also argue that the irony and hence the monologue is distinguished by its extreme and chaste obliquity, that the lyric harmony between Lippo and ourselves is untuned by our imaginations, not our morals, and that the resulting disharmony is so slight as to be barely audible. On the one hand, Lippo tries to reconcile the disparate elements of his life and aesthetics; on the other, the reader tries to gauge his failure to do so. Lippo is aware of his attempt; his reader, however, is aware of both attempt and failure. So far the monologue conforms to the genre. "Fra Lippo Lippi" particularizes this generic pattern by inviting its *reader* to repeat Lippo's attempt to reconcile life and art. Of course, we fail, and this failure confirms not only the difficulties of the poem's reading but the generic hubris of our presumed superiority.

I am arguing, then, that the poet, like his speaker, has set out to discover and then push back the limits of his chosen genre. Like his speaker, he succeeds. As readers our vision is finally ironic—despite virtually total empathy we do discover and fault Lippo's imperfection—but the irony is curiously benign, our superiority suspiciously hesitant. We have already learned that to fault the speaker of a Browning monologue for imperfection is to risk faulting ourselves, to risk our judgment's transfiguration into a self-judgment. But "Fra Lippo Lippi" compounds this risk by taking as its topic the very interpretive dynamics used in its reading. The interpretive history has identified Lippo's aesthetics as essentially Browning's,[45] and a case for his ethics being Browning's could be made as well. But it is not generally recognized, even among the majority who read Browning as consistently attacking the perfecting desire of representation, that *Lippo* is not, at least knowingly, mounting such an attack.[46] Indeed, his self-proclaimed aesthetics is almost palpably mimetic:

> This world's no blot for us,
> Nor blank; it means intensely, and means good:
> To find its meaning is my meat and drink.
>
> (ll. 313-15)

As a theoretical aesthetician (whose practice, not incidentally, is at odds with his preaching), Lippo would *find* rather than *make*. He argues that meaning is "out there," already and "intensely" inherent in the world, and that the business of the artist is discovering and copying that meaning rather than inventing worlds whose incompletion invites the beholder to contribute his completing share, thereby substantiating their reality. Lippo's rejection of the "blot" method of making meaning is a characteristically mimetic denial of the schema, a denial glossed two centuries ago by Alexander Cozens in Lippo's own terms: "to blot is to make varied spots . . . producing accidental forms . . . from which ideas are presented to the mind. . . . To sketch is to delineate ideas; blotting suggests them."[47]

Given that Browning wrote this poem, Lippo's representational hermeneutics not surprisingly contains its own potential correction. Having painted himself into his painting—"I, in this presence, this pure company!" (l. 368)—he fears the imperfection or strange loop thus created: "Where's a hole, where's a corner for escape?" (l. 369). Lippo's self-imagined tutor answers that his anxiety is an artifact of thinking mimetically, in terms of "sketching" or copying rather than of "blotting" or creating:

> Then steps a sweet angelic slip of a thing
> Forward, puts out a soft palm—"Not so fast!"
> —Addresses the celestial presence, "nay—
> He made you and devised you, after all,
> Though he's none of you! Could St. John there draw—
> His camel-hair make up a painting-brush?
> We come to brother Lippo for all that,
> *Iste perfecit opus!*"
>
> (ll. 370-77)

This "angelic" answer, analogous to Lippo's self-representation in the painting we know as the *Coronation of the Virgin*, draws our attention to and thereby opacifies the verisimilar fabric of the text. The answer is a lesson that exists both within the speech and without the poem, alluding at once to Lippo as maker and to the maker of Lippo: "He made you and devised you, after all,/Though he's none of you!" The ambivalence of the word "*perfecit*," meaning both "he made" and "he finished or perfected," draws our attention to the poem's radical redefinition of "perfection": it is a wording that defines not closure but beginning, not finitude but "the infinite within the finite." Hofstadter's appropriation of Gödel, Gombrich's critique of literalized representation, and Browning's own poetic practice—all teach that "putting the infinite within the finite" is accomplished not by copying ever more fastidiously with an ever more transparent medium but by *suggesting* with ever greater strength and subtlety. And the most powerful suggestion of this kind is self-reference, the transfigured blotting that acknowledges its own beginnings, the transgression that includes its own doubt.

But the "angelic" lesson of suggested infinitude is apparently lost on Lippo. Obliquely escaping or, perhaps, deliberately evading his hermeneutic enlightenment—"I shuffle sideways with my blushing face/Under the cover of a hundred wings" (ll. 378–79)—he announces his preference for an erotic entrapment, an eternized playing at "hot cockles." Lippo, of course, reads his epitaphic self-inscription otherwise: "And so all's saved for me." But *his* readers learn the "angelic" lesson of making and imperfection and put their learning to good use by correcting and thereby "perfecting" Lippo's vision. Yet immediately we notice the contradiction between what we have learned and how we have learned it, the "perfection" of our vision becomes itself shot through with irony, an irony that slantingly illumines all Browning's imperfect speakers and readers but perhaps nowhere with more curious benignity than here. For the irony of "Fra Lippo Lippi," like that of "The Bishop Orders His Tomb" only more so, resides less in its irrepressible speaker than in our shared human and hermeneutic predicaments. Our barely audible laughter, like our subtly rendered judgment, is, once again, aimed less at the speaker than at ourselves.

Madness, Melodrama, and the Monologue: The Problem of Genre Revisited

Mad speakers are favorites of the apprentice monologist. The garish outlines of madness are easily sketched, the reader's superiority easily secured. The early efforts of even Browning and Tennyson concentrate on simulating madness: St. Simeon Stylites, Johannes Agricola, Porphyria's lover, and, as some have argued, the Duke. But Frost's "A Servant to Servants" argues against such melodramatic necessity, demonstrating that dramatized madness can probe and write the speaker's self no less precisely and profoundly than do Andrea's unwindings of self-deception. Discussion of this monologue will at once complete testing of the genre as here defined and suggest the need for and definition of a new genre.

The conversational opening of "A Servant to Servants" is disarming. Only retrospectively does the speaker's linguistic and emotional exhaustion portend madness: "It seems to me/I can't express my feelings anymore" (ll. 6–7); "It's got so I don't even know for sure/Whether I *am* glad, sorry, or anything" (ll. 11–12). And only with repetition and elaboration does this exhaustion grow ominous:

> There's nothing but a voice-like left inside
> That seems to tell me how I ought to feel,
> And would feel if I wasn't all gone wrong.
> You take the lake. I look and look at it.
> I see it's a fair, pretty sheet of water.
> I stand and make myself repeat out loud
> The advantages it has . . .
>
> (ll. 13–19)

Such foreshadowings deepen into the shadow itself as the speaker relates the story of her mad uncle endlessly rattling the bars of his cage, shouting into the night "Until the strength was shouted out of him,/And his voice died down slowly from exhaustion" (ll. 132–33). The violence of this episode contradicts the quiet surface of its recitation and the "normal" world in which it is embedded, a contradiction that by its resistance to resolution generates the poem's power. For "A Servant to Servants," unlike "Karshish," does not invite its reader to distinguish and choose between two worlds, the one ordinary and the other extraordinary, but rather to discover and then accept their paradoxical coexistence. This paradox is shaped by the artifice of the poem's studied artlessness, by its deceptively conversational ease and merely surface control. The speaker's very inarticulateness is designed to express inexpressible tension and the nervousness of her self-restraint to presage its loss:

> Bless you, of course, you're keeping me from work,
> But the thing of it is, I need to *be* kept.
> There's work enough to do—there's always that;
> But behind's behind. The worst that you can do
> Is set me back a little more behind.
> I shan't catch up in this world, anyway.
> I'd *rather* you'd not go unless you must.
>
> (ll. 171–77)

But this drama of madness in a world of "doughnuts and soda biscuit" is powerful not only because it refuses our resolution but also because it would, in typical monologic fashion, implicate us in the speaker's condition. This implication is a consequence of her madness being played out on a stage of disturbing familiarity:

> He thinks I'll be all right
> With doctoring. But it's not medicine—
> Lowe is the only doctor's dared to say so—
> It's rest I want—there, I have said it out—
> From cooking meals for hungry hired men
> And washing dishes after them—from doing
> Things over and over that just won't stay done.
>
> (ll. 46–52)

Because the borderlines between exhaustion and madness, between domestic tedium and untamed intensity are exactingly obscured throughout, our involvement is made easy and distance difficult. Curiously, her madness does not make this speaker seem strange. Rather, she seems to be writing the liminal darkness of our daylight lives, much as Andrea's self-deception and the Bishop's fear of dissolution seem to be writing our own.

Nevertheless, the poem does not reward discussion as a lyric for the same reason that these others do not: it invites us to know the speaker in a way that she cannot know herself. To the Servant all is flattened, accepted, unremarkable, but the reader is reading a poem as well as a speech and so sees foreshadowings of which the Servant is unaware and a *non sum dignus* that is beyond her capacity to know, if not to enact. But the critical reader also notes another and more specifically textual flattening: among monologues this is remarkable for its tropological inertness. Bloom's theses—"*Defenses can be said to trope against death*" and "*tropes can be said to defend against literal meaning*"— suggest that the speaker's imminent madness results from an imagination not overwrought but unused. Like her uncle's voice, hers also dies "down slowly from exhaustion," a dying down that we began tracing in "Cleon" and that here finally fulfills the desire of all representational striving: the complete submergence of *verba* in *res*, the death of metaphor—and mind—into the thing itself.

Not all poems traditionally deemed dramatic monologues are as subtly compelling and indirectly ironic as those just discussed. Indeed, the genre seems most readily to achieve effects more properly deemed melodramatic: to parade striking but simplified speakers, to beget designs that thrill and amuse rather than move and disturb. Even Tennyson's monologues, as well as many of Browning's earliest, avoid the complication of sympathy and strive instead for the boldest irony, the least complex distance between speaker and reader.

Browning's "Soliloquy of the Spanish Cloister" is a case in point. The speaker's difference from us is maximized, the inanity of his impotent hatred for Brother Lawrence exaggerated, the comedy protected from the dilutions of both apprehension and sympathy. The speaker is a nuisance, not a menace:

> How go on your flowers? None double?
> Not one fruit-sort can you spy?
> Strange!—And I, too, at such trouble
> Keep them close-nipped on the sly!
>   (ll. 45–48)

He unwittingly confutes his own slander:

> —Can't I see his dead eye glow,
> Bright as 'twere a Barbary corsair's?
> (That is, if he'd let it show!)
>   (ll. 30–32)

And his last words seal our unhesitating judgment: as he growls his hatred— "Gr-r-r——you swine!"—he names Brother Lawrence the beast. The poem's comic power, in short, is Jonsonian. It lacks the implicating and therefore salvational ironies of Browning's greatest monologues, but its undiluted ridicule is itself a perfectly polished if minor effect.

As is the effect of Tennyson's "St. Simeon Stylites." Its speaker, a self-satisfied ascetic and self-styled martyr, pursues sainthood with a fervor whose excess defeats his end—although not the poet's. Confined to his pillar, he revels in "Rain, wind, frost, heat, hail, damp, and sleet, and snow" (l. 16). He treasures the decades spent "In hungers and in thrists, fevers and cold,/In coughs, aches, stitches, ulcerous throes and cramps" (ll. 12–13). His is a tropology run amuk, and, indeed, FitzGerald tells us that "this is one of the Poems A. T. would read with grotesque Grimness, especially at such passages as 'Coughs, Aches, Stitches, etc.,' laughing aloud at times."[48]

But it is this very grotesquery that makes the monologue critically instructive, its unwittingly hyperbolic speaker and mannerist perspective glorifying by contrast the subtle and redemptive powers of Browning's best. In "St. Simeon Stylites" we find no defused objections, no atoning virtues, no seductive interiority, no temptation to feel Simeon's madness as if it were our own. These strategies are the instruments of emotional and ethical complexity, their absence the cause and consequence of caricature. We diagnosed the Servant's madness as a radical failure of the figurative, of the power to imagine and to word that imagining. Simeon's madness is in one sense exactly different: it is a hypertrophy of the figurative, an exhaustion of the imagination through the explosion of fancy. But in another sense it is no different: both hermeneutic states are similarly diseased in being unwittingly entered and beyond the speaker's control. Unlike the Servant, however, Simeon is not only mad, he is also ridiculous: he sees neither his absurdity nor the contradiction inherent in a sainthood consciously sought. Whereas the pathology of the Servant is tempered throughout by pathos, in "Simeon" as in "Soliloquy" there is no such tempering. Instead, we are handed the dubious luxury of a perfectly unambiguous triumph.

Except in the hands of a master the monologue invites such comic exaggeration as well as the gaudy sensationalism all too readily purchased by mad, criminal, degenerate, or even nonhuman speakers.[49] Both invitations shunt drama in the direction of melodrama. "Soliloquy of the Spanish Cloister" and "St. Simeon Stylites" work this melodramatic potential into a species of minor perfection, but their example is exceptional, very nearly unique. The best monologues work in a radically different way, which minimizes the melodramatic and engages the difficult. The generic dilemma, then, is this: if the poet would progress beyond caricature, satire, and melodrama, to more complex and hence more seemingly "real" speakers, the ironic structure of the genre stands in his way. Because the monologic speaker always ends as the object of our irony, his stature and complexity are inevitably less than they might be. We and the implied poet always stand together in conclusion, apart from the speaker, so we always have the illusion of knowing more and, thereby, of *being* more. In sum, the irony that distinguishes the genre is in itself limiting: it restricts the richness and variety of its speakers; it checks the depth, range, and heuristic power of our response.

Browning's fecundity and inventiveness countered the generic limitation and left us these varied and complex poems. But so great was his success that the seeming reality of his speakers and their speeches has tended to obscure and thereby diminish his art. Hence Langbaum: "the dramatic monologue has no *necessary* beginning and end but only arbitrary limits" (p. 144). Hence Miller: "the only thing certain is that the inner dialogue will go on indefinitely, only arbitrarily brought to a conclusion, and chopped off into a poem."[50] Thus does the genre's interpretive history deny Browning his art even as its very success prompts this denial. I have argued otherwise: that these monologues are far from arbitrary, but because their design in each instance must simultaneously meet the seemingly incompatible demands of verisimilar speech and artful poem, the very ambidexterity of that design has seemed to argue its absence. Just as the speaker's naturalistic "excess" has seemed to signal its insignificance, the poem's tropological "excess" has seemed a gratuitous adornment on an otherwise mimetically chaste content. In short, the better the monologue, the more difficult its explanation.

My readings have endeavored to answer these objections—either there is too much reality or there is too much art—by showing how they issue from the mimetic language habitually used to discuss the monologue and how the very characteristics objected to are precisely those responsible for the genre's distinctive power. I answered the first objection, to the monologue's much admired but critically elusive "realism," by arguing that, as Burke has said, a character strikes us as "real" only if he has more traits than he needs. He is a convincing person when he is *not* perfectly adapted to his function, to the suasive exigencies of his immediate situation. The bulk of any good monologue is in this sense gratuitous, at times even at odds with the speaker's attempt to persuade the narratee. But these speakers are imperfect in another and no less life-giving way: when considered as people rather than as characters, they are always defective, particularly in self-knowledge. As we read we infer and correct this defect, much as in everyday life, and these acts of inference and correction lend life to the speaker, rounding him, filling the gaps in his self-textualization with the substance of unuttered but thoroughly imagined thought. In Gombrich's words, we enact the beholder's share, and this enactment, no less in literature than in painting, is what makes the illusion possible. I answered the second objection, to the genre's artifice or, more precisely, to its refusal to reject its art and marry the real, by connecting the two rhetorics, by showing that the speaker's problems with tropes are indistinguishable from his suasive and self-inscriptional dilemmas. To be sure, the genre is designedly arbitrary—hence Miller's observation and Laugbaum's—but it also insists on this design, on the reason why it is so and not otherwise. In short, it equivocates. But this equivocation is neither incidental to the genre nor a lamentable fault. Rather, it is the essence of the genre, its enabling and distinguishing virtue. It creates both the feel of reality and the finish of the ideal. It invites the reader to read "as if" and rewards our performance of this paradox: we are at once immersed in belief and without that belief, both lost in the play and watchful of our own performance.

This study has aimed to unfold this formal and affective ambidexterity, to display the ways in which the best monologues challenge the traditional limitations of the genre and, by so doing, challenge our capacity to read "as if." I have argued that the imaginative lure of the monologue, the experience of matching with minds extraordinary and diverse, is one with its heuristic power to exercise this capacity: to join the speaking voice to the written word, to fuse our perceptions of the speaker as person and the speaker as words, as himself spoken. More than any other literary genre, monologues invite us to a conscious illusion and to a criticism that is the unfolding of that illusion as well as its recapitulation: let us read this poem as if it were at once made and said, as if we could "match" simultaneously with the speaker implied by the speech and the poet implied by the poem, as if this poem were like this genre and unlike that.

We are thus returned to our opening assertions about genre: that it is the critic's deductive, provisional, and heuristic tool. It is his primary and powerful way of explaining. As always, it is tempting to hypostatize genre, particularly when the genre in question is substantiated by a long interpretive history. As a corrective to such temptation in the case of the monologue, we need only remind ourselves that Browning, as far as we know, never used the term "dramatic monologue."[51] First encountered in 1857, it appeared only intermittently until Tennyson's dedication to *Locksley Hall Sixty Years After* (1886) established its currency. In 1894 Stopford Brooke grouped poems of Tennyson and Browning as "dramatic monologues," and in 1897 Austin Dobson gave the term critical legitimacy by listing it in his *Handbook of English Literature*. The monologue held a particular fascination for critics in the early decades of this century, who poured their conceptual energy into codification and definition. Ironically, this project embedded the genre yet more deeply in the poems, making it seem intrinsic, covering over the fact of its retrospective definition. Subsequent critics treated the genre accordingly, debating the probable rightness rather than the explanatory usefulness of defining any particular poem as a monologue. Definitions of the genre have been similarly debated, their justification mounted in representational rather than rhetorical and pragmatic terms.

In the last chapter I argued that genre is a metaphoric and syllogistic way of talking, a conceptual language that enables us to discuss texts "in terms of what they are not." Modern criticism has nevertheless preferred to treat genre as intrinsic or transparent to the literary text, denying and concealing their ineluctable difference. I also argued that foregrounding this difference makes it useful: that "discovering" the genre's difference from the poem is a powerful way of explaining why the poem is as it is and not otherwise. But there is a limit to the usefulness of such generic difference, a limit reached here in the readings of "Fra Lippo Lippi" and "A Servant to Servants." When the speaker is even less distanced from poet and reader than Fra Lippo and the Servant, we shall find that the poem fails as a monologue.

The next chapter will accordingly propose another generic model: the mask lyric. It is expressly designed to "correct" the monologic model in discussions of poems like "Ulysses" and "Prufrock," poems that confute rather than reward the reader's attempts to distinguish the speaker's meaning from the poem's. From this definition a sequence of generic distinctions readily unfolds: whereas the monologue invites us to know its speaker analytically and agonistically, the mask lyric invites a synthetic and sympathetic knowing; whereas the monologue invites us to infer inner "truth" from outer "evidence," the mask lyric invites us to know its speaker from within, as if we were seeing with his eyes; whereas the monologue is finally monist, implying the singular truth of our concluding and antagonistic stance, the mask lyric is pluralist, implying the relative truth of many if not all stances. The mask lyric accordingly offers a larger repertory of complex speakers, whose greater inwardness of conception assists both their complexity and that of the poem. Not surprisingly, the explanation of these complexities itself grows complex.

Chapter 3
The Mask Lyric

Tell all the Truth but tell it slant—
Success in Circuit lies.

Emily Dickinson

Maintenant, je suis juge-pénitent.

Albert Camus

Complicating the Rhetoric of Lyricism: Wordsworth, Pound, and the Mask Lyric

In 1802 Wordsworth wrote "The Emigrant Mother." Deservedly unknown, the poem nevertheless deserves our attention here because the poet-speaker's statement of poetic strategy in the opening lines articulates the enabling imaginative supposition of all mask lyrics:

Once in a lonely hamlet I sojourned
In which a Lady driven from France did dwell;
The big and lesser griefs with which she mourned,
In friendship she to me would often tell.

This Lady, dwelling upon British ground,
Where she was childless, daily would repair
To a poor neighbouring cottage; as I found,
For sake of a young Child whose home was there.

Once having seen her clasp with fond embrace
This Child, I chanted to myself a lay,
Endeavouring, in our English tongue, to trace
Such things as she unto the Babe might say:
And thus, from what I heard and knew, or guessed,
My song the workings of her heart expressed.

I

"Dear Babe, thou daughter of another,
One moment let me be thy mother!
An infant's face and looks are thine
And sure a mother's heart is mine:
Thy own dear mother's far away,
At labour in the harvest field:
Thy little sister is at play;—
What warmth, what comfort would it yield
To my poor heart, if thou wouldst be
One little hour a child to me!"

(ll. 1–24)

By prefacing the mother's song with his own words, the poet-speaker lends his authority to that song, intensifying its pathos and, however paradoxically, heightening its intimacy. These words open the conventionally closed space between lyric speaker and poet, but they do so only to collapse this artificially articulated distance into a self-conscious proximity not otherwise possible. The effect is striking, distinctive of the genre. It is also a difficult effect, one unusually dependent on the reader and, in particular, on his mastery of conscious illusion. Hence the tutorial function of the preface: telling us that he has matched with the thoughts and feelings of the mother, the poet-speaker invites us to match similarly, both with her and, by implication, with him. As we read we have the illusion that the poet is speaking, overtly in the frame, implicitly in the song, so that when the mother begins to speak we seem to hear the poet-speaker as well. The two speakings are conflated rather than distinguished as they are in the monologue, and the imaginative acts that create and recreate them—his, hers, and ours—are taken as one.

Remove the opening frame and the imaginative strategy of "The Emigrant Mother" becomes indistinguishable from that of Coleridge's "Frost at Midnight" or Yeats's "A Prayer for My Daughter." The poet in the opening stanza represents himself in the act of writing a poem through a speaker whom he professes to know as if that speaker were himself, but this self-representation or, as Hofstadter would say, "strange loop" does not so much change the status and strategy of the poem as complicate it.[1] Because the poet foregrounds his imaginative or "as if" supposition, the poem remains lyric, albeit complexly so, and the reader in his reenactment of the poet's lyric act accordingly "discovers" no distance between himself and the speaker. He does not perform the reconstructive activity definitive of monologic reading but, rather, hears the speaker's words just as the speaker seems to have intended them.

Like all mask-lyric speakers and unlike all monologic speakers, the emigrant mother is neither written nor read as a full-bodied, free-standing "other."

Rather, she is a strategic device that frees the poet from the confines of his more usual voice, enabling him to speak more variously and complexly even as this more various and complex voice continues to seem his own. She and all mask-lyric speakers are personae in the strict etymological sense: they are that through which the poet seems to speak. But these speakers are manifest not simply as sound but also as texts, and, as such, they exhibit neither the opacity of the monologic speaker, whom we seem to look at, nor the transparence of the lyric speaker, whom we seem to look through, but rather a studied translucence. They are a special case of conscious illusion.

The imaginative and critical complexities of the mask lyric have been most simply laid out by Pound's early lyrics: such poems from *Personae* as "La Fraisne," "Cino," "Na Audiart," "Marvoil," "Sestina: Altaforte," "Piere Vidal Old," and "Ballad of the Goodly Fere"; such translation-poems from *Cathay* as "The River-Merchant's Wife: A Letter," "Lament of the Frontier Guard," and "Exile's Letter." Like all poems here defined as mask lyrics, these, despite their relative simplicity, have consistently been treated as generically problematic. Their interpretive history has been plotted by a sequence of unresolved conflicts, the unanswered question of how they are like and unlike the dramatic monologue repeatedly raising further questions, which have in turn gone unanswered—as to their intentional and historical origin, the affective dynamics of their reading, their aesthetic and ethical value. The emergent lesson of this history is that a prior, well-formulated, and metaphorically dead critical genre—in this case, the dramatic monologue—has enormous territorial power, tending to dominate discussions not only of those poems for which it was designed but also of those that resemble them only superficially. Even the poet's own statements, the critic's intuitive response, and the text's resulting devaluation have not sufficed to make us question a genre to which we have grown accustomed and for which we can readily find textual "evidence."

Virtually every critic of Pound's early poetry quotes the poet's own generic definition:

> To me the short so-called dramatic lyric—at any rate the sort of thing I do—is the poetic part of a drama the rest of which (to me the prose part) is left to the reader's imagination or implied or set in a short note. I catch the character I happen to be interested in at the moment of song, self-analysis, or sudden understanding or revelation. And the rest of the play would bore me and presumably the reader. I paint my man as I *conceive* him. Et voila tout![2]

Such commentary, as Eliot has said, "takes its significance from the fact that it is the writing of a poet about poetry; it must be read in the light of his own poetry."[3] Conversely, the poetry is profitably read in the light of this commentary, which gives us the poet's own generic definition. Nevertheless, Browning's monologues have for several reasons continued to dominate our reading of these lyric-like poems: their common use of characterized and often historical speakers; Browning's conspicuous influence on Pound's early poetry; the fact that each called his poems "dramatic lyrics"; the inertia of critical habit; the representational strategy of schematic self-erasure, which makes changing genres difficult.[4] The less than satisfactory consequences of this habit have not, however, been lost on us: they are at once the force behind our repeated reading and a reminder of that reading's repeated failure.

Dissatisfaction with the strictly Browningesque has most frequently led Pound's critics to posit the additional and complicating influence of Yeats, of both his lyricism and his strategic masks, and to solve the generic problem posed by such radically different "fathers" by arranging Pound's poems along a continuum between the two. Thus N. Christoph de Nagy finds that Pound's personae "stand somewhere between Browning's dramatic monologues and Yeats's masks," and Hugh Witemeyer finds that "by a sort of useful oversimplification, we may think of Yeats and Browning as opposite ends of a spectrum along which Pound's dramatic monologues can be ranged."[5] Such arrangements give us a way of reading Pound's poems in terms of Browning's dramatic energy, verbal precision, rhythmic roughness, colloquial diction, and "unpoetical" matter. They also give us a way of reading in terms of the late Romantic deliquescence of Yeats's lyricism: its song-like epiphany and languorous lilt. But such arrangements beg the generic and valuative question: Are Pound's early poems rough-and-ready lyrics or wilting monologues? We still have no way of discussing how these poems are *affectively* like and unlike those of their two "fathers," nor do we have a way of discussing the radically different self-perspectives taken by speakers of monologues and lyrics. Whereas the monologue, as Bagehot observed, catches its speaker "*in difficulties* . . . amid the circumstances least favorable . . . struggling with obstacles . . . encumbered with incongruities,"[6] Pound catches his speaker "at the moment of song, self-analysis, or sudden understanding or revelation." Whereas the monologic speaker fails to know himself as we know him, the speaker of a mask lyric succeeds: he is represented at a moment of successful self-representation, caught in the act of fluent self-writing. To make sense of these differences and of the critical perplexities caused by their inarticulation, we need a new generic definition, one more precisely and radically responsive to our questioning.

Although only rarely made explicit, this need is felt throughout the interpretive history. De Nagy, for example, compares the speakers of Pound and Browning at length, reluctant to relinquish the monologic genre and yet cognizant of the essential lyricism of Pound's poems: "The masks of Pound were largely created to voice what Pound himself had to say in a personal way" (p.

131); "the lyrical verve of the mask occasionally breaks through the framework of the dramatic monologue that has been imposed on him" (p. 114); "the emphasis [in "Piere Vidal Old"] is laid on the lyrical element" (p. 123). Such repeated emphasis on the "lyrical element," both in the poetry and in its criticism, at once casts doubt on the old genre and suggests the beginnings of a new. So also do the distinctions made between Browning and Pound: "whereas Browning presents artists of various groups, the painters being the most numerous, all of Pound's major masks, with the exception of 'La Fraisne,' are poets" (p. 112); "Pound makes it a rule what with Browning was the exception," telling in his lengthy epigraphs what "in an orthodox monologue it would be the poet's task to 'bring in' step by step" (p. 116).

The "lyrical element" or "verve," the use of poets as speakers, the dependence on the epigraph to set the stage for the epiphany—all these characteristics can be discussed by the monologic genre only as gratuitous anomalies, and yet their repetition in the interpretive history argues their explanatory importance—as does the repeated gesture toward a new genre. J. P. Sullivan, for one, suggests that "Pound uses other poets to widen the range and deepen the effects of his own poetic personality. The method allows almost infinite nuances and shades of feeling, of irony and ambiguity, but above all an accuracy and a concision of expression for certain things he felt."[7] Pound himself made a similar suggestion:

> I have written "Heather," which represents a state of consciousness, or implies, or "implicates" it.
>
> A Russian correspondent, after having called it a symbolist poem, and having been convinced that it was not symbolism, said slowly; "I see, you wish to give people new eyes, not to make them see some new particular thing."[8]

Once again, we do well to let Pound's critical insight suggest ours: the speaker of a mask lyric is these "new eyes," and the consequent complication of our vision defines the distinctive power of the genre. Unlike the monologic speaker, he is designed not to seem opaquely autonomous, distinct from and independent of the poet who made him but, rather, to transfigure the poet's more usual voice and our more usual vision. Yet among Pound critics only Hugh Kenner has explicitly indicated the process of composing and understanding these poems to be this empathetic extension of self:

> The first poem he has chosen to have us read . . . is about how it feels to become a tree and thus understand many a thing "that was rank folly to my head before." The next poem in *Personae* imagines how it feels to be Tristram and beyond passion because dead; . . . the next, "Na Audiart," imagines how it feels to be Bertrans de Born who had been hurt

by two women at least, and is contriving in homage to one of them an ideal
lady whose torso is the other's; and when Audiart of the torso, who wishes
him ill, shall have grown old, she will soften, remembering his homage.[9]

Unfortunately, the locution—the *poem* imagines—obscures the critical problem
we are exploring, a problem that readily comes into focus with rephrasing: it
is the poet-speaker who has imagined himself feeling as if he were an other and
who has verbalized this imaginative act so that we can do likewise. Writing from
the point of view of someone else, just as did the poet-speaker of "The Emigrant
Mother," he enables us to see and feel as if we were that someone.

It is no accident that for Pound this someone else is typically a poet: Cino,
Villon, Marvoil, Bertrans de Born. In contrast with monologic speakers, who
reveal themselves unawares and, what is much the same, are unaware that they
are themselves written, speakers of mask lyrics are definitively self-conscious
and aware of themselves as written. Hence Prufrock's conspicuous concern with
the inadequacies of his appearance and his utterance: he has a bald spot in the
middle of his hair; he finds it impossible to say just what he means. Speakers
of mask lyrics are distanced from themselves, fully aware of the ironies of their
situations and actions, sensitive to the implications of their (usually verbal)
gestures. They see themselves as if they were their own readers and, in a sense,
they are just that: like the poet, they anticipate and thus perform their own reading. Pound's choice of the poet-persona thus makes perfect imaginative sense,
the poetic act being the paradigm of such self-consciously "as if" or imaginative
performances. His choice to speak through poets of other times and places is no
less justifiable, for such speakers deftly collapse otherness and oneness, distance
and intimacy, irony and sympathy, the act of seeing and the act of saying. In
other words, they make possible a characteristically modern kind of poem: the
mask lyric.

Recall that the monologue invites us to distinguish two voices and visions.
The Poundian mask lyric issues a contrary invitation, asking us to conflate two
voices and visions, those of the modern poet and those of the ancient, asking
us to read the poem as if it were a lyric while simultaneously recognizing its difference from that more traditional genre. M. L. Rosenthal's comment on the
Cathay poems suggests just such a conflation and complexity: "If the original
poet were alive today, writing in *our* language and with *our* experience behind
him, how would he do this poem? This is the problem Pound sets himself in his
translation-adaptations."[10] The solution to this problem, which defines the
experiment of not only the *Cathay* poems but of all mask lyrics, is a strategically
translucent and self-aware lamination of times, places, and personalities. Selectively transparent and opaque, the visions of speaker and poet remain distinctive
and yet are treated as if they were indistinguishable. The speaker is at once himself and outside himself, a dweller within his time and beyond it, a self that

writes and a self that is written about. This paradox is the enabling trope of the genre.

Like the dramatic monologue, then, the mask lyric issues its "as if" invitation in terms of a particular personality, but unlike the monologue it frees its speaker from the particulars of time and place. As is suggested by the monologue's sheer proliferation in the last century, the Victorians preferred its archaism and diachronic distance to the layered synchronism of the mask lyric. But by the century's turn this preference had reversed.[11] Eliot's remarks in "Tradition and the Individual Talent" (1917) gloss the consequences of this reversal:

> The historical sense involves a perception, not only of the pastness of the past, but of its presence; the historical sense compels a man to write not merely with his own generation in his bones, but with a feeling that the whole of the literature of his country has a simultaneous existence and composes a simultaneous order. This historical sense, which is a sense of the timeless as well as of the temporal and of the timeless and of the temporal together, is what makes a writer traditional. And it is at the same time what makes a writer most acutely conscious of his place in time, of his own contemporaneity.[12]

As do Pound's less well-known but no less pertinent remarks in *The Spirit of Romance* (1910):

> It is dawn at Jerusalem while midnight hovers above the Pillars of Hercules. All ages are contemporaneous. . . . This is particularly true of literature, where the real time is independent of the apparent, and where many dead men are our grandchildren's contemporaries, while many of our contemporaries have been already gathered into Abraham's bosom.[13]

Not surprisingly, most of Eliot's own early poems, like Pound's, are mask lyrics. Yet in his criticism Eliot does not connect the modernity of his temporal insight to the modernity of his poetic genre, nor do his critics. And while Langbaum does remark this synchronism, he identifies it as a peculiarity of the monologue:

> Pound actually makes dramatic monologues of his paraphrases from the personal utterances of ancient poets by intruding into them a modern consciousness. By employing an idiom and a tone so unmistakably contemporary as to give us an historical view of the utterance that the ancient poet could not himself have had, Pound uses the ancient poet as the speaker of a dramatic monologue.[14]

We do, as Langbaum suggests, have a perspective unavailable to the ancient poets, but the added perspective does not, as in "Cleon" and "Karshish," engender a separate and superior stance. Langbaum begins to make this point:

> The past becomes . . . a means for achieving another extraordinary
> point of view. . . . For the modern sense of the past involves, on the one
> hand, a sympathy for the past, a willingness to understand it in its own
> terms as different from the present; and on the other hand it involves a crit-
> ical awareness of our own modernity. . . . Sympathy frees us for the
> widest possible range of experience, while the critical reservation keeps
> us aware of how far we are departing. (P. 96)

The interest and value of these reading experiences does indeed lie in our awareness of "how far we are departing" from our own vision. This awareness, however, leads us to depart from the *speaker*'s vision only if his vision, like Cleon's
or Karshish's, is delimited by willful blindness as well as by time. Whereas all
extraordinary perspectives, not only those that are historical, both strain our
imaginative capacity and make us aware of that strain, only those that the
speaker could have shared and yet refuses to share invite our irony. Difference
per se tends to be not damning but intriguing.

Nevertheless, our modernity undeniably threatens our lyric union with the
speaker, a threat that Pound and other makers of mask lyrics minimize by building our "modern sense of the past" not merely into the poem, as Browning does
in "Cleon" and "Karshish," but into the speaker as well. The two visions, his
and ours, are thus conflated, each made invulnerable to the other's perspective.
In "Na Audiart," for example, the ironies are emphatic, but because they issue
from the speaker they parry our discounting, making us feel that his vision is
no less clear or knowing than ours:

> Yea though thou wish me ill,
> Audiart, Audiart.
> Thy loveliness is here writ till,
> Audiart,
> Oh, till thou come again.
>
>   . . .
>
> Thou shalt then soften,
> Knowing, I know not how,
> Thou wert once she . . .
>   (ll. 33–37; 50–52)

Projecting himself into the future, the time that is our present, the speaker
shares even as he creates our double vision. This doubleness makes the poem
ironic, but because the irony's victim is not the speaker but Audiart the poem
remains lyric as well. Witemeyer, however, reads "Na Audiart" in mimetic
terms, as "the portrait of a detached, sophisticated, and ironic character," and
thus concludes that the poem "approaches the Browningesque end of our spectrum in being a portrait of some psychological complexity" (p. 75). Irony and

complexity, that is, are once again taken as generic signs of the monologue. Yet because this polyvocality characterizes both genres, it is also necessary to note its strategic function, to note that the ironies and complexities of "Na Audiart" or any mask lyric do not sever the speaker's meaning from the poem's but, rather, are cause and consequence of the speaker's variegated vision, of the way his eyes refract the world for our edification and pleasure. The monologic speaker may be no less complex and his vision no less distinctive, but our "seeing" him from two different perspectives, his and the poet's, makes his vision or character seem opaque, possessed of an almost tactile reality. The complexity of the mask lyric speaker works differently: it is taken as a sign of the speaker's artificiality or, put otherwise, of his symbiotic connection with the poet who made him. Browning's monologic speakers thus seem to be what we see, whereas Pound's seem that through which we see.

This distinction is perhaps most clearly exemplified by "Ballad of the Goodly Fere," a poem written, as Pound has told us, to protest "a certain sort of cheap irreverence."[15] The poem indeed seems as intently persuasive—its announced purpose is to make the reader see Jesus as "a man o' men"—as any of Browning's monologues. The difference is that Pound does not focus on his speaker, the Apostle Simon Zelotes, and his failure to see but, rather, on what he sees and the accuracy of his vision:

> He cried no cry when they drave the nails
> And the blood gushed hot and free,
> The hounds of the crimson sky gave tongue
> But never a cry cried he.
> I ha' seen him cow a thousand men
> On the hills o' Galilee,
> They whined as he walked out calm between,
> Wi' his eyes like the grey o' the sea.
>   (ll. 37–44)

The emotional and perceptual confines of this vision are difficult to escape, our assent to what we seem to see difficult to withhold. The very details that appall—"the blood *gushed* hot and free"—simultaneously compel, intensifying this difficulty and, thereby, Pound's protest. We accordingly unlearn our traditional conception of Jesus and learn instead that his palpable physicality and vigor confirm rather than deny his spiritual stature.

Hopkins' "The Windhover" is proof that eyewitness accounts can be powerfully persuasive, but when the "eye" is characterized the vision becomes vulnerable, the account open to question. No longer an implicitly universal and flawless seer, the speaker of a mask lyric runs the risk of any explicitly particular and hence partial vision. Makers of these poems must accordingly work overtime to protect the lyric alliance from the very irony its "masking" or configuration creates. Thus Pound has his speaker project himself forward in time, anticipating and thereby joining our modern and more knowing vision:

> If they think they ha' slain our Goodly Fere
> They are fools eternally.
>
> (ll. 52–53)

Whatever the state of our religious belief, the very endurance of Christianity as a historical phenomenon here supports the speaker's case against those who "are fools eternally." As always happens in the mask lyric, the prophecy is self-fulfilling and hence strategic. More precisely, it is proleptic: it protects the speaker from our historical discounting and thus our irony. In "Ballad of the Goodly Fere" these defensive maneuvers combine with the novelty of an explicitly physical Jesus and the speaker's linguistic vigor to propel our imaginative belief toward and through the transcendent vision that concludes the poem:

> I ha' seen him eat o' the honey-comb
> Sin' they nailed him to the tree.
>
> (ll. 53–54)

To realize the vulnerability of this imaginative leap and recognize Pound's achievement, we have only to consider how these lines would strike us if displaced to the poem's opening. There we would accept or reject them as we might personally be inclined. But it is the very duration of reading *as if* this speaker saw him that builds our belief in the seer and, by an imaginative back formation, in what is seen.

Compared to Browning's monologues, wherein our ironic judgment of the speaker insistently argues the poet's vision, Pound's poem is a gentler persuasion. This gentleness has its advantages: by lending the speaker his articulate vision, the poet opens up a range, depth, and complexity of verbal imagining unavailable in the monologue; by presenting rather than denying a vision, he specifies particulars that otherwise must be left unsaid. It also has its disadvantages: making the speaker's vision so visible creates the possibility of our rejecting it and, as well, the poet's verbal vision or poem. We found that the rhetorical obliquity of the monologue makes such rejection difficult, that the very implicitness of the poet's values and vision confers a devious protection. But because the *en plein jour* guise of the mask lyric is relatively defenseless against the reader, the generic strategy must be double, at once working to seduce us to the speaker's vision and guarding that vision against our rejection. Insofar as this strategy works, insofar as the speaker's vision not only captures but carries us through the conclusion, the poem succeeds. But even these successes, which are both many and varied, seem vulnerable when contrasted with those of the bolder genre within whose historical and conceptual shadow they struggle to define themselves. The aesthetic and heuristic power of the mask lyric is finally equal to if not greater than that of the monologue, but its subtlety has undeniably put it at a critical disadvantage. Its power, in short, has seemed either invisible or suspect.

I have dwelt on the generic dilemma presented by Pound's early poems because the failure of its traditional solution typifies the pattern of all mask-lyric criticism: the critic remarks the essential lyricism of the poem and our response, but the received generic model deems this lyricism gratuitous, even inappropriate, an inexplicable if Yeatsian dilution of the ironic thrust so esteemed in Browning's monologues. Our recorded response to the poem thus becomes discontinuous with the poem's supposed generic structure, and the poems themselves lose value, seemingly burdened with inexplicable deadwood, spoken by speakers too self-knowing for the poems' ironic good, if not their own. I have been arguing that discussing these poems in terms of the mask-lyric model enables us to justify them aesthetically and ethically beyond what is possible when speaking in terms of the monologic model. It might, of course, be argued in reply that the poems continue to mean as they do no matter what we call them. But the interpretive history of mask lyrics strongly supports Gombrich's insistence on the importance of the "initial schema."[16] De Nagy, for example, qualifies his "initial schema" virtually out of existence in order to reconcile his intuition to his readings, but his intuitive insights nevertheless remain dangling, thereby confirming Gombrich's point: if the schema has "no provisions for certain kinds of information we consider essential, it is just too bad for the information" (p. 73). As we move to more intricate and powerful mask lyrics, we discover that their very intricacy and power proceed from the simultaneous presence of matter that seems to support the monologic model and matter for which this model has "no provisions." The critical problems increase accordingly.

But first let us define generally, as it were, the differences between the two genres. We have seen that the built-in discounting of the speaker's vision and the implicitness of the poet's render the dramatic monologue relatively invulnerable to further ironic discounting by the reader. It is difficult to undo implicit affirmations, those realized by our own reconstructing activity or "beholder's share," and it is redundant to undo what is already undone within the poem. As long as our alliance is with Cleon, it is open to the ironic upset that finally occurs. Once we adopt the poet's ironic stance, however, the poem neither rewards further discounting nor invites a return to the lyric vision with which we began. Although some literature invites and rewards endless discounting, the dramatic monologue does not: it is, to use Booth's terms, covert (it does not overtly invite our discounting), finite (the poet's implied assertion does not presume to comment on all men or all discourse), and stable (it does not reward further discounting).[17] Its persuasions are at once bold and controlled.

The mask lyric uses a radically different suasive strategy. Like the lyric, it weaves a vision unwarped by an external perspective. Invited to take the speaker as he takes himself, we take the speaker's meaning as the poem's. But the characterization of the mask-lyric speaker transfigures the transparence of his eye, thereby creating opportunities for speaker-directed irony. The conspicuously personal vision may offer, as Langbaum has argued, the only convincing validity in a post-Cartesian world, but it also is particularly open to the charge of idiosyncrasy. It will probably seem interesting, but it may also seem wrong.

Our strategies for making sense do, of course, have a certain inertia. In the last chapter we found that the very duration of lyric matching increases the difficulty of ironic closure, that Cleon's extensive and intensive hold on us could be broken only violently, by a conclusion so abrupt it borders on self-parody. But inertia alone cannot protect the patently idiosyncratic speaker. Such speakers engender reading experiences whose delicate balance of involvement and awareness tips at the first touch of judgment, however long deferred. The mask-lyric speaker accordingly performs the steps of ironic reconstruction himself: he takes a perspective on his meaning; he judges and, not infrequently, damns himself; he makes his self-writing critical, conscious of and thus protected against the consequences of its reading.

The New Criticism argued that all lyrics, whether "masked" or not, are similarly vulnerable and are ideally protected by this strategy. To purchase integrity and yet contain the multifariousness of life, the poem must not only see the ironies of that life but also the irony of its own vision. Thus Cleanth Brooks in "The Heresy of Paraphrase": the poem "preserves the unity of experience and . . . at its higher and more serious levels, triumphs over the apparently contradictory and conflicting elements of experience by unifying them into a new pattern."[18] And Robert Penn Warren: "the poet wishes to indicate that his vision has been earned, that it can survive reference to the complexities and contradictions of experience."[19] And Brooks once more, approving I. A. Richards's "poetry of synthesis": it is "a poetry which does not leave out what is apparently hostile to its dominant tone, and which, because it is able to fuse the irrelevant and discordant, has come to terms with itself and is invulnerable to irony."[20]

These statements exemplify a formalist definition of lyric strategy: the poem protects itself from our irony by making itself ironic, from our superior awareness by making itself self-aware, from the charge of limitation by implicitly deflecting limitless discounting. The argument is a literary phrasing of Vaihinger's thesis: express self-contradiction is the driving force of thought.[21] And of Hofstadter's: "what else is a loop but a way of representing an endless process in a finite way?" (p. 15). And of Browning's: all poetry is "a putting the infinite within the finite."[22] By "looping" back on itself, by making its self-contradictory or tropological nature explicit, writing both protects itself against extramural attack and creates the illusion of fullness or self-completion. In poetry, the most explicitly and densely tropological of all writing, this "strange looping" is the enabling rule rather than the disabling exception, and in monologues and mask lyrics this "strange looping" assumes the particular cognitive shape of irony. The two genres differ primarily in whether the irony is performed by the poet at the expense of the speaker or by both in unison.

For Brooks this irony is the infallible test of the lyric vision:

> Does the speaker seem carried away with his own emotions? Does he seem to oversimplify the situation? Or does he, on the other hand, seem to have won to a kind of detachment and objectivity? In other words, we are forced to raise the question as to whether the statement . . . acknowledges the pressure of the context; whether it is "ironical"—or merely callow, glib, and sentimental.[23]

Brooks lays out the defensive strength of the richly inclusive vision, the vision tempered by its self-contradiction, but the obvious bias of his questioning—irony is good, being "carried away" with emotion is bad—also cautions us to look more closely. We do indeed take the ironic or self-tempered vision seriously, but are we not also, even frequently, taken by emotion freed from all constraint, sensibility untempered by even a self-begotten sense? When the speaker of "Western Wind" cries "Christ, if my love were in my armes,/And I in my bed againe," we are swept up precisely because his emotion is unqualified. When the speaker of "The Windhover" confides that his "heart in hiding/Stirred for a bird,—the achieve of, the mastery of the thing," the unqualified depth of this stirring is what moves us. And in "Karshish" we join the speaker's vision precisely insofar as it breaks the bounds of everyday caution: "The very God! think, Abib, dost thou think?" These speakers are, to be sure, carried away with their own emotion, but no one would judge them callow, glib, or sentimental. Brooks would have all our lyrics be proof against our judgment, but such tempering does not necessitate an emotionless detachment, nor is such detachment necessarily a criterion of poetic value. The lyric's seemingly simple rhetoric is, even at its simplest, more complex. Unqualified emotion can be compelling as well as distancing, as much a summons to lyric involvement as to ironic chill. Moreover, the self-directed irony that protects the speaker's vision may simultaneously stem the outpouring of his emotion, itself powerfully seductive.

The mask lyric solves the problem posed by these contraries by refusing to choose between them, by preferring Schlegelian or, as it is usually known, romantic irony.[24] The reading experience of the mask lyric is at once an immersion and a withdrawal, a reveling in the powers of self-writing and a writing of its limits, a glimpse of the infinite that opens with every entry into an other and a grounding in the finite that closes with every reminder of our selfhood. As we have found, the dramatic monologue at its subtle best also works recognized limitation into felt plenitude, but the dynamics are different, the loci of awareness

differently organized. The monologic speaker matches our knowing only intermittently if at all. He tutors us in the ways of romantic irony, but always at his
own expense. His lesson is always inadvert and never masterly, although, of
course, it is his inadvertence that composes the very substance of the poet's
masterly design. It is his failure to know himself that makes our edification and
pleasure possible.

The speaker of a mask lyric, however, is himself a romantic ironist, a practitioner of becoming rather than a seeker after being. His aim is not the reconciliation, obliteration, or even transcendence of opposites but rather their designed
coexistence *as opposites*.[25] He, like the poem he speaks, from which he cannot
be distinguished, balances what Schlegel called *Selbstschöpfung* or self-making
and *Selbstvernichtung* or self-erasure. His achievement is a kind of *Selbstbe-
schränkung*, a self-limiting that constitutes not a limitation of self-knowledge so
much as the very stuff of its fashioning—and the condition of its invulnerability.[26] He has made his text ironical, so it cannot be accused of being callow,
glib, sentimental, or self-ignorant. As Schlegel put it, "Irony is self-polemic
overcome."[27] But this overcoming does not mean for Schlegel what it means for
Brooks: a triumph of "unity" and a reduction of passion into "a kind of detachment and objectivity." The romantic ironist has it, which is to say himself, both
ways: at once carried away and in control of his own transport. He is a master
of conscious illusion.

The Rhetoric of Self-Conscious Imaginings: "Tithonus" and "Ulysses"

Given that lyric sympathy is a more unstable literary emotion than ironic detachment and that the figured "eye" of the characterized speaker redoubles this
instability, it should come as little surprise that the most daring of mask lyrics
are repeatedly pronounced failures. Tennyson's "Ulysses" is just such a victim
of its own rhetorical daring, but its "failure" is best examined indirectly, by
way of its less problematic companion poem "Tithonus." Let us use Tennyson's
own words to tell the story behind what Pound calls the speaker's moment of
"sudden understanding or revelation": Tithonus was "beloved by Aurora, who
gave him eternal life but not eternal youth. He grew old and infirm, and as he
could not die, according to legend, was turned into a grasshopper."[28] The story
promises an extraordinary perspective and an extraordinary poem. But it also
promises problems: the speaker is potentially foolish, pathetic, even ludicrous
as he withers toward his demeaning metamorphosis. Criticism of the poem
accordingly remarks not only the poem's lyricism but also its irony and comedy.
James Kincaid first lays out the problems and strategies of the poem's lyricism:

Tithonus is made a slave to life, not death, suggesting the grotesque argument that man is born to shun the single friendly act of nature, his destruction.

Such an argument calls up very strong instinctive resistance, and the major artistic problem here is to generate sympathy in order to bypass our urgent need to judge. Most generally, Tennyson manages to do this by making the poem one of the most impassioned and self-absorbed of dramatic monologues. The speaker has very little perspective on his own situation and is mastered by his single obsession with release. Thus, we are not ourselves encouraged to find the detachment that more self-control or variety would allow. Even more important, perhaps, is the effect of the fine opening, where the "pure" poetry of incantation subversively draws us into the poem.[29]

He then argues for a monologic reading:

The tension between sympathy and judgment is further increased by incongruous echoes from the comedy of manners. The whole poem is cast as a lover's quarrel, filled with bizarre flattery and sly wheedling. The simplest logic behind Tithonus' argument is the strategy of pure pressure: keeping up a steady stream of words, even the same words, until the opponent yields from exhaustion. . . . The echo of the comedy of manners and its accompanying comfortable and assured values jars horribly with the genuine sound of Tithonus' anguish. . . . He is tauntingly placed at the center of comedy.[30]

Langbaum's argument runs parallel:

There is the same tension between sympathy and judgment; our experience of a longing to evade experience becomes itself the most intense of experiences to the extent that we realize how far from the norm we are departing. Sympathy adapts the dramatic monologue for making the "impossible" case and for dealing with the forbidden region of the emotions, because we must suspend moral judgment, we must sympathize in order to read the poem. (Pp. 92–93)

The poem's interpretive history has deemed its lyricism as problematic as it is necessary and hard-won: "the major artistic problem here is to generate sympathy"; "we must suspend moral judgment, we must sympathize in order to read the poem." Whether Tennyson failed to realize his creative intention is, of course, always open to question, as is that intention itself, but his revisions suggest that he was trying to keep the potential comedy and our potential judgment from becoming actualities. Consider that in Tennyson's early handling of the myth, "The Grasshopper," Tithonus completes his metamorphosis and that this finale, which presents an insuperable threat to the speaker's dignity, is absent from "Tithonus." Consider also that the emphases of the poem, in particular what Seymour Chatman would call the proportion of discourse-time to story-time, all support the case for a lyric reading:[31]

> Ay me! ay me! with what another heart
> In days far-off, and with what other eyes
> I used to watch—if I be he that watched—
> The lucid outline forming round thee; saw
> The dim curls kindle into sunny rings;
> Changed with thy mystic change, and felt my blood
> Glow with the glow that slowly crimsoned all
> Thy presence and thy portals, while I lay,
> Mouth, forehead, eyelids, growing dewy-warm
> With kisses balmier than half-opening buds
> Of April, and could hear the lips that kissed
> Whispering I know not what of wild and sweet,
> Like that strange song I heard Apollo sing,
> While Ilion like a mist rose into towers.
>
> (ll. 50–63)

By its extension and particularity this paean to Aurora's seductiveness becomes itself seductive, empowered to persuade us that Tithonus' temptation was irresistible, that we also could not have chosen otherwise than to spend eternity with the Goddess of Dawn. Thus tempted, we do not presume to find his situation comic. We understand it as an inevitable consequence of an unavoidable act, and we see Tithonus not as a fool but as a man undone in contest with the gods, an unfortunate but, again, an inevitable and not dishonorable fate. To argue otherwise is, of course, possible, but this passage would then become not only a gratuitous beauty but also an inexplicable dilution of the supposed comic effect. The reason for preferring one reading or one genre over another is, as always in explicitly deductive generic reasoning, less inherent than valuative: which reading or which genre unfolds the best poem?

Like all successful mask lyrics, then, "Tithonus" risks a devaluing or monologic reading. The characterization of the speaker and his bizarre predicament lend themselves to ironic discounting or even, as Kincaid argues, to comedy. But such risk-taking is valued most highly by discussing these poems not as monologues but as mask lyrics: concentrating on Tennyson's attempts to "generate sympathy," to counter "our urgent need to judge," to finesse our amusement, to seduce us into reading as if we were Tithonus. This sympathetic seduction, which drives not only the particular suasion of "Tithonus" but also that of the genre, may be defined thus:

> Looking at the object aesthetically would require that we be locked into the rapturous exploration of its discernible elements as they relate to each other. What would characterize the experience as aesthetic rather than either cognitive or moral would be its self-sufficiency, its capacity to trap us within itself, to keep us from moving beyond it to further knowledge or to practical effects.[32]

Murray Krieger's quintessentially formalist definition of "aesthetic" experience suggests that immersion in a perspective persuades us to value that perspective, that the text enfolds us by making explicit its own infolding, that reflexivity, autonomy, and coherence are not inert textual properties but active rhetorical strategies, ways of drawing us into the poem and keeping us there. In "Tithonus" the conflated infoldings of speaker and poet repeat the seductive strategy endemic to all lyrics—hence the formalist preoccupation with that form—but the unusual suasive riskiness of this and other mask lyrics places unusual strategic weight on the seductiveness of these infoldings. Packed with matter that threatens our imaginative involvement, these poems depend more than traditional lyrics on the tropologically dense textual surface and on the speaker's inward gaze. They aim to attract our attention to that surface and to trap it in that vision. This aim, however, is accomplished only when inner vision and poetic surface unite, when the speaker seems to generate both. Hence the genre's need for a self-conscious and articulate speaker, a poetic speaker, or, indeed, a poet.

It is no accident, then, that "Tithonus" reminds us throughout that it is a poem as well as a speech. This reminder is in part a matter of incantatory rhythms, in part a matter of tropological counterpoint: light against dark, warmth against coldness, youth against age, rose against white and silver, fire against ashes. Tithonus names himself a "white-haired shadow" who longs for "that dark world" where he was born but who is trapped forever in the "gleaming halls of morn." He has become "ashes" while Aurora's team continues to beat "the twilight into flakes of fire." Such express contradictions attract attention to themselves, focusing our gaze on the text and making our experience "aesthetic." But because in "Tithonus" this tropological attraction joins with a tactile sensuousness, our "as if" dwelling in the speaker's Thanatotic predicament becomes an erotic experience as well:

> Yet hold me not forever in thine East:
> How can my nature longer mix with thine?
> Coldly thy rosy shadows bathe me, cold

Are all thy lights, and cold my wrinkled feet
Upon thy glimmering thresholds . . .

(ll. 64–68)

The predicament, in other words, is at once knowingly ironic and passion-ately pathetic: seeking an *eros* bereft of *thanatos*, Tithonus finds a *thanatos* so conspicuously marked by *eros* that it has become exquisitely reminiscent of his loss. But like all speakers of mask lyrics, he is nothing if not self-aware. Indeed, it is his act of self-awareness, his adoption of a detached perspective on his predicament, that alone enables him to inscribe his self against a background of circumambient nothingness. He thereby achieves a Brooksian "detachment." He is free from "sentimentality," although he is not free from passion. He at once defines himself by wording his desire, and guards that definition and desire against our irony and redefinition. This transcendence of self, what Hofstadter would call "strange looping," the speaker's knowing himself *as if* he were an other, pervades the poem but is particularly conspicuous as it opens and closes, as Tithonus ponders the "I" that "used to watch—if I be he that watched" (l. 52), as he envies the "happy men that have the power to die,/And grassy bar-rows of the happier dead" (ll. 70–71). Moreover, the absence of these last lines in the original version of the poem—"Tithon" was written in 1833, some twenty-six years before "Tithonus"—suggests that in revision Tennyson sought to emphasize further not only the mortuary cast of Tithonus' displaced erotic longing but also his awareness of that displacement and its attendant self-ironic pathos.

Thus does "Tithonus" transform the implicit Brooksian conflict between intense emotion and ironic detachment into an express self-contradiction, the emotional and imaginative paradox that lies at the heart of romantic irony. As we shall see, this self-contradiction is generically definitive, the intense and yet self-detached emotion of mask-lyric speakers making possible an illusion that, unlike the illusion generated by the dramatic monologue, is conscious not only for the reader but also for the speaker. In "Tithonus," however, the self-contra-diction proves uniquely definitive as well, the speaker's gelid self-detachment being in this poem the emotion that is intensely felt.

It is also the emotion that makes the poem seem modern, more kin to Eliot than to Wordsworth. Like much Romantic poetry, "Tithonus" is a postlapsarian lament: the speaker mourns his fall away from a previous time and self; he longs to reverse or, at least, console himself for that fall by wording it. But Tithonus knowingly ironizes this Romantic lament: recovery or even consolation is pre-sented as finally and forever impossible; his ennui is a consciously cultivated weariness that is less a loss of ardor than its exhaustive celebration; he has fallen not away from but into heaven. To be sure, the splendor of this particular heaven is a torment. It mocks, even as it elicits, his variously erotic and mortuary desires. But it is also the very condition of his self-knowledge, the landscape of his salvation. The resulting self-detachment may feel cold to the emotional touch, but that assessment holds only momentarily, until we see the intensity with which it is felt and, what is finally the same, the thoroughness with which it is imagined.

Tennyson spoke of "Tithonus" as a pendant to "Ulysses," a metaphor that at once confirms their biographical kinship—both were conceived in the immediate aftermath of Hallam's death—and predicts the greater complexity of the latter poem's interpretive history.[33] It is generally agreed that both poems are attempts to manage a death-longing, but whereas for Tithonus this longing is unadulterated by any internal resistance, Ulysses contradicts his longing, fictionalizing it into a stance so intricate that it has engendered not only its readers' enduring fascination but an equally enduring interpretive conflict. Once again, Tennyson's own remarks, repeatedly quoted in the interpretive history, predict as much. In the *Memoir* we read that "Ulysses" was "written soon after Arthur Hallam's death, and gave my feeling about the need of going forward, and braving the struggle of life perhaps more simply than anything in 'In Memoriam.' "[34] And to James Knowles Tennyson said that it "was written under the sense of loss and that all had gone by, but that still life must be fought out to the end."[35]

The conflict dramatized in the poem's interpretive history reenacts that dramatized in the poem and glossed by Tennyson's remarks—between giving in and going on—but it more specifically reenacts the ethical dubiety of the attitudes adopted by Ulysses as resolving strategies. Should we read Ulysses as a "villainous other" or as a "lyrically sympathetic old warrior"?[36] Or, phrased in the generic terms of its history, should we read the poem as a fatigued monologue or as a fractured lyric? Either reading can be and has been argued for, but each has proven similarly and unacceptably reductive, capable of making sense only by ignoring large blocks of the text, by defining the "essence" of the poem either in terms of the following two passages or in spite of them. First, the opening wherein Ulysses repudiates his people and his wife:

> It little profits that an idle king,
> By this still hearth, among these barren crags,
> Matched with an agèd wife, I mete and dole
> Unequal laws unto a savage race,
> That hoard, and sleep, and feed, and know not me.
>
> (ll. 1–5)

Second, the lines in which he abdicates:

> This is my son, mine own Telemachus,
> To whom I leave the sceptre and the isle—

Well-loved of me, discerning to fulfil
This labour, by slow prudence to make mild
A rugged people, and through soft degrees
Subdue them to the useful and the good.
Most blameless is he, centred in the sphere
Of common duties, decent not to fail
In offices of tenderness, and pay
Meet adoration to my household gods,
When I am gone. He works his work, I mine.

(ll. 33–43)

These passages must trouble attempts to read the poem lyrically. The "agèd wife" is Penelope, whose rejection recalls a mythic fidelity and thus invites our condemnation. His aristocratic condescension is distasteful. His praise of his son is stunning in its blandness. Not surprisingly, many dispute the lyric reading. E. J. Chiasson finds Ulysses rhetorical in the least flattering sense, the overwhelming close being a "burst of oratory," and John Perry finds the poem "satiric of the vainglorious posturings of the aged Ulysses."[37] Yet even those who thus argue end by conceding the poem's lyric power—despite the cost to their own arguments. Thus Chiasson: "Drinking life to the lees, drinking delight of battle with his peers, following knowledge like a sinking star—all render him abundantly lyrical."[38] And Perry: "Ulysses' very words can be said by the author without irony."[39]

The oft-quoted comment of W. H. Auden, however, casts a more subtle light on the interpretive conflict: "And what is *Ulysses* but a covert—the weakness of the poem is its indirection—refusal to be a responsible and useful person, a glorification of the heroic dandy?"[40] Auden condemns the poem not for its failure to accomplish what we infer to have been Tennyson's affective intention but for succeeding all too well. In other words, he confirms the poem's aesthetic achievement—Tennyson successfully seduces us with an ethically dubious speaker—but finds in this achievement an ethical fault: he shouldn't have. Perhaps not. But Auden's point suggests that the interpretive history, like Auden, has judged Tennyson's achieved intention in terms of the extramural ethical value of that intention. That is, "Ulysses" has engendered interpretive conflict not only because the text allows and even encourages critical readers to justify two views of its speaker but also because, as with dramatic monologues, those same readers have implicitly treated its speaker as if he were designed not with affective purpose but with aesthetic purposelessness. This treatment virtually requires the critic to interpret a poem in terms of its speaker and, in the case of "Ulysses," to fault it for the supposed ethical faults of that speaker.

The interpretive history of "Ulysses," then, has been plotted by a distinctive struggle, by the attempt to decide a perplexity prefigured in the poem itself: Which part of the poem—or its speaker—is more powerful? Does Ulysses' arrogance and abdication of social responsibility cancel his lyric seductiveness or does this seductiveness, rightly or wrongly, overwhelm the two passages quoted above, quelling irony and inviting the reader's empathy? We can, I think, more successfully argue the latter reading, proceeding as follows. We might begin with Tennyson's glosses on the poem, arguing the harmony of elegiac mood and lyrical mode. We might note that even ironic and satiric readings find it impossible to deny the poem's lyrical power and that those readers who attempt to read the poem both ways readily concede that "the splendor is undeniably all with Ulysses."[41] We might further observe that in the "lyrical" passages the lines are densely tropological and euphonious, whereas in the "ironic" passages they are flatly literal and tonally dead, an observation that suggests that the poem is selectively invoking the beholder's share and soliciting our aesthetic admiration—all in the service of a lyric reading. Because godlike questing is incompatible with connubial bliss, we might argue that neither Ulysses nor the poem should be faulted for his making a necessary if difficult choice. Indeed, we might argue that the two troublesome passages show Ulysses' awareness of this difficulty and, thereby, serve to deflect our ironic discounting and protect the lyric reading. And we might observe that poetry is not "properly" faulted Auden-style, by mounting an extramural attack on intramural values. And finally, we might refer to the original manuscript, observing that the entire Telemachus passage is a compositional afterthought, separated from the poem's end by a considerable space.[42] And from this observation we might conclude that the poem was originally conceived as a sustained lyric outburst and that it is best read as just that.[43]

I have sketched this justification of the lyrical reading in a suppositional mode in part to remind us that, like all interpretations, its superiority is relative and rhetorical, in part to imply its provisional status in this discussion. For despite what I would argue is its explanatory superiority to the ironic reading, the lyric reading, particularly if concentrated on the poem's aesthetic beauty, only meagerly justifies the affective risk incurred by the troublesome passages and falls mute before more particular questioning. Read thus, "Ulysses" is undeniably "beautiful" but is no less undeniably a compositional failure, a perhaps overly poetic poem in which "details are inconsistent, the reasoning specious, the whole a kind of brilliantly whited sepulchre."[44] Such a poem cannot justify the attention we have paid it because it disdains that attention, refusing our questions. Why, we would like to know, does Ulysses speak in shifting space and indeterminate time? Or does he speak at all? Who listens, if anyone? Such questions rarely arise in discussing dramatic monologues, and it is interesting to ponder why they do so here. Why the emphasis on seeking and finding? What is he looking for? Why does the object of his desire, whatever it is, recede at his approach? And why are we never told what it is? Such questioning, as well as the larger and unresolved question of how to take the Telemachus passage, suggests a need for a reading that would incorporate the either-or readings canonized in the interpretive history, justify the troublesome passages without subverting or compromising the rest of the poem, and explain the particulars of the poem's affective design.

I have argued that critical reading begins with the choice of a beginning premise, an assertion from which further explanatory assertions may be deduced. In the case of Tennyson's "Ulysses," I suggest we begin by asserting that Tennyson intended his compositional afterthought to complicate rather than confute the lyric poem into which it was inserted. And because the insertion was accomplished without any transitional smoothing—in the poem as we now have it the fragment rasps against its adjoining textual edges—we may further assert that the affective impression of fragmentation and dissonance was designed. The reason, once again, for making such assertions is pragmatic rather than representational: we cannot know or represent Tennyson's intention, but we can use the compositional evidence to posit an intention that will enable us to make a superior sense of the poem or, what is the same, enable us to read a superior poem.

Let us, then, look more closely at what Ulysses is doing in the two passages in question. The Telemachus passage, as noted above, is distinguished from the rest of the poem by its tropological inertness and by the not-unrelated blandness of Ulysses' praise. Nevertheless, as oratorical suasion—the oratorical cast of "Ulysses" is routinely, if not approvingly, recognized in the interpretive history—this passage readily falls into the epideictic category, in which the orator ceremoniously praises or blames, as contrasted with the forensic, in which he decides past action, or the deliberative, in which he decides future action.[45] Aristotle's analysis of the three categories is useful here, and we may justify its relevance biographically by recalling the thoroughly rhetorical foundation of nineteenth-century education, particularly Tennyson's early habit of writing lyric poems as prosopopoeiae, rhetorical exercises in which the student writes as if he were an other, an other who is represented as speaking but who is known in lyrical fashion, as if from within.[46]

Aristotle observes that the starting point in all three modes is the interpreter's suasive occasion and purpose rather than his uninterpreted encounter with an unavoidable Truth. He further observes that whereas deliberative discourse is primarily political and forensic discourse is primarily legal, epideictic discourse is ethical both in topic and affective purpose. The epideictic speaker whose goal is praise accordingly proceeds by invoking a set of particular ethical values and intensifying the adherence of his audience to those values and thereby to their embodiment, the person praised. Finally, Aristotle observes that whereas the forensic ponders past action and the deliberative future action, the epideictic ponders or, to be precise, performs present action. Thus, when we consider that in the other two modes the discourse action attempts to represent an action prior to or posterior to itself, the epideictic acquires the additional distinction of being coextensive with itself, of being what we might call the most "literary" because the most self-substantiating of the three rhetorical modes.

Reading the Telemachus passage in epideictic terms, we find that it is indeed ethically enumerative: Telemachus is "well-loved of me," "most blameless," "decent not to fail/In offices of tenderness"; his adoration of the household gods is "meet," his prudence "slow." There is no overt blame here—indeed, Telemachus is explicitly deemed "most blameless"—but the seeming faintness of Ulysses' praise sounds puzzling if not suspicious to our ears and, perhaps more than anything else in the poem, has been responsible for the "villainous other" readings. Yet if we consider that only in the twentieth century did Ulysses come to seem less than perfectly admirable and that Telemachus here expresses Tennyson's gradualist philosophy of the early thirties, we should begin to doubt our post-Romantic ethical values and categories of reading rather than Tennyson's way of writing, which was ineluctably Romantic to be sure but, perhaps more to the point, was classical and rhetorical as well.[47] Turning again to Aristotle's *Rhetoric*, which Tennyson doubtless knew, we find the "virtues" listed: "justice, courage, temperance, magnificence, magnanimity, liberality, gentleness, prudence, wisdom."[48] The list is particularly interesting for our purposes because all nine virtues are found in the poem, but not all are found in the speaker. Indeed, Aristotle values most highly those assigned the speaker's son: "If virtue is a faculty of beneficence, the highest kinds of it must be those which are most useful to others."[49] This older ethics thus corrects the interpretive distortion wrought by our contemporary devaluation of "the useful and the good," helping us to see that for Tennyson and his readers "the useful" *was* "the good" and that our distaste for Telemachus is primarily just that: a matter of contemporary taste.

Nevertheless, the tropological and tonal inertness of the Telemachus passage must give pause to any attempt to value the son *over* the father—particularly when we recall that the epideictic mode has historically been remarkable for its verbal ornamentation, so much so that the absence of such ornament, particularly in the eighteenth and nineteenth centuries, must be itself conspicuous, occasion for questioning. And if we again return to Aristotle, we find yet further reason to complicate our developing stance: "All actions are noble that are appropriate to the man who does them: if, for instance, they are worthy of his ancestors or of his own past career."[50] Or, as Ulysses puts it, "Some work of noble note, may yet be done,/Not unbecoming men that strove with Gods" (ll. 52–53).

We can, in other words, argue the value structure of the poem both ways. Like Aristotle's list, the poem performs a double counterpoint: virtues of limitation are set against those of limitlessness, virtues of self-sacrifice against those of self-fulfillment. The critical benefit of reading the passage against its background of classical ethics and rhetoric is that such reading liberates us from the either-or terms that plot the poem's interpretive history and empowers us to make sense in terms of the comparative discrimination announced in the poem itself: "He works his work, I mine" (1. 43). Read thus, Ulysses' purpose would seem to be not the damnation with faint praise canonized in the interpretive history but, rather, a more interesting and difficult attempt: to discriminate and choose between the socially impeccable values of his son, and those of intellectual and imaginative adventure. Seen thus, the faintness and inertness of the passage become conceptually and strategically indispensable: they simultaneously enable Ulysses to define his ethics and win our adherence to his definition.

Like the Telemachus episode, the poem as a whole rewards reading in epideictic terms. Pondering and performing a set of ethical evaluations, Ulysses is intent on increasing adherence to the person praised. But because this person is Ulysses himself, because the mode of praise is here transfigured to the risky mode of self-praise, the poem and its speaker on this count also invite the adverse judgments recorded in its interpretive history. Although the accuracy of his self-definition—he is, after all, truly extraordinary—helps to keep the charge of arrogance at bay, it cannot cancel the risk incurred by the poet's attempts to persuade us to value that definition. But by having Ulysses seem to speak to himself and the reader seem to overhear, his rhetoricity is minimized and his sincerity increased: hence the rhetorical importance of the critically troublesome indeterminacies of space, time, and audience.

By no accident is this last vagueness a characteristic and enabling strategy of Romanticism, of both its poetry and its poetics: "A poet is a nightingale, who sits in darkness and sings to cheer its own solitude with sweet sounds; his auditors are as men entranced by the melody of an unseen musician, who feel that they are moved and softened, yet know not whence or why."[51] Shelley's famous definition of poetic suasion suggests that for Tennyson's Romantically trained audience Ulysses seemed, if not a poet, at least poet-like in his seeming disregard of all "rhetorical" ethos except the one called "sincerity." Shelley also concisely states Romanticism's "philosophic" justification for the other indeterminacies typical of its poetic speakers: "A poet participates in the eternal, the infinite, and the one; as far as relates to his conceptions, time and place and number are not."[52] Tennyson may or may not have known Shelley's *Defense* while writing "Ulysses." The *Defense* was first published seven years later, in 1840, but the fact that sixteen of the twenty names mentioned in *The Palace of Art* (1832 version) occur in the *Defense* suggests that Tennyson may have read the essay in manuscript.[53] The point, however, is that the poetic strategies of Romanticism, documented paradigmatically but far from exclusively by Shelley, conspicuously inform the poem and its reception.

I would argue, then, that we can best justify the art of "Ulysses" by treating its speaker as engaged in the project of verbal self-definition, as defining himself by writing himself: "I am," he announces, "become a name" (l. 11). In one sense Ulysses becomes a name simply by announcing that he has, but in another he must argue the significance of this announcement, enact the connection between naming and knowing. One way of doing this is for Ulysses to say what he is not. Hence the Telemachus passage and the passage that opens the poem. He there divests himself of his social self-definition, his identity as an "idle king"; he departs a landscape of imaginative deadness, the "still hearth" and "barren crags"; he abandons the delimiting activities of meting and doling; he abjures the quotidian and its unconscious actors, those who "hoard, and sleep, and feed, and know not me."

But self-definition also requires that Ulysses say what he *is*. For the rhetorical thinker, such self-articulation is not a matter of discovering some inner essence but rather of performing a conceptual activity, and for that, as Vaihinger argues, Ulysses must choose and make use of a conceptual fiction that will "drive" or make possible his thought. The fiction he chooses, paradoxically enough, is that of representational questing:

> And this gray spirit yearning in desire
> To follow knowledge like a sinking star,
> Beyond the utmost bound of human thought.
>
> (ll. 30–32)

Ulysses self-consciously imagines himself performing the Faustian quest of representational knowledge, but the quest is uncharacteristically played out in explicitly imaginative or "as if" fashion, in full recognition of its tropological status. Hence the infinite recession of the object of knowledge, the "sinking star" that dwells "beyond the utmost bound of human thought"; hence the "world whose margin fades/For ever and for ever when I move" (ll. 20–21); hence his purpose, "To sail beyond the sunset, and the baths/Of all the western stars, until I die" (ll. 60–61). He seeks, but it is a search undertaken for its own sake; he would find, but the object to be found is not only never specified, it is deliberately imagined as permanently hidden, definitively elusive, forever beyond his grasp.

Tennyson thus both follows and departs from what we believe to be his primary source. Dante's Ulysses, it will be recalled, also speaks to his mariners, also is "old and tardy," also is driven by intellectual curiosity:

> "O brother!" I said, "who through a hundred thousand dangers have
> reached the West, deny not, to this the brief vigil
> of your senses that remains, experience of the unpeopled world behind
> the Sun.

Consider your origin: ye were not formed to live like brutes, but to follow virtue and knowledge."[54]

Dante's Ulysses, it should be noted, speaks after-the-fact and, not incidentally,
from the eighth circle of hell. He presents himself as actually having sailed in
pursuit of his goal, whereas Tennyson's Ulysses presents himself as performing
a purely anticipatory voyage, to be speaking before-the-fact. This presentational
antithesis, however, itself requires revision, for the Victorian Ulysses does not
in fact speak *before* he quests. Rather, his questing is coincident with his speaking. Not only, then, is his goal permanently beyond him, his quest is permanently imaginary and present tense.[55] The two changes rung on the Dantean
source cleanse such questing of medieval suspicion and enable Tennyson to present *curiositas* as not sin but virtue.

His Ulysses thus indefinitely defers fulfillment of the most basic representational desire: a face-to-face encounter with the object of knowledge, meaning
his "essence." This deferral, however, is not imposed from without. It is a self-
consciously chosen strategy, which drives his thought, enabling him to act or
write his existence by acting *as if* he seeks his essence. The poem thus dramatizes how the characteristic activity of one tradition of knowledge, the representational search for the object of knowledge, can, when performed in "as if"
fashion, be made to serve the purpose of a different and nascent tradition of
knowledge, the writer's existentialist writing of his existence. Ulysses' search
is thus in one sense suppositional and purposeless: he acts as if there is an essence or interpretive ground and as if he can find it. Yet in another sense it is
quite real and purposeful: he is actually performing an act of imagination in
order to make his self.

We might at this point usefully compare the attempts of monologic speakers
to define themselves, attempts that, however varied, characteristically end in
imaginative death. Recall Cleon's "will to interpretive closure," which drives
him to fulfill representational desire literally and which ends, as all such fulfillments end, in a perfected completion that is also a silence and a death. Having
successfully inscribed a series of closures—temporal and traditional, human and
divine—Cleon completes their logic: he imagines himself forever asleep in the
enclosure of his well wrought urn. Recall also the Bishop's intense imaginative
activity as well as its failure to defend against death. Like Cleon, he ends en-
tombed precisely because he has literalized his imaginative activity and, thus,
failed to purchase its redemptive power. While it is true that Cleon did, as he
tells us,

> dare at times imagine to his need
> Some future state revealed to us by Zeus,
> Unlimited in capability

> For joy, as this is in desire for joy,
> (ll. 325-28)

he ends by repudiating his imagining, much as Andrea ends by repudiating his. And we found that Andrea, whose reach was deliberately toned down to his grasp, who deliberately dwelt in a hermeneutic landscape of twilight stasis, was as surely doomed by his perfection to self-embalmment as were Cleon and the Bishop.

Bloom argues that "a poem is written to escape dying."[56] But we found that monologic speakers cannot manage such an escape precisely because they refuse to know their poetic self-inscription as such, as a strategy that enables the activity of self-definition, rather than as a transparent window on their essence. Ulysses, however, is knowing in just this way, and he accordingly does "escape dying." Unlike the speakers of even Browning's most complex monologues, he deliberately defers representational fulfillment, leaving himself open to future re-writing, successfully "putting the infinite in the finite," thereby becoming in yet another way poet-like.

The landscape of Longinian sublimity through which Ulysses imaginatively moves seduces our imaginations as surely as his definitively "poetic" if ethically dubious eloquence. The landscape also dramatizes just this infinitude of human and hermeneutic possibility. Gaston Bachelard in *The Poetics of Space* defines the drama thus:

> Immensity is a philosophical category of daydream. Daydream undoubtedly feeds on all kinds of sights, but through a sort of natural inclination, it contemplates grandeur. And this contemplation . . . transports the dreamer outside the immediate world to a world that bears the mark of infinity. . . . works of art are the *by-products* of this existentialism of the imagining being. In this direction of daydreams of immensity, the real *product* is consciousness of enlargement.[57]

Bachelard's poetics suggests an explanatory metaphor: the imaginative activity of Ulysses and his reader is like a free-floating state of consciousness in which envisioned immensity invites the dreamer's expansion of self, his perpetual open-endedness. Ulysses and his reader are like the daydreamer who "sees himself liberated from his cares and thoughts [the "still hearth," the "agèd wife," the "common duties"] . . . he is no longer . . . the prisoner of his own being."[58] He fuses with the world, its horizon moving "for ever and for ever" as he moves within it. It is precisely through such transactions, Bachelard writes, that "these two kinds of space—the space of intimacy and world space blend. When human solitude deepens, then the two immensities touch and become identical."[59]

And so they seem to in "Ulysses." This fusion of intimate and infinite space, a fusion repeated as the poem concentrates its vast intertextual "origins" into this lyric or intimate space, was present in the first draft and was intensified by Tennyson's revisions, the lines

> Yet all experience is an arch thro wh[ich]
> Gleams the untravelled world[60]

becoming

> Yet all experience is an arch wherethrough
> Gleams that untravelled world, whose margin fades
> For ever and for ever when I move.
>
> (ll. 19–21)

Freed of time and space, Ulysses, like all speakers of mask lyrics, accepts the risk of dwelling in an infinite universe. Unlike the monologic speaker, he refuses "to store and hoard" himself. He is willing, even eager, to take a dramatic risk, "to perform the self as fragmented perceptions and desires."[61] The distinctive triumph of "Ulysses" is that the performance is enacted on the stages of two distinct traditions.

This dramatic ambidexterity, however, has further vexed the poem's interpretive history, adding to the "villainous-virtuous" question yet another: whether Ulysses would live intensely until arbitrarily stopped by death or whether death is what he seeks. Undeniably, the presence of *thanatos* increasingly shadows this "as if" quest for *logos*: Ulysses is a "gray spirit," the star is "sinking," "the long day wanes," he would sail until he dies. Langbaum finds Ulysses' death-longing to be the "central fact" of the poem, and even those who, like A. Dwight Culler, read Ulysses as longing for intellectual knowledge cannot avoid *thanatos*: "It is a voyage into all that is obscure upon the map, all that is dark and mysterious in the human consciousness, all that is shadowy either in this world or the next. It is certainly a voyage into Death."[62] Well, yes, but the question remains unanswered: Does Ulysses seek death or is death an incidental if inevitable consequence of his search? Culler's answer is very nearly satisfying: "Those readers who find this element incompatible with the rest of Ulysses' quest seem to me to interpret that quest too narrowly, for it is not a real voyage but a visionary voyage, and, like Browning's '*Childe Roland to the Dark Tower Came*,' includes the 'last curiosity' of death."[63] But if we fully recognize the visionary or "as if" nature of this voyage, we also recognize that this "last curiosity" or ultimate *logos* is itself an enabling, even salvational fiction, the self-contradiction that "drives" Ulysses' thought and perpetuates his life. His literal death is inevitable but only incidental to that life. His imaginative death, as our repeated rewritings of his self-writing testify, is perpetually deferred.

The Rhetoric of Nightmare Questing: " 'Childe Roland to the Dark Tower Came' "

Like Ulysses, the speaker of Browning's " 'Childe Roland to the Dark Tower Came' " enacts a quest, and the reader of this poem, like the reader of "Ulysses" and of all mask lyrics, reenacts this quest in his reading, experiencing the speaker's experience as if it were his own.[64] But the two poems share a particular as well as a generic kinship: their speakers similarly use representational questing as a metatrope, an imaginative stylus with which to inscribe the self. And because their kinship is so particular, we can also particularize their difference: whereas the experience of Ulysses is analogous to daydream, that of Roland is analogous to nightmare.[65]

Ulysses quests in a mood of Edenic nostalgia. The landscapes of world and mind seduce not only by their conflated infinitudes, the horizonal distances of the one speaking the retrospection of the other, but also by their euphony and twilight shimmer:

> The lights begin to twinkle from the rocks;
> The long day wanes; the slow moon climbs; the deep
> Moans round with many voices.
>
> (ll. 54–56)

"Childe Roland" shows the lurid underside of such idyllic questing, dramatizing the manifest animus that threatens speaker and reader alike:

> All the day
> Had been a dreary one at best, and dim
> Was settling to its close, yet shot one grim
> Red leer to see the plain catch its estray.
>
> (ll. 45–48)

Imaginative dwelling in such a world is accomplished only with a strain whose extremity marks it as deliberate or defining, as the critical pattern of the poem's power. For the significance of Roland's concluding gesture—

> Dauntless the slug-horn to my lips I set,
> And blew. "*Childe Roland to the Dark Tower Came.*"
>
> (ll. 203–4)

—becomes manifest only if we have become his questing companions and if that quest is *with difficulty* accomplished. Insofar as the loathsomeness and threat of Roland's world are mitigated, the gesture loses force; insofar as they are intensified, the poem risks our withdrawal. Nightmares, that is, tend to be neither pleasing nor ultimately edifying, yet because "Childe Roland" is finally both, the critical question is how Browning has managed this end, how he has led us to reenact Roland's seemingly purposeless quest and, as well, to know its purpose and pleasure.

Roland presents himself as the victim of the world he and we enter. We never learn why or how he is victimized—this mystery lies at the heart of the nightmare—but from the beginning we have no doubt that he is:

> My first thought was, he lied in every word,
>   That hoary cripple, with malicious eye
>   Askance to watch the working of his lie
> On mine, and mouth scarce able to afford
> Suppression of the glee, that pursed and scored
>   Its edge, at one more victim gained thereby.
>   (ll. 1–6)

These lines do not invite us to join Roland; they insist. We read, "My first thought was," and ask: Whose first thought? And what is the implied second thought? We read, "he lied in every word," and ask: Who lied? Why? Such incompleteness is bewildering, and our bewilderment both makes us depend on Roland as a source of information about his world and heightens our curiosity, not only about his world but also about his quest. Moreover, we learn from this first line both that our reading, like Roland's, must be mistaken and that those mistakes, like Roland's, must nevertheless be made. Even as it is told, we know that the "first thought" is wrong, that the cripple did not lie, yet we believe in the man Roland encounters because we know that our belief is the coin needed to purchase Roland's experience, whose value is assumed at the poem's beginning but is not confirmed till the poem's end. More than most, this poem depends on the conventional economics of the reader's willing suspension of disbelief: believe in Roland's experience and in return you get that experience—for whatever it's worth, and the difficulty of its acquisition makes us think that it is worth a great deal indeed. To read "Childe Roland" as a dramatic monologue—severing Roland's meaning from the poem's, doubting his knowing of his world and self—is, then, to diminish the poem: to distance its weirdness, to dull its wit, to render its conclusion inexplicably lame. "Childe Roland" is best justified in mask-lyric terms, by a generic explanation that affirms rather than denies the clarity of Roland's retrospective vision and, what is the same, shows the fusion of that vision with ours.

We may posit, then, that the poet's problem was how to sustain the hermeneutic anxiety generated by the text's knowing error, its strategic admixture of mistake and self-retrospection, while neither undercutting the emotional immediacy of Roland's narration nor the bizarre reality of the world it bodies forth. The following passage exemplifies Browning's solution:

> One stiff blind horse, his every bone a-stare,
>   Stood stupefied, however he came there:

Thrust out past service from the devil's stud!

Alive? he might be dead for aught I know,
   With that red gaunt and colloped neck a-strain,
   And shut eyes underneath the rusty mane;
Seldom went such grotesqueness with such woe;
I never saw a brute I hated so;
He must be wicked to deserve such pain.

                 (ll. 76–84)

By detailing sight, sound, color, texture, horse, and tree in discourse time, the poet creates a world that seems less read than real. It is also a world that persistently defeats our expectations and Roland's, that seems, like the world we live in, to be beyond imagining or, once again, real. In part this defeat is accomplished syntactically, as in the opening lines where the difficulty and retrospective uncertainty of our parsing recapitulate Roland's questing. But our normal ways of reading and of making our way in a normal world are also defeated by the defamiliarizing strangeness of this particular world and the disorienting suddenness with which we come upon it:

   A sudden little river crossed my path
   As unexpected as a serpent comes.
   No sluggish tide congenial to the glooms;
                (ll. 109–11)

Its sheer unexpectedness makes the river seem real and Roland's vision seem true. The relationship between this seeming reality and our imaginative belief in Roland's vision is reflexive, Roland's world and his reading of that world being so wedded that its every incident and his every reading seem mutually authenticating and increasingly inevitable. Because we have no clue to what horror comes next, Roland's world seems, as it must for the poem to disturb and disorient, to be beyond his control. But because the poem simultaneously would have us see the world in the way he sees it, his every reading is informed by the response it would elicit in its reader. To continue with the river:

   This, as it frothed by, might have been a bath
   For the fiend's glowing hoof—to see the wrath
      Of its black eddy bespate with flakes and spumes.

   So petty yet so spiteful! All along,
      Low scrubby alders kneeled down over it;
      Drenched willows flung them headlong in a fit
   Of mute despair, a suicidal throng:
   The river which had done them all the wrong,
      Whate'er that was, rolled by, deterred no whit.

Which, while I forded,—good saints, how I feared
To set my foot upon a dead man's cheek,
Each step, or feel the spear I thrust to seek
For hollows, tangled in his hair or beard!
—It may have been a water-rat I speared,
But, ugh! it sounded like a baby's shriek.

(ll. 112–26)

Roland's reading seems to fit or mirror his world in large part because it informs that world. But the constitutive power of his mind is strategically camouflaged by Roland's manifest surprise at what he encounters and by the dramatic resistance that that world presents to his understanding ("The river which had done them all the wrong,/Whate'er that was."). Roland's world corroborates his vision precisely because it is fully but not noticeably authored by that vision.

As we read, then, Roland's vision accrues credibility, growing increasingly invulnerable to our discounting. As does Roland himself. We are told virtually nothing about him. We reexperience only the exhaustion and torturous progression of his quest. The pasts of his questing predecessors were marred by disgrace, but Roland's implicitly similar past and guilt remain strategically implicit, sufficient to shade his vision to the translucence typical of mask-lyric speakers but insufficient to darken that vision toward monologic opacity. We learn enough to wonder but not enough to judge. Moreover, his quest lacks explicit cause for the same reason that the Ancient Mariner's shooting of the Albatross lacks cause: a known reason can be deemed unworthy, a cause not plausibly ours. Its unsaid origin gives Roland's narration, like the Mariner's, the power to attract and implicate the reader.

The absence of bases for judgment, the intense and self-confirming inwardness of the vision as it covertly creates what it seems to see, our apprehensive fascination with Roland's world as he and we negotiate its unexpectedness, Roland's retrospective or "written" awareness of his present or "lived" predicament—all fuse our vision to his as we read. Even the grotesquery of Roland's world is finally seductive, a triumph of invention over disgust. As in much Romantic poetry, particularly Wordsworth's and Shelley's, the topography of "Childe Roland" is as mental as it is physical. The speaker shows his mind by seeing or, more precisely, penning his world. But the grotesquery of Roland's world is neither merely decorative nor simply a way of speaking his mind. For the reader, as for Roland, it intensifies *curiositas*, the desire to reach the end and *know*. But of course this end, even when reached, is impossible to word or know. Once again, the rhetoric of a "masked" lyricism is shown to be a matter of balancing contraries, of saying and sustaining the contradictions of emotion and thought, of language and world, of desire and its fulfillment.

As in "Ulysses," the tropological and the topographical, the word and the world, are intimately bound. From its first line "Childe Roland" both promises understanding—the tower and *logos* that will explain this imaginative world and text—and promises that that understanding will be frustrated, first by deferral, then by enigma. Roland's epiphany, the insight that simultaneously ends and is the end of his quest, coincides with his accepting that this frustration is inherent in the nature of worlds, minds, and texts. He and we learn that the path from here to there must be torturous to be true. But Roland's insight also coincides with and, indeed, *is* his act of self-writing and strange looping. The sentence that concludes both poem and quest, "*Childe Roland to the Dark Tower Came*," is an explicit self-inscription, one that is, moreover, self-consciously literary and intertextual. (In his headnote to the poem Browning explicitly instructs us to read intertextually—"See Edgar's song in *Lear*"—and thereby to anticipate this con-clusion.) It is also the point at which the poem turns back on itself, "putting the infinite within the finite" by incorporating within itself a verbal perspective on itself, namely, its title. Unlike Browning's monologic speakers, Childe Roland is aware of himself as self-written. He is also aware that by knowing the ultimate unknowability of the object known, a "dark tower" located as much within as without, he gives his narration its plot, his self-definition its possibility. And because we seem to have seen with his eyes and thought with his words we seem to have undergone his ordeal. We know the strength and significance of his gesture as he knows it: as an act whose seeming emptiness is precisely what fig-ures forth its self-redemptive power.

The Rhetoric of Implication: "The Love Song of J. Alfred Prufrock"

Moving to the twentieth century, we increasingly encounter texts that, like "Childe Roland," torture our reading and yet succeed in making that torture not only edifying but pleasurable:

> S'io credesse che mia risposta fosse
> A persona che mai tornasse al mondo,
> Questa fiamma staria senza piu scosse.
> Ma perciocche giammai di questo fondo
> Non torno vivo alcun, s'i'odo il vero,
> Senza tema d'infamia ti rispondo.

> Let us go then, you and I,
> When the evening is spread out against the sky
> Like a patient etherised upon a table;
> Let us go, through certain half-deserted streets,
> The muttering retreats
> Of restless nights in one-night cheap hotels

> And sawdust restaurants with oyster-shells:
> Streets that follow like a tedious argument
> Of insidious intent
> To lead you to an overwhelming question . . .
> Oh, do not ask, "what is it?"
> Let us go and make our visit.
>
> (ll. 1–12)

"If I believed," speaks the damned soul of the epigraph, which like all epigraphs is explicitly addressed to the reader, "that I were speaking to someone who would return to the world, I would remain silent. But since no one ever has returned from such a depth alive, I will answer you without fear of disgrace." As we know, Count Guido da Montefeltro was mistaken: Dante not only returned, he returned with the answer to his question. Prufrock begins his utterance by repeating the Dantean landscape, translated as a world of "restless nights in one-night cheap hotels," and this repetition leads us to expect another, that the older answer will itself be translated. We are initially if not ultimately disappointed, for, unlike Guido, Prufrock defers answering the "overwhelming question"—"Oh, do not ask, 'What is it?'"—and suggests instead that we "go and make our visit." Despite its sordid edges, the poem opens with high seriousness and impeccable credentials. But the opening also warns that the announced genre is wrong: the speaker's name is inauspicious for a lover, and his "song" is conspicuously unsonglike. We are being asked, it would seem, to be of two minds at once: to take speaker and song both seriously and satirically. The poem's interpretive history has routinely refused this invitation by choosing to read the poem either as a lyric or as a monologue, the more frequent choice being the latter: to find Prufrock the object of irony, to reject his vision, to read the poem as congeneric with monologues like "Andrea del Sarto." The named and characterized speaker, the implication of setting and audience, the colloquial tone, the present-tense immediacy, the opacities of Prufrock's vision—all immediately suggest Browning's monologues as the natural generic ancestors, and scarcely a discussion of "Prufrock" begins without their *a priori* presence. Sometimes the monologue suffers by comparison:

> If we compare "Prufrock" with Browning's "Andrea del Sarto," another dramatic monologue in which a self-proclaimed failure tries to explain "exactly what I mean," "Prufrock" emerges—from a psychological standpoint, and apart from other merits—as more *precise* than Browning's poem. The supposedly "subjective" method gets us more convincingly close to the "inexpressible" and at the same time gets the whole reality of Prufrock's predicament down in a way which Browning's approach does not allow. . . . For Eliot the literal stage setting and scene of the

traditional dramatic monologue is initially indispensable, but only to trigger the psychological mechanism which then moves the poem out into new dimensions.[66]

But more frequently the mask lyric suffers as the critic drastically modifies the starting schema, attempting to justify the value placed on the poem by its interpretive history:

> The poem . . . reads as though it has sprung directly from a wish to set down as precisely as possible what it feels like to be Prufrock; but as this does not feel comfortable, the question of possible change is inherent in the subject. Very likely such a theme was not part of Eliot's first conscious intention, for he had evidently set out to do a portrait modeled upon the pattern of Browning's dramatic monologues, with time, place, and revealing situation conscientiously set forth through the character's speech.[67]

Elisabeth Schneider's reading recalls Hugh Kenner's comment on Pound's early poems—the poem does indeed record "as precisely as possible what it feels like to be Prufrock"—but the monologic schema necessarily leaves this insight dangling. It separates Eliot's creative "wish" from his "conscious intention," thereby denying the possibility and power of verbal design, whether aesthetic or heuristic. This denial, repeated throughout the poem's interpretive history, joins with the high seriousness of both opening and conclusion to suggest that we can better justify "Prufrock" otherwise: by reading it as a mask lyric, as congeneric with "Ulysses" and "Childe Roland."

We begin with the poem's end, for, as Barbara Herrnstein Smith has observed, closure in a poem "often depends upon the class of forms with which we identify it. We will know that a sonnet is complete *as such* only if we know what sonnets are."[68] Conversely, we know that a poem is a sonnet in part by the way it closes. In terms of our present discussion, we can often best define a poem's generic design by defining the way it closes: a monologue by confirming or even creating our severance from the speaker, a mask lyric by foreclosing even the possibility of such severance. The irony sufficiently prodigious to tear us from Roland after he blows the horn or from Tithonus as he "earth in earth" forgets "these empty courts" is difficult to imagine, and, more to the point, the poem's value would suffer from our effort. "Prufrock" repeats this generic pattern by explicitly conflating our vision with the speaker's, by creating in conclusion the greatest possible resistance to imaginative divorce:

> I have seen them riding seaward on the waves
> Combing the white hair of the waves blown back
> When the wind blows the water white and black.
>
> We have lingered in the chambers of the sea

By sea-girls wreathed with seaweed red and brown
Till human voices wake us, and we drown.
                                    (ll. 124–31)

A poet-speaker's entrance into a dreamlike, even epiphanic state is a typically lyric drama, but it is the sudden rupture of that state that makes the drama powerful. Hence the conclusions of Milton's "Sonnet XXIII" ("Me thought I saw my late espoused Saint")—

But O, as to embrace me she inclin'd,
I wak'd, she fled, and day brought back my night.
                                    (ll. 13–14)

—and of Keats's "Ode to a Nightingale":

Forlorn! the very word is like a bell
    To toll me back from thee to my sole self!
Adieu! the fancy cannot cheat so well
    As she is fam'd to do, deceiving elf.
Adieu! adieu! thy plaintive anthem fades
Past the near meadows, over the still stream,
    Up the hill-side; and now 'tis buried deep
        In the next valley-glades:
Was it a vision, or a waking dream?
Fled is that music:—Do I wake or sleep?
                                    (ll. 71–80)

In all three poems the speaker's loss remains lyric because the irony of his situation is as fully recognized by him as by us. Painfully aware that the world he imagines has given way to the world he must live in, that the possibility of fulfillment has been replaced by the taunt of impossible fulfillment, the speaker's awareness not only matches ours but is its source. Such an ending would be explicable in a dramatic monologue only as a curious and devaluing solecism. Yet endings are a poet's last word. Any explanation that can account for a text's ending only by labeling it a flaw is itself devalued, perhaps the least convincing explanation possible. That the ending of "Prufrock" implies that we understand Prufrock from within, that we are not invited to distinguish his meaning from the poem's, that we experience his fate as if it were our own—these affective implications are properly the substance rather than the detritus of the poem's critical readings.

Yet anyone who has taught the poem knows its potential for generating speaker-directed irony. Prufrock's flaws are obvious: he is indecisive, impotent, neurotically self-conscious, devitalized, the butt of his own sardonic humor and ours. Moreover, these flaws remain emphatic until the concluding vision. If we assume that Eliot meant us to stay with Prufrock throughout—and the elegiac lyricism of the concluding vision implies that he did—then we must ask why he chose to dramatize these flaws at such length and with such particularity, thereby risking the reader's irony. The creative and critical problem generically resembles that of "Childe Roland," in which the protracted and inexplicably dreadful vision of the speaker threatens the lyric alliance in order to secure the heuristic force of his concluding gesture. Similarly, we might reason that the display of Prufrock's topographical and tropological hell threatens the lyric alliance in order to implicate us more deeply in his self-inscribed doom.

We are drawn into Prufrock's shaded vision by strategies typical of the genre: the speaker's isolation, both formally and in his world, makes us feel his predicament as poignant; the inwardness of his gaze turns our gaze inward as well, even as it figures the world he sees; the tropological cast of his self-inscription interests our imagination even as its explicitness anticipates and counters our discounting; his verbal grace under pressure dignifies even as it seduces. But "Prufrock" poses problems of significance as well as of seduction: because we can make sense of the conclusion only if we take Prufrock's despair as seriously as we take another speaker's windhover-inspired exaltation, Prufrock's predicament must seem to signify beyond the particular occasion. The problem is that creating such significance is difficult in the mask lyric, the perplexed proximities of its speaker's interior mental space obscuring our vision of this "beyond."

The problem of larger significance, albeit in less urgent form, is endemic to the lyric itself. The emotions of speakers of Romantic and post-Romantic lyrics are typically presented as responses of particular men to particular occasions—a point that returns us to Langbaum and the poetry of experience—but we can make sense of the intensity and implicit import of such responses only by taking them at more than face value, as defining or inscribing not just the particular moment and self but the speaker's particular way of being, what we might call his particular style of self-writing. "Prufrock" is like "Tithonus," "Ulysses," and "Childe Roland" in that it both continues and concentrates this tradition: it stages its speaker's dilemma by presenting him in the act of describing an outer landscape, an act that simultaneously creates his inner landscape or self. This drama has been repeatedly performed since "Tintern Abbey" and "Dejection: An Ode." Even such contemporary self-writings as James Wright's "Gambling in Stateline, Nevada," however stylized their restagings of the drama, still depend on its metaphoric logic, on the reflexive revelations of the phenomenal and the noumenal:

> The great cracked shadow of the Sierra Nevada
> Hoods over the last road.
>
> I came down here from the side of
> A cold cairn where a girl named Rachel

Just made it inside California
And died of bad luck.

Here, across from the keno board,
An old woman
Has been beating a strange machine
In its face all day.

Dusk limps past in the street.
I step outside.
It's gone.
I finger a worthless agate
In my pocket.

(ll. 1-15)

The connections between style and the man, between the world within and
the world without, between the speaker who speaks the poem and the poet who
writes the poem—these connections have informed poetics since Wordsworth
announced a new poetry, defined in terms of a new use of language, and a new
poet, defined also in terms of that use and in terms of his innate power to reflect
the natural world: "He considers man and nature as essentially adapted to each
other, and the mind of man as naturally the mirror of the fairest and most interesting properties of nature."[69] The contemporary poet continues to use this
grand metatrope of the Romantic tradition to write his poem: he inscribes his
self by describing "the great cracked shadow of the Sierra Nevada," the dusk
that "limps past in the street." And the contemporary poet-theoretician similarly reaffirms the contemporaneity of Romanticism's fusion of poem and poet,
of the acts of inscribing the self and describing its world. As Gregory Corso has
said, "Poetry and the poet are inseparable—I cannot write about poetry without
writing about the poet. In fact I, as poet, am the poetry I write."[70]

Nevertheless, the sordid and lackluster particulars of Prufrock's world are
undeniably insufficient to support the speaker's and reader's epiphanic conclusion. Wright's poem, not incidentally, does not attempt such a conclusion: it
ends at a point emotionally coincident with Prufrock's "I do not think that they
will sing to me." Hence the magnified strategic problem of the mask lyric and,
in particular, Eliot's poem: How is the reader led to recognize the significance
of Prufrock's failure? Precisely by the mass of allusion that ironically substan-
tiates Prufrock's seduction and that remains inexplicable deadwood in a monologic reading. Thus does Prufrock repeatedly define his passionless present
against a passionate past: Michaelangelo is set against idle chatter, the assertive
desire of the Duke in *Twelfth Night* against Prufrock's lack thereof, the head of
John the Baptist against Prufrock's own, "grown slightly bald." Most persistent
is the tolling counterpoint of "To His Coy Mistress":

And would it have been worth it, after all,
After the cups, the marmalade, the tea,
Among the porcelain, among some talk of you and me,
Would it have been worth while,
To have bitten off the matter with a smile,
To have squeezed the universe into a ball
To roll it toward some overwhelming question,
To say: "I am Lazarus, come from the dead,
Come back to tell you all, I shall tell you all"—
If one, settling a pillow by her head,
    Should say: "That is not what I meant at all.
    That is not it, at all."

                                    (ll. 87–98)

This intertextual resonance works: it deepens the significance of Prufrock's failure. Yet the irony generated has been often read as diminishing rather than deepening the speaker. The risk of this reading is the price of significance, but the risk is minimized by showing Prufrock to be the source of the irony, thereby forestalling the reader's distinction between Prufrock and the implied poet. This, then, is Eliot's primary strategy. For even more than most mask-lyric speakers, Prufrock is presented as poet-like: as self-consciously engaged in the act of writing himself, as knowingly allusive or intertextual, as fully capable of defining himself in terms of his poetic tradition. In short, he resembles Eliot's ideal poet in "Tradition and the Individual Talent." And because Prufrock's allusions can be read as if they were simultaneously his and the poet's, we take his identification with Lazarus as recapitulating in "strange loop" fashion the situation dramatized by epigraph and poem alike: the departed soul returning to tell an indifferent audience (the reader, the "you" of the poem) his tale. At such points the three discourses—that of the speaker, the poet, and the epigraph—unite, making our illusion conscious.

But we have yet to explain how the poem deflects our potential discounting of Prufrock's flaws. Simon O. Lesser suggests an answer: "Correspondence between a reader and a fictional character facilitates identification, but differences in situation, age and sex do not preclude it. Nor do differences in personality structure, unless they are so pronounced that a reader finds the motivations and thought processes of a character incomprehensible."[71] Lesser implies that a speaker's inadequate perception, not his flaws, impels our rejection of his meaning, our search for alternatives, our positing of a covert speaker. He implies, in other words, that we reject the monologic speaker for reasons less moral than intellectual: his vision seems inadequate to the facts as he presents them. Put rhetorically, his self-writing does not acknowledge its tropological dynamics. The further implication of Lesser's remarks is that the creation of a flawed lyric speaker is only difficult, not impossible, and that the difficulty is managed by dramatizing the accuracy of the speaker's self-perception or, what is paradoxically the same, his awareness of the tropological warping of his discourse. The primary defensive strategy of "Prufrock," then, which both enables Prufrock's intensively allusive exploration of his failure and protects the significance of that failure from our discounting, is the strategy of all good mask lyrics: it is the speaker's self-conscious or "romantic" irony, his manifest power to see his feelings as we see them.

Note that nowhere do we perceive an irony that he has not himself anticipated. We see him as a fop, but so does he: "Shall I part my hair behind?" We see him as a coward, but so does he:

> I have seen the moment of my greatness flicker,
> And I have seen the eternal Footman hold my coat, and snicker,
> And in short, I was afraid.
>
> (ll. 84–86)

The Hamlet stanza is only the most extensive of such anticipations:

> No! I am not Prince Hamlet, nor was meant to be;
> Am an attendant lord, one that will do
> To swell a progress, start a scene or two,
> Advise the prince; no doubt, an easy tool,
> Deferential, glad to be of use,
> Politic, cautious, and meticulous;
> Full of high sentence, but a bit obtuse;
> At times, indeed, almost ridiculous—
> Almost, at times, the Fool.
>
> (ll. 111–19)

Curiously, Pound had objected to this passage: "I dislike the paragraph about Hamlet, but it is an early and cherished bit and T. E. won't give it up, and as it is the only portion of the poem that most readers will like at first reading, I don't see that it will do much harm."[72] The decision of the usually deferential Eliot to let it stand establishes him, at least this once, as *il miglior fabbro*, for placing Prufrock's most detailed and castigating self-attack just prior to the epiphany is precisely what forestalls our separate judgment and confirms the sufficient lucidity of Prufrock's vision.

I have throughout been discussing such anticipatory irony purely as a defensive strategy: it conspires to keep us from abandoning the speaker's vision and retreating to our own. But "Prufrock" suggests that this defensive trope also works constructively, that it not only prevents separation but creates bonding. Hence Edith Wharton, analyzing her friendship with Henry James: "The real marriage of true minds is for any two people to possess a sense of humour or irony pitched in exactly the same key, so that their joint glances at any subject cross like interarching search-lights. I have had good friends between whom and myself that bond was lacking, but they were never really intimate friends; and in that sense Henry James was perhaps the most intimate friend I ever had, though in many ways we were so different.[73] Wharton's insight readily transfers to the distinctly literary affinities we are here considering, for the alliance of reader and speaker in a mask lyric triumphs over their inevitable difference precisely insofar as it is constructed from "a sense of humour or irony pitched in exactly the same key." Closely scrutinized, the oblique affinity between the reader and speaker of any mask lyric will be found to depend on this coincident pitch, but the exactness of pitch is more than usually crucial in "Prufrock," a mask lyric that insists on the bizarre and off-putting confines of its speaker's mental world even as it beguiles us with the proffer of intimacy.

Returning to the problem initially posed, we can now justify the protracted prelude to the lyric coda as well as the unsparing delineation of Prufrock's flaws as necessary if risky strategies. As in many lyrics, the speaker here soars into a state of heightened consciousness that begins and ends in the ordinariness of daytime reality. "Prufrock" is peculiar among lyrics only in its distortion of this pattern, but this distortion is largely what defines its distinctive emotional power—and its distinctive modernity. What in Milton's sonnet and Keats's ode is the frame here becomes the substance, the soaring vision shrinking to a vestigial epiphany while the speaker's banal existence expands to fill the poem. This shift skews Prufrock's world toward the hell of the epigraph, but its extended, particularized, and exactly pitched presentation keeps it compelling, causing us to enter into Prufrock's life at such length and in such detail that despite its unnerving perplexities we feel it as if it were our own. The switch in the final tercet from "I" to "we" confirms this imaginative fusion. Having dwelt at length in both the speaker's quotidian world and his Laforgueian mockery of that world, we dwell by imaginative right and necessity in his epiphany and doom: "human voices wake us and we drown."

We may justify the presence of Prufrock's flaws similarly. To state an obvious but generally ignored fact, Eliot, like all makers of mask lyrics, did not find his speaker but, rather, made him. He interwove poetic fluency with self-irony to produce Prufrock's disinterested perspective on his "lyric" passion. Hence his resemblance to Tithonus. Eliot also chose Prufrock's flaws and chose to make them emphatic. We are effectively seduced, but because this emphasis makes us know our seduction for what it is, we are implicated as well. Once again, our imaginative illusion grows conscious, even conceptual, and, once again, the mask-lyric speaker, like the monologic speaker in this, is revealed to be his maker's most powerful heuristic strategy.

Reading "Prufrock" as a mask lyric, then, we find that we share Prufrock's realization of his flaws and his failure, but because this realization or writing is simultaneously our self-realization or self-writing, we also find that the poet has anticipated our resistance, working to counter our threatening slip into speaker-directed irony even as he constantly exposes his poem to the threat. In other words, the ironic or monologic reading of "Prufrock," like that of all powerful mask lyrics, is an unavoidable potentiality of the premised lyric intention. To make his poem powerful, the poet must risk this reading's becoming an actuality, and that it sometimes does argues less his failure than his daring.

Lyric knowing is stretched very far indeed in "Prufrock," and it is precisely such stretching that sets "Prufrock" and other mask lyrics apart from more traditional lyrics with characterized speakers: the first and last ecologues of Spenser's *The Shepheardes Calender*, the countless laments spoken since Theocritus and Vergil by indistinguishable shepherds and lovers. In such poems the characterized speaker tends to be little more than a stereotypical convention, an articulated and sometimes named stance. He tends to have few if any specific traits beyond his generic type and is often deliberately made uninteresting, a dead metaphor that focuses the lyric vision without subjecting it to the stresses characteristic of the mask lyric.

But the imaginative stress that distinguishes the reader's experience in this genre does not necessarily require speakers as noticeably flawed as Ulysses and Prufrock. As in "Ballad of the Goodly Fere" and "Tithonus," such stress may also result from an unflawed but extraordinary perspective. Thus in Edward Arlington Robinson's "Ben Jonson Entertains a Man from Stratford," we find no reason to judge Jonson, the speaker, but are nevertheless acutely conscious of seeing strangely. We have acquired Jacobean eyes, a way of seeing Shakespeare as a contemporary, a way previously impossible and therefore presently fascinating. And this acquisition is made possible precisely because the dramatic particularization of the speaker has created our belief in his vision.

This last point suggests that the generic experience may be had without the obviously extraordinary speaker, that what matters is less the speaker's "character" than the mode of its display. Indeed, this turns out to be the case, for we find that speakers who seem to be quite ordinary also have the power to exercise our "as if" capacity and, as they do so, come to seem themselves extraordinary. In other words, the lyric poet's power to make the seemingly familiar seem strange readily translates into a generic power, into the "masking" of the lyric. Thus in Robert Lowell's "Mother Marie Therese," the speaker, an old nun who remains unnamed, reminisces without subjecting us to either the stress of flawed vision or the seduction of the obviously strange. Through her eyes we see not Aurora, Jesus, or Shakespeare but a drowned mother superior and a vanishing way of life. "Piling on more driftwood/And stooping with the poker" while she talks, she reveals the power of a cloistered yet mundane life. She also reveals the extraordinary power of the genre. We learn that her vision, however unspectacular, is transfigured by the specifics of personality, a transfiguration that demands the imaginative exertion we have come to associate with the mask-lyric. We also learn that this exertion is necessary to achieve a precise intimacy with any distinctly "other" mind, whether spectacular or subtle or both. This power to make us see the fine turnings of the ordinary, the tropes upon which the writing of the everyday depends, is the most elusive and ethically significant power of the mask lyric. It tutors us not in the extraordinary or bizarre nature of that with which we match but *in the process of matching itself*, a process that, when exercised with proficiency, transmutes our attempt to know even the ordinary into an edification of our ordinary selves.

Epilogue

> If we cannot imagine ourselves as different from what
> we are . . . we cannot impose a discipline upon
> ourselves though we may accept one from others. Ac-
> tive virtue, as distinguished from the passive accep-
> tance of a code, is therefore theatrical, consciously
> dramatic, the wearing of a mask.
>
> William Butler Yeats

> I am interested in language because it wounds or
> seduces me.
>
> Roland Barthes

Eloquence denying itself is always a curious spectacle:

Mrs. Ramsay sat silent. She was glad, Lily thought, to rest in silence, uncommunicative; to rest in the extreme obscurity of human relationships. Who knows what we are, what we feel? Who knows even at the moment of intimacy, This is knowledge? Aren't things spoilt then, Mrs. Ramsay may have asked (it seemed to have happened so often, this silence by her side) by saying them? Aren't we more expressive thus?[1]

Recent criticism has sought out such assertions of imaginative isolation and verbal impotence, assertions invariably linked and increasingly common since the Romantics, and has used them to argue that all texts, whether explicitly or not, thus deny their own potency.[2] But the poems just read eloquently speak against such programmatic skepticism—both about our capacity to know others, including conspicuously textualized others, and about the power of words to enable this knowing. This defense is distinctively but not exclusively a property of modern texts. When Dante's encounter with Beatrice at the end of *The Divine Comedy* leaves him mute, he says so in so many words: "As children, dumb with shame, stand listening with eyes to earth, self-confessing and repentant, such stood I."[3] Similarly, when a more recent self-confessor laments that "it is impossible to say just what I mean," his lament fulfills his and the poet's desire precisely because it articulates the inner spaces of their purported impotence. This hollowness is at once human and hermeneutic, and the law of its composition can be worded only because the poet, like Laocoon hurling his spear, possesses a tropological license traditionally denied the prosaic world: "uteroque recusso insonuere cavae gemitumque dedere cavernae."[4]

Yet the poet's words are powerful not only because they wound but because they wound *in order* to heal. This paradoxical power is itself captured in the word "bless," which interweaves a host of Jewish, heathen, and Christian etymological threads: crossing "consecrate with blood" with "speaking well" (from analogy with *benedicere*), "sacrifice" with "bliss."[5] This "speaking well" is undeniably difficult, hardly bliss:

> Words strain,
> Crack and sometimes break, under the burden,
> Under the tension, slip, slide, perish,
> Decay with imprecision, will not stay in place,
> Will not stay still.
>
>> T. S. Eliot, *Burnt Norton*

By thus expressly contradicting or "speaking against" themselves, such lines struggle to solve the very problem that they pose. They would overcome "the intolerable wrestle/With words and meanings" (Eliot, *East Coker*) by wording it. This is not to say that language by itself fulfills the desire that it articulates but, rather, that it defines an adjacent and distinctly verbal space, one that with the practice of indwelling becomes a landscape no less consolatory than it is strange.

The complex rhetoric of dramatic monologues and mask lyrics is both cause and consequence of such a wrestle, of the attempt to hollow out an imaginative space that, with the repetition of reading, particularly the critical reading that is itself a writing, becomes substantial. In both genres speakers and poets are actively engaged in the act of self-writing, of wielding tropes in order to make themselves, and in both the reader's experience recapitulates their struggle. Both genres refuse "to rest in silence," to concede "the extreme obscurity of human relationships," and both affirm the possibility and ethical value of such poetic or explicitly tropological writing of the self. This refusal and affirmation, however, take definitively different shapes in each genre.

We have found that the power of the dramatic monologue is best explained by discussing it as an analytic and antagonistic drama: it invites and rewards our attempts to correct the speaker's imagination or, to be precise, lack thereof. I defined this power by crossing Bagehot's observation about the speaker—the monologue "takes the type . . . . *in difficulties*. It gives a representation of it . . . . just while it is struggling with obstacles, just where it is encumbered with incongruities"[6]—with Adams' observation about the reader: "our whole tendency is . . . to struggle out of his perspective into some other. It is this tension between encasement in the form and our desire to escape to a position of vantage which strikes us so intensely."[7] The readings deduced from this definition show that both speaker and reader are indeed engaged in an active wrestle with words, but whereas the speaker fails to struggle to "a position of vantage," the reader succeeds in doing just that: he takes a perspective on the speaker that the speaker desires but lacks. We accordingly come away from our reading of a dramatic monologue convinced that we have seen deeply and clearly, a conviction that proceeds from our seeming to have seen more deeply and clearly than the speaker. Such superiority presents a temptation to the reader's hubris *as a reader* and thus threatens the genre's heuristic power. But the monologue manages this threat by teaching us to fault the monologic speaker not for his imperfection, a state that is in any human case unavoidable, but for not making a knowing use of that imperfection: the speaker fails to recognize his imaginative or "as if" fictions as such; he misuses and denies the very tropes that he needs to write his self and, ultimately, to live.

We learned, in other words, that the failure of the monologic speaker is typically not moral but imaginative. He literalizes the play of his mind, idealizing himself as passive and essentially fixed, as capable of self-description but not of self-creation, as closed to change, growth, and rewriting. We learned that Cleon and Andrea, who among monologic speakers are remarkable for their self-consciousness, are nevertheless and for this very reason the most subtly and profoundly erroneous of all. Each connects his self-proclaimed "perfection" to his self-inscribed doom, but each fails to understand that connection as fully as he might. The monologic speaker never learns that the fault of the "faultless" self-writer lies in his use of tropes to delimit and finish rather than to open. His text or self is accordingly urn-like, however well wrought. It entombs rather than frees.

For the reader these poems provide stages for enacting an inverse drama. Unlike the speaker, we do struggle to "a position of vantage," not only because we have a speaker to struggle with but because this very struggle instructs us in the wages of fulfilled representational desire. "I'll pay my fancy," Andrea announces, and we answer in the spirit and words of Coleridge: that the price of a Lockean or representational fancy is too high, that the only tolerable alternative to the "essentially fixed and dead" fancy is the "vital" and self-aware imagination.[8] Still, our struggle to such knowledge is difficult and deliberately so. To explain these poems in order to justify the value accorded them by their interpretive history, we must learn to imagine not only intensely but ambidextrously, to read the monologue as if it were at once made and said, as if we could match simultaneously with the speaker implied by the speech and the poet implied by the poem. Although we finally do struggle out of the speaker's perspective and into the poet's, we do so by means of our own inferential efforts, which are contradicted intermittently by the seductiveness of the speaker's vision. It is this very difficulty, however, that engenders the heuristic power of the genre. Were our victory over the speaker easy, we would remain ignorant, for the knowledge our reading yields is less a matter of knowing-that than of knowing-how, less a matter of knowing that any particular speaker's vision is erroneous than of knowing how to correct such error—in monologue after monologue.

The difficulty of the mask lyric is at once different and similar. While the monologue is most fruitfully discussed in analytic and antagonistic terms, the mask lyric is best discussed as a synthetic and sympathetic drama: it invites and rewards conflation of our vision and the speaker's. Whereas we know the speakers of monologues much as we know others, inferentially and from without, we know the speakers of mask lyrics much as we know ourselves, intuitively and from within. When reading a monologue we at once understand the speaker's words as if they were his and understand this understanding to be itself an illusion, a finely wrought and magical consequence of the poet's art. When reading a mask lyric we understand the speaker's words both as if the poet were speaking them and as if they were our own, an understanding that we again take as a consequence of the poet's art. When reading a monologue we accordingly align ourselves with the poet against the speaker, whereas when reading a mask lyric we lose ourselves in alliance with both.

The use of a characterized speaker multiplies the possibilities of the lyric voice, but this multiplication throws the speaker's otherness into prominence and so initially seems to work against the genre's fundamentally lyric dynamics. I accordingly argued that the distinctively modern rhetoric of the mask lyric was effectively defined in terms of its capacity to sustain this paradox of otherness and oneness. This definition was particularized as a complex of certain strategies: the speaker's self-consciousness enables him to anticipate and thereby counter our desire for severance; his isolation solicits our sympathy; the inwardness of his gaze guides ours; his inventive power forestalls the potentially distancing monotony of solipsistic complaint; his eloquence, however ethically dubious, nevertheless seduces. But the most powerful strategy was his knowing use of tropes. Whereas the monologic speaker seeks to "write" himself as a transparent window on an essential and fixed self, the mask lyric speaker acknowledges and delights in his textuality. He seeks to write a provisional and dynamic self by weaving a text selectively opaque to our literalizing efforts to see through and thereby reduce him to the not-himself. This triumph depends upon his recognizing his defining fictions or tropes, upon his displaying his self-woven textuality. "I am," Ulysses announces, "become a name," and this becoming is seemingly accomplished by his own imaginative effort, which is formally indistinguishable from that of the poet who actually wrote him and from that of the reader who actually reads the text thus written.

As a result the mask lyric neither invites nor rewards attempts to distinguish the speaker's meaning from the poem's meaning. Its speakers are poets or poet-like, and their speeches are accordingly poems or poem-like: hence Prufrock's "song." Like monologic speakers, they imagine themselves performing actions, but unlike monologic speakers their imaginings are self-conscious and verbal. Childe Roland's concluding act is a particularly explicit instance of such self-writing, of a speaker's knowingly assuming an intertextual and "strange loop" perspective on himself: "Dauntless the slug-horn to my lips I set,/And blew. '*Childe Roland to the Dark Tower Came.*' "

Nor does the mask lyric invite and reward discussion of its speaker as if he were a real person. We found that the monologue's characteristic specification of time, place, situation, and personality encourages just such discussion, the specificity or realistic staging of the speaking self creating an illusion of taut coherence and indelibly inscribed borders. In contrast, the mask-lyric speaker is free from or, more precisely, frees himself from such limitations, his knowing use of the linguistic imagination enabling him to move in time, space, and texts that, strictly or representationally speaking, are not his own. Ulysses, Childe Roland, and Prufrock readily diffuse their selves into a circumambient universe, a diffusion accomplished both topographically and tropologically. Hence the difficulty of orienting the mask-lyric speaker in physical space: the oft-remarked vagueness, the disturbing undecidability of his whereabouts.[9] He is no less difficult to orient in intertextual space, for he readily appropriates other texts, rewriting the self-writings of others so as to enrich and open his own: Roland uses the line from *King Lear* and Prufrock reworks "To His Coy Mistress" in order to escape the rigor of unidirectional chronology and the confines of unitary personality. These difficulties of orientation actively tutor us in the act of synchronic imagining. Insofar as we learn this lesson, to cope with and make sense of the speaker's textual allusiveness and real-world elusiveness, our eyes become sensitive to the tropologically dense textual surface. We learn to see its opacity. Or, what these poems imply is the same, we come to know the speaker's uniqueness, his vital strangeness.

I have argued that our perspective on the mask-lyric speaker and his perspective on himself are finally indistinguishable: the text he writes and the text we read are conflated both sympathetically and hermeneutically. The speaker's meaning and the poem's meaning are one. Yet this conflation does not mean that we lose sight of the speaker's otherness, his distinguishing opacities. Quite the contrary: we are reminded throughout of his difference from our usual selves and throughout made aware of the difficulty of our human and hermeneutic struggle to match with him or, what is again the same, to make a rich and coherent sense of the text that he speaks and the poet writes. The generic design of the mask lyric maximizes this palimpsestic reminder, thus intensifying our struggle to make sense, while it simultaneously works to insure conflation. Conversely, the generic design of the monologue minimizes this reminder, thus seducing us to read the speaker's words as if they were spoken, while it simultaneously works to insure final separation, the conclusive and compressed sense made by our gathering attempts to sever ourselves from the speaker and, what is the same, to sever the speaker's meaning from the poem's.

I have discussed these two genres primarily in terms of difference because their similarities have dominated the interpretive history, encouraging us to treat poems like ''Ulysses'' and ''Prufrock'' as if they were congeneric with poems like ''Cleon'' and to devalue them for failing to match the monologic type. We found that discussing mask lyrics otherwise, as if they were like each other and unlike monologues, more fully justified the received value of poems in both genres. But the genres are finally alike as well as different: both invite and reward our matching with the not-ourselves, whether speaker, poet, or some combination thereof, and both strive to make this matching or making of sense difficult. That we and most readers recorded in the interpretive history of these poems find them difficult comments not only on the poems but on the criteria that post-Kantian criticism has most frequently used to assign value. That is ''*most* beautiful,'' Coleridge announced to the ensuing century and a half, ''where the most obstacles to a full manifestation have been most perfectly overcome.''[10] And standing behind Coleridge we repeatedly hear Kant announcing that the beautiful has ''at its basis a merely formal purposiveness, *i.e.*, a purposiveness without purpose.''[11] In other words, the poem has aesthetic value insofar as it unites strikingly disparate matter and insofar as this union is accomplished seemingly disinterestedly, as if done for its own sake. The interpretive history of dramatic monologues and mask lyrics has repeatedly affirmed their aesthetic value in precisely this sense.

But our readings have shown these poems to be ethically valuable for much the same reason. Whereas the interpretive history contains only hints of such valuation—''what we took for obscurity in him,'' George Eliot wrote of Browning, ''was superficiality in ourselves''—the preceding pages have repeatedly explained these complex acts of ''as if'' supposition in terms not only of beauty and pleasure but of heuristic power.[12] For the effort of matching—of making human and hermeneutic metaphors for thought, of straining to discover likenesses in the midst of difference—is far more than a purely aesthetic effort. As Gombrich has observed, ''it is only in making things and trying to make them like something else that man can extend his awareness of the visible world.''[13] And, we might conclude, of written worlds as well.

Notes

Editions of Poems Cited

Anon. "Western Wind." *Medieval English Lyrics: A Critical Anthology*. Edited by R. T. Davies. London: Faber and Faber, 1964.

Robert Browning. *The Complete Works of Robert Browning with Variant Readings and Annotations*. Edited by Roma A. King, Jr., et al. Athens, Ohio: Ohio University Press, 1969–73. Poems not contained in King's edition are cited from *The Works of Robert Browning*. Edited by F. G. Kenyon, London: Smith, Elder, 1912.

T. S. Eliot. *The Complete Poems and Plays: 1909–1950*. New York: Harcourt, Brace & World, 1952.

Robert Frost. *The Poetry of Robert Frost*. Edited by Edward Connery Latham. New York: Holt, Rinehart and Winston, 1967.

Gerard Manley Hopkins. *Poems of Gerard Manley Hopkins*. 3d ed., ed. W. H. Gardner. New York: Oxford University Press, 1948.

John Keats. *The Poetical Works of John Keats*. Edited by H. W. Garrod. London: Oxford University Press, 1956.

Robert Lowell. *The Mills of the Kavanaughs*. New York: Harcourt, Brace, 1946.

John Milton. *Complete Poems and Major Prose*. Edited by Merritt Y. Hughes. New York: Odyssey Press, 1957.

Ezra Pound. *Personae: The Collected Shorter Poems of Ezra Pound*. New York: New Directions, 1926.

Alfred, Lord Tennyson. *The Poems of Tennyson*. Edited by Christopher Ricks. New York: W. W. Norton, 1969.

James Wright. *Collected Poems*. Middletown, Conn.: Wesleyan University Press, 1971.

Notes

A Theoretical Introduction

1. For two examples among many, see the opening pages of Ralph W. Rader, "Fact, Theory, and Literary Explanation," *Critical Inquiry* 1 (1974): 245–72, and Stanley Fish, "Interpreting the *Variorum*," *Critical Inquiry* 2 (1976); rpt. in *Is There a Text in This Class? The Authority of Interpretive Communities* (Cambridge, Mass.: Harvard University Press, 1980), pp. 147–73.

2. For theoretical analyses of the reader-text conflict see Fish's "Introduction" in *Is There a Text in This Class?* and Steven Mailloux, *Interpretive Conventions: The Reader in the Study of American Fiction* (Ithaca: Cornell University Press, 1982), chaps. 1 and 2. For an exemplary enactment of the conflict, see J. Hillis Miller, who initially supported the reader, arguing with Nietzsche that "each reader takes possession of the work . . . and imposes on it a certain pattern of meaning" ("Tradition and Difference," *Diacritics* 2 [1972]: 12). More recently, he has supported the text, arguing that "the readings of deconstructive criticism are not the willful imposition by a subjectivity of theory on the texts but are coerced by the texts themselves" ("Theory and Practice: Response to Vincent Leitch," *Critical Inquiry* 6 [1980]: 611). Miller's change of mind is strategic: his earlier argument assists deconstruction's usurpation of text-oriented criticism; the later assists its institutional validation.

3. J. Hillis Miller, *Fiction and Repetition: Seven English Novels* (Cambridge, Mass.: Harvard University Press, 1982). In his first chapter, "Two Forms of Repetition," Miller lays out his premises and makes a prefatory argument for their explanatory power. Each of the following seven chapters "practices" these premises in terms of a different novel. For a different kind of theoretical criticism, see David Carroll, *The Subject in Question: The Languages of Theory and the Strategies of Fiction* (Chicago: University of Chicago Press, 1982). (See also chap. 1, n. 7, of the present study.) The most sustained union of theory and practice, however, has been Murray Krieger's. Krieger has consistently worked to make criticism aware of its premises and to weave that awareness, as a strengthening warp, into the fabric of the critical text. For a recent instance of Krieger's theoretical criticism, see "Poetic Presence and Illusion: Renaissance Theory and the Duplicity of Metaphor," *Critical Inquiry* 5 (1979): 597–619. See also *The Classic Vision: The Retreat from Extremity in*

Modern Literature (Baltimore: Johns Hopkins University Press, 1971), in which Krieger takes a stand on the problem of genre: "I must somehow defend the usefulness of thematic genres even as I defend the uniqueness of the work and its vision. But I believe my formulation shows how we may evade this dilemma. We need only admit frankly that these thematic genres, like others, operate for the critic, indeed are largely invented in the act of criticism" (p. 15).

4. See "Theory," *The Compact Edition of the Oxford English Dictionary* (Oxford: Oxford University Press, 1971).

5. Quoted in "Theory."

6. The phrase, part of Matthew Arnold's definition of "disinterestedness," is taken from *The Function of Criticism at the Present Time* (1864), in *The Complete Prose Works of Matthew Arnold* (Ann Arbor: University of Michigan Press, 1962), III, 270. Arnold, of course, is discussing "criticism," but his ideal is virtually indistinguishable from that of contemporary theory: "theoretical criticism is criticism in its own right: its existence assumes that when we have read and reacted to a poem, it is natural and proper to ask, disinterestedly, what we have done" (Brewster Rogerson, "Criticism: Functions," *Princeton Encyclopedia of Poetry and Practice*, ed. Alex Preminger [Princeton: Princeton University Press, 1974], p. 161).

7. Paul de Man, "The Resistance to Theory," *Yale French Studies* 63 (1982): 4.

8. The New Criticism, or more generally, formalism, is distinguished by its taking what is in sight, namely, the text's features of irony, paradox, ambiguity, and so forth, as its ground. But even as it sought to collapse surface and ground, the New Criticism was simultaneously wrestling with the problems caused by this collapse: the lack of "objective" constraint and the attempt to define such a constraint in spite of its larger program. See W. K. Wimsatt, Jr., and Monroe C. Beardsley, "The Intentional Fallacy," *Sewanee Review* 54 (1946); rpt. in *The Verbal Icon: Studies in the Meaning of Poetry* (Lexington: University Press of Kentucky, 1954), pp. 3-18. The authors finally settle upon the public norms of language as the critic's constraint or ground.

9. Richard Rorty, *Philosophy and the Mirror of Nature* (Princeton: Princeton University Press, 1979).

10. Michael McCanles, "The Authentic Discourse of the Renaissance," *Diacritics* 10 (1980): 79-80.

11. Steven Knapp and Walter Benn Michaels, "Against Theory," *Critical Inquiry* 8 (1982): 723-42. See also my response: Adena Rosmarin, "On the Theory of 'Against Theory,' " *Critical Inquiry* 9 (1983): 775-83. Both essays are reprinted in W. J. T. Mitchell, ed., *Against Theory: Literary Studies and the New Pragmatism* (Chicago: University of Chicago Press, 1985).

12. Knapp and Michaels, "Against Theory," p. 742.

13. Paul de Man, "Sign and Symbol in Hegel's *Aesthetics*," *Critical Inquiry* 8 (1982): 761-75.

14. Ibid., p. 761.

15. Ibid., p. 775.

16. Kenneth Burke, "Terministic Screens," *Proceedings of the American Catholic Philosophical Association* 39 (1965); rpt. in *Language as Symbolic Action: Essays on Life, Literature, and Method* (Berkeley: University of California Press, 1966), pp. 44-62.

17. Benedetto Croce, *Aesthetic as Science of Expression and General Linguistic*, trans. Douglas Ainslie (London: Macmillan, 1922), p. 188.

18. Rorty, *Philosophy and the Mirror of Nature*, p. 31.

19. Burke, "Terministic Screens," p. 49.

20. The contemporary literary theory distinguishes itself from its predecessors in part by its habit of displaying and analyzing its critical strategies. See Jonathan Culler, *On Deconstruction: Theory and Criticism after Structuralism* (Ithaca: Cornell University Press, 1982), particularly the section "Critical Consequences," pp. 180-225, and chap. 3, "Deconstructive Criticism," pp. 227-80. Also see Steven Mailloux, "Learning to Read: Interpretation and Reader-Response Criticism," in *American Critics at Work*, ed., Victor Kramer (Troy: Whitston, 1985) pp. 296-315.

21. See Robert Langbaum's analysis of the Romantic and contemporary resistance to genre, a resistance exemplified in Blanchot's argument (quoted below in the text): "The dissolution of genres, as well as the dissolution of the distinction between the poet and his material and the poet and his reader, are best explained by what has been called the organic theory of poetry—the theory, which begins with romanticism, that a poem is not a deliberate rhetorical construction but a quasi-natural organism, a 'birth' as Nietzsche calls it, a kind of plant which the mind puts forth in accordance with the laws of its own nature. Such a theory is destructive of the older theory of genres. For it suggests, on the one hand, that there must be as many genres as poets and even poems; and, on the other hand, that there can be only one genre, since the dramatic movement from poet into poem and the lyrical movement from poem back into poet remain always the same" (Robert Langbaum, *The Poetry of Experience: The Dramatic Monologue in Modern Literary Tradition* [New York: W. W. Norton, 1957], pp. 232–33). The strangeness of this repeatedly stated position becomes immediately manifest as soon as one considers that Langbaum, like many post-Romantic critics, is centrally concerned with genre and, moreover, that the very genre with which Langbaum is concerned—the dramatic monologue—is itself not only much discussed but also subject to deliberate generic experimentation (see Donald S. Hair, *Browning's Experiments with Genre* [Toronto: University of Toronto Press, 1972], pp. 73–115). The position becomes stranger yet when one tries to think of a literary genre that has not since the beginning of the nineteenth century been subject to such experimentation, from the odes of Wordsworth and Keats, the "Female Quixote" and gothic novels of Austen (*Emma* and *Northanger Abbey*), and the monodramas of Southey to the yet more conspicuous experimentations of our own century. It would seem that the "dissolution of genres" is a phenomenon that happens neither in the literature of the time nor in its criticism (see Richard Stang, *The Theory of the Novel in England, 1850–1870* [New York: Columbia University Press, 1959]) but in its—and our—poetics. From its beginning, which is to say Wordsworth's "Preface," the dissolution has been programmatic and polemical. As Langbaum notes, it is connected to other dissolutions: between the poet and his reader, the poet and his material, and, we might add, the poet and his medium. But all are strategies of Romanticism's rhetoric of sincerity, which characteristically if paradoxically expresses itself in generic terms. Hence John Stuart Mill's praise of the lyric as being "more eminently and peculiarly poetry than any other" because it is "most natural to a really poetic temperament" ("The Two Kinds of Poetry," in John Stuart Mill, *Literary Essays*, ed. Edward Alexander [Indianapolis: Bobbs-Merrill, 1967], p. 71). See also Fredric Jameson's Marxist explanation of the "dissolution of genres": it is a "strategic feature of what must be called the *ideology of modernism*" ("Magical Narratives: Romance as Genre," *New Literary History* 7 [1975]: 135).

22. Maurice Blanchot, *Le livre à venir* (Paris: Gallimard, 1959), p. 293. I here give the French text:

> Seul importe le livre, tel qu'il est, loin des genres, en dehors des rubriques, prose, poésie, roman, témoignage, sous lesquelles il refuse de se ranger et auxquelles il dénie le pouvoir de lui fixer sa place et de déterminer sa forme. Un livre n'appartient plus à un genre, tout livre relève de la seule littérature, comme si celle-ci détenait par avance, dans leur généralité, les secrets et les formules qui permettent seuls de donner à ce qui s'écrit réalité de livre. Tout se passerait donc comme si, les genres s'étant dissipés, la littérature s'affirmait seule, brillait seule dans la clarté mystérieuse qu'elle propage et que chaque création littéraire lui renvoie en la multipliant,—comme s'il y avait donc une "essence" de la littérature.

I cite the translation (slightly amended) to which Todorov (see note 23) refers. However, the page numbers given in Todorov's text (pp. 136, 243–44) are incorrect.

23. Tzvetan Todorov, "The Origin of Genres," trans. Richard M. Berrong, *New Literary History* 8 (1976): 160.

24. Michel Foucault, for one, answers this question in the negative. See *The Archaeology of*

Knowledge, trans. A. M. Sheridan Smith (New York: Harper and Row, 1972), particularly pt. IV, chap. 1, "Archaeology and the History of Ideas." Todorov answers similarly, if for different reasons, concerning "literature" in "The Notion of Literature," trans. Lynn Moss and Bruno Braunrot, *New Literary History* 5 (1973): 5–16. The argument that the notions of "book" and "literature" are conventional does not, however, impinge on their usefulness. As Gustavo Pérez Firmat has observed, we cannot have theories and criticism of genres without some such notions, particularly a *specific* notion such as the "book." First, "there would be nothing left to classify," and, second, "if one does not think in terms of books, one cannot think about novels" ("The Novel as Genres," *Genre* 12 [1979]: 284).

25. For examples of such awakening see Rorty, *Philosophy and the Mirror of Nature*, and Paul de Man, *"The Epistemology of Metaphor,"* *Critical Inquiry* 5 (1978): 13–30.

26. See Edmund Husserl, *Experience and Judgment: Investigations in a Genealogy of Logic*, ed. Ludwig Landgrebe, trans. James S. Churchill and Karl Ameriks (Evanston: Northwestern University Press, 1973), pp. 31–40. For use of this concept in contemporary literary theory see E. D. Hirsch, Jr., "Objective Interpretation," *PMLA* 75 (1960); rpt. as an appendix in Hirsch, *Validity in Interpretation* (New Haven: Yale University Press, 1967), pp. 212–24. See also Hans Robert Jauss, *Toward an Aesthetic of Reception*, trans. Timothy Bahti (Minneapolis: University of Minnesota Press, 1982), particularly pp. 25–32 (in "Literary History as a Challenge to Literary Theory"), p. 88 (in "Theory of Genres and Medieval Literature"), and pp. 139–85 ("The Poetic Text within the Change of Horizons of Reading: The Example of Baudelaire's 'Spleen II' ").

27. E. H. Gombrich, *Art and Illusion: A Study in the Psychology of Pictorial Representation* (Princeton: Princeton University Press, 1960), chap. 4, "Reflections on the Greek Revolution." Further citations will be included in the text. Gombrich uses "schema" in its Kantian sense, as meaning a mental category, but he complicates that sense throughout *Art and Illusion*. For Gombrich, the schema is both a mental and a visual category: it exists both within and without the mind, the circle with which the artist begins his drawing of a face existing both as a notion of a circle and as the circle drawn on the page. But Gombrich's schema differs from the Kantian also in its rhetorical and pragmatic definition: it is a tool *used* by the artist in order to persuade his audience to have a visual illusion. The language of representation is, for Gombrich, just that—a language—and schemata are "the starting points of the artist's vocabulary" (p. 183). These starting points may be highly codified, as in Egyptian art, or they may be *ad hoc* beginnings, such as inkblots, or the irregularities that, on a cave wall, suggest a bison. The schema is necessary in the sense that *some* schema must be used to begin the process of representation, but the choice of a *particular* schema is necessary only in the sense that it is determined by the artist's judgment of which among those possible will best serve his painterly purpose. Its choice, in short, is pragmatic and rhetorical.

28. The art of children is invariably "conceptual" rather than illusionistic, but the analogy between the conceptualism of the child and, for example, that of the Egyptian painter is not exact: the motives of the former tend to be more mixed and less deliberate. See Gombrich, *Art and Illusion*, p. 119.

29. For the distinction between "knowing-that" something is so and "knowing-how" to perform an activity see Gilbert Ryle, *The Concept of Mind* (London: Hutchinson, 1949), pp. 25–61.

30. David Hume, "Of the Standard of Taste," in *Of the Standard of Taste and Other Essays*, ed. John W. Len (New York: Bobbs-Merrill, 1965), p. 17.

31. Hirsch, "Objective Interpretation," p. 222.

32. Barbara Johnson, "Nothing Fails Like Success," *SCE Reports* 8 (1980): 15.

33. Fish, "Introduction," p. 13. For my analysis of Fish's position, see Adena Rosmarin, "Reading Stanley Fish," *Denver Quarterly* 16 (1981): 100–105. For my analysis of the different kinds of "readers" defined by the reader-response movement, see Adena Rosmarin, "Reading the Readers," *Denver Quarterly*, in press.

34. The conflict between text and schema, between what is read and the manner of reading, is

our discipline's version of philosophy's realist-idealist debate. Rorty discusses this debate intermittently throughout *Philosophy and the Mirror of Nature*, but for literary studies the most pertinent discussions are Knapp and Michaels' critique of Fish's idealist position ("Against Theory," pp. 737–42) and Steven Mailloux's critique of their critique ("Truth or Consequences: On Being against Theory," *Critical Inquiry* 9 [1983], 760–66); rpt. in Mitchell, ed., *Against Theory*, pp. 65–71.

35. I will be arguing that genre serves the critic as just such a starting place, that it is a premise or beginning assertion from which the ends of argumentation are deduced. The connection to ancient rhetoric is through the notion of *loci*, the use and value of which was determined not by their truth, since they are all "true" but not always or even often compatible, but by their potential utility in the argumentative situation. Thus something might be valued because it is common, as in a "commonly held" opinion or "common sense," *or* because it is not, as in that which is rare or "original." The locus of quantity enables us to value the normal, the locus of quality the unique. As has been noted, these two *loci* form major axes of argumentation and, not incidentally, map the conflict between genre and the literary text. See Chaim Perelman and L. Olbrechts-Tyteca, *The New Rhetoric: A Treatise on Argumentation* (Notre Dame: University of Notre Dame Press, 1969), pt. 2, "The Starting Point of Argument."

36. I. A. Richards, *The Philosophy of Rhetoric* (New York: Oxford University Press, 1936), p. 30.

37. Ibid., p. 31.

38. For further discussion of this point see Fish, "Interpreting the *Variorum*," in *Is There a Text in This Class?* p. 171.

39. John Canaday's analysis of Picasso's *Guernica* (1937) exemplifies both the painter's and the critic's use of the schema: "The large space is organized on one of the oldest schemes in Western art. It is essentially a triptych on the formula of a Renaissance altarpiece with a central portion and two folding wings. Its two wing-like side elements, which would once have been occupied by flanking saints, show on one side a mother who screeches as she holds the body of her child, and on the other a woman who falls through the floor of a burning building. The triangular motif, which in the altarpiece would have built up to a madonna enthroned among adoring saints, is packed with mangled human and animal forms including a symbolical severed arm and hand still grasping a broken sword. A comparison of the completed picture with a preliminary composition study shows that Picasso built the central triangular mass, and flanked it by the two 'wings,' by reorganizing a more chaotic scheme composed of the same elements" (*Mainstreams of Modern Art* [New York: Holt, Rinehart and Winston, 1964], pp. 486–87). Picasso may or may not have been painting in terms of the triptych. However, Canaday's analysis depends not on its correspondence to authorial or painterly intention but on whether the schema used makes a "good" (meaning, in this particular case, "coherent") sense of a seemingly chaotic yet indisputably great text. In chap. 3 I will use Tennyson's revisions of "Ulysses" much as Canaday here uses Picasso's: not to validate explanation but to flesh it out, displaying the organizing and affective power of the schema being used to make critical sense. For Miller's reading of *Wuthering Heights* see *Fiction and Repetition*, chap. 3, "*Wuthering Heights*: Repetition and the 'Uncanny,' " pp. 42–72.

40. Even those theorists who use "context" to answer the question of interpretive constraint argue its ultimate insufficiency as an answer. As Jonathan Culler puts it, "Meaning is context-bound, but context is boundless" ("Convention and Meaning: Derrida and Austin," *New Literary History* 13 [1981]: 24). See also Stanley Fish, "Normal Circumstances, Literal Language, Direct Speech Acts, the Ordinary, the Everyday, the Obvious, What Goes Without Saying, and Other Special Cases," in *Is There a Text in This Class?* pp. 268–92; and Steven Mailloux, "Convention and Context," *New Literary History* 14 (1983): 399–407.

41. Aristotle, *Rhetorica*, trans. W. Rhys Roberts, in *The Works of Aristotle*, ed. W. D. Ross (Oxford: Clarendon Press, 1960), XI, 1355b. For a concise and penetrating analysis of the pragmatism of rhetoric, see Terry Eagleton, *Walter Benjamin or Towards a Revolutionary Criticism*

(London: Verso Editions, 1981), pp. 101-13. Eagleton traces the history of "rhetoric," meaning "both the theory of effective discourse and the practice of it" (p. 102). He formulates his analysis in political terms—"Its intention, quite consciously, was systematically to theorize the articulations of discourse and power, and to do so in the name of political practice: to enrich the political effectivity of signification" (p. 101)—but this formulation readily transfers to the institutional enterprise of literary studies. Note also the fusion of theory and practice, a fusion that is cause and consequence of the pragmatism of rhetorical theory.

42. The strength of Miller's argument is in part due to the explicitness of his premises and purpose. For example, he argues that "one of the most obvious characteristics of works of literature is their manifest strangeness as integuments of words. Poets, novelists, and playwrights say things which are exceedingly odd by most everyday standards of normality. Any way of interpreting literature would need to account for that oddness" (p. 18). What makes an explanation "good" is already implicit here, but Miller immediately makes it explicit: "A critical hypothesis, it may be, has more or less value as it facilitates or inhibits this noticing [of oddness]" (p. 18). The test of a hypothesis, in other words, is analogous to the "test of an image": "not its likeness but its efficacy within a context of action" (Gombrich, *Art and Illusion*, p. 110).

43. For further definition and discussion of the notion of "interpretive history" see Adena Rosmarin, "Misreading' *Emma*: The Powers and Perils of Interpretive History," *ELH* 51 (Summer 1984): 315-42, and Adena Rosmarin, "Hermeneutics versus Erotics: Shakespeare's *Sonnets* and Interpretive History," *PMLA* 100 (January 1985): 20-37.

44. Harold Bloom, *A Map of Misreading* (New York: Oxford University Press, 1975), p. 3; de Man is cited above (n. 7).

45. "Misreading," like the notion of "inevitable error" (Jonathan Culler's interpretation of de Man's position in Culler, *The Pursuit of Signs: Semiotics, Literature, Deconstruction* [Ithaca: Cornell University Press, 1981], p. 14), is a common way of phrasing the process of painting or writing texts. This contemporary locution is useful in its emphasis on the selecting and shaping that compose this process, but it is unfortunate in its implications that there is something "wrong" with the resulting text and, moreover, that there could be a "correct" text, one that reads either its topic or previous texts without selecting and shaping. It also implies that such selecting and shaping is to be lamented, rather than welcomed as a powerful aesthetic and conceptual tool.

46. Hans Vaihinger, *The Philosophy of "As If": A System of the Theoretical, Practical and Religious Fictions of Mankind*, trans. C. K. Ogden (London: Routledge & Kegan Paul, 1924).

47. Ibid., p. 108.

48. Ibid.

49. For further discussion of this point, see Adena Rosmarin, "Theory and Practice: From Ideally Separate to Pragmatically Joined," *Journal of Aesthetics and Art Criticism* 43 (1984): 31-40.

50. Gombrich, *Art and Illusion*, p. 101. Gombrich refers us to Nikolas Tinbergen, *The Study of Instinct* (Oxford: Oxford University Press, 1951), but for a fuller inquiry into these avian "mistakes" see Tinbergen's later study, *The Herring Gull's World: A Study of the Social Behavior of Birds* (New York: Doubleday, 1960), chap. 17.

51. For two important instances of reading novels as if they were poems see Mark Schorer, "Technique as Discovery," *Hudson Review* 1 (1948), and "Fiction and the 'Analogical Matrix,' " *Kenyon Review* 11 (1949); both rpt. in *The World We Imagine: Selected Essays by Mark Schorer* (New York: Farrar, Straus and Giroux, 1968), pp. 3-45.

Chapter 1. Defining a Theory of Genre

1. E. H. Gombrich, *Art and Illusion: A Study in the Psychology of Pictorial Representation* (Princeton: Princeton University Press, 1960), p. 301; I. A. Richards, *The Philosophy of Rhetoric* (New York: Oxford University Press, 1936), p. 30. Further citations will be included in the text.

See also Hayden White, *Tropics of Discourse: Essays in Cultural Criticism* (Baltimore: Johns Hopkins University Press, 1978): "the beginning of all understanding is classification" (p. 22).

2. Aristotle, *Poetics*, in *Critical Theory Since Plato*, ed. Hazard Adams (New York: Harcourt, Brace and Jovanovich, 1971), p. 62. The connection between the biologist's attempts at classification and the critic's may be said to originate with Aristotle, who was a naturalist and who begins his *Poetics* by announcing just such an attempt: "I propose to treat of poetry in itself and of its various kinds, noting the essential quality of each . . . " (p. 48). In post-Linnaean times, the genus has become the biologist's way of organizing its member species and the species his way of organizing its member individuals. The analogy with literary genres and their member texts is, strictly speaking, with the latter pairing, and, indeed, such eighteenth-century writers as Samuel Johnson and Hugh Blair referred to "genres" as "species," the term "genre" not coming into use until the nineteenth century. This change, however, did not affect the analogy since the general-particular relationship repeats on all levels of bionomial nomenclature.

The field of literary studies characteristically distinguishes its use of classification from that of the natural sciences. The distinction, however, typically depends upon a misunderstanding of the status and function of classification in both disciplines, a misunderstanding exemplified by Tzvetan Todorov's analysis in the opening chapter of *The Fantastic*, trans. Richard Howard (Cleveland: Press of Case Western University, 1973): 'the birth of a new tiger does not modify the species in its definition. The impact of individual organisms on the evolution of the species is so slow that we can discount it in practice" (p. 6). Although it is true that evolutionary changes are reflected in the bionomial nomenclature, they account for only a small percentage of biology's ongoing and multitudinous reclassifications. In avian nomenclature, for example, 84 percent (674 of 798) of North American species have, on some taxonomic level, been reclassified between the fifth (1957) and sixth (1983) editions of the *Checklist of North American Birds*. Purely nomenclatural changes—corrections made to conform to the grammar of the classical languages, those made to accord with the principle of historical priority of names, those made to eliminate the inadvertent duplication of names—account for twenty changes. The rest, which involve either "lumping" groups previously classed as separate or "splitting" groups previously classed as one, reflect new opinion on the actual or potential breeding behavior of the groups involved, opinion that is variously based on morphological, ethological, or biochemical data. Moreover, individual populations not infrequently undergo multiple reclassifications. The Thayer's Gull, for example, was not distinguished from the Herring Gull till 1915, when it was granted full species status. In 1925 it was demoted to a subspecies of the Herring Gull, then in 1973 once again was granted full species status. And at present, "there exists some feeling that Thayer's Gull should, again, be lumped—this time with Iceland" (Paul Lehman, "The Identification of Thayer's Gull in the Field," *Birding* 12 [1980]: 198). My point is that biological classification is itself an explanatory system, which has been devised primarily to make sense of an otherwise disparate group of individuals and which is changed primarily in order to improve that sense. While robins and poems are obviously different, the attempt to make a reasoned sense similarly dominates their study.

3. Aristotle, *Poetics*, p. 48.

4. Percy Bysshe Shelley, *A Defense of Poetry*, in Adams, *Critical Theory Since Plato*, p. 499.

5. Kenneth Burke, *Counter-Statement* (Berkeley: University of California Press, 1968), p. 125.

6. Barbara Herrnstein Smith, *Poetic Closure: A Study of How Poems End* (Chicago: University of Chicago Press, 1968), p. 38.

7. Avigdor Arikha, *TIME*, 30 July 1979, 71. A recent attempt to perform "both the transgression and the inclusion of doubt" is David Carroll's *The Subject in Question: The Languages of Theory and the Strategies of Fiction* (Chicago: The University of Chicago Press, 1982). Carroll opens by stating his premise and purpose: "Rather than place theory and literature (in this case theory and fiction) against each other in sterile opposition, in this book I use fiction strategically to indicate the limitations of theory and theory to indicate the limitations of fiction—each revealing the

premises, interests, and implications of the other. Each is not so much opposed to the other as always already implicated in the other'' (p. 2).

8. My distinction between the two repetitions, which an expressly deductive genre theory and practice interweaves, has its most immediate theoretical antecedents in Jacques Derrida, "Differance," *Bulletin de la Société française de philosophie* 62 (1968); rpt. in *Speech and Phenomena: And Other Essays on Husserl's Theory of Signs* (Evanston: Northwestern University Press, 1973), pp. 129-60, and Gilles Deleuze, *Logique du Sens* (Paris: Les Editions de Minuit, 1969). Derrida phrases the two repetitions in terms of difference and delay—"In the one case 'to differ' signifies nonidentity; in the other case it signifies the order of the *same*' (p. 129)—and then joins them in the term *differance*. Deleuze phrases the two repetitions thus: "Let us consider two formulations: 'only that which resembles itself differs,' 'only differences resemble one another.' It is a question of two readings of the world in that one asks us to think of difference on the basis of preestablished similitude or identity, while the other invites us on the contrary to think of similitude and even identity as the product of a fundamental disparity'' (p. 302). My most immediate practical antecedent is J. Hillis Miller's use of these two repetitions in *Fiction and Repetition: Seven English Novels* (Cambridge, Mass.: Harvard University Press, 1982). Miller opens with their theoretical definition (he invokes Deleuze's definition, among others, and I accordingly cite his translation) and proceeds to use that definition to perform critical practice. This usage transfers in the present study to the practices of both genre theory and genre criticism. See also Derrida's "The Law of Genre," trans. Avital Ronell, *Critical Inquiry* 7 (1980): 55-81, one of the theses of which is that "every text participates in one or several genres, there is no genreless text; there is always a genre and genres, yet such participation never amounts to belonging'' (p. 65).

9. Barbara Johnson observes that in deconstructionist criticism "truth is preserved in the notion of error'' ("Nothing Fails like Success," *SCE Reports* 8 [1980]: 14). Richard Rorty makes a similar point (about Derrida's notion of "trace") in "Philosophy as a Kind of Writing: An Essay on Derrida," *New Literary History* 10 (1978-79); rpt. in Rorty, *Consequences of Pragmatism (Essays: 1972-1980)* (Minneapolis: University of Minnesota Press, 1982), pp. 90-109.

10. Gustavo Pérez Firmat argues similarly: that "the genre achieves textual existence in the present-day critic's own discourse" ("The Novel as Genres," *Genre* 12 [1979]: 276). I find Firmat's study, although on several points it differs from my own, to be the most insightful recent inquiry into genre. Especially valuable is his analysis of Todorov and the inductive-deductive problem (pp. 277-84). See also Stanley Fish's argument that "the claims of independence and priority are the same" in "Interpreting the *Variorum*," *Critical Inquiry* 2 (1976); rpt. in *Is There a Text in This Class? The Authority of Interpretive Communities* (Cambridge, Mass.: Harvard University Press, 1980), p. 162. In other words, to claim that the genre preexists the critic's description is to claim that it is independent of that description.

11. E. D. Hirsch, Jr., *Validity in Interpretation* (New Haven: Yale University Press, 1967). Further citations will be included in the text.

12. E. D. Hirsch, Jr., "Objective Interpretation," *PMLA* 75 (1960); rpt. in ibid., pp. 209-44. Hirsch argues the stated points in chap. 3 of *Validity*.

13. The best contemporary example of this blend is Stanley Fish's theory of interpretive strategies (see chaps. 13 through 16 of *Is There a Text in This Class?*). Like Kant, Fish takes a category or, as he says, "interpretive strategy" as his object of description. He emphasizes the constitutive power of this "strategy," its power to make meaning, but he also assumes the power of his metatheory to describe that "strategy" accurately, without contamination from its own strategies. This latter power is paradoxical, being a power of powerlessness: it is that of the perfectly polished mirror, the perfectly transparent lens. Conceived thus, the theoretical medium neither causes nor constitutes meaning but, rather, reflects critical meaning, enabling the theorist to *describe* how our critical strategies cause or constitute the literary meaning that they, in like fashion, present themselves as describing. Kant's categories differ from Fish's primarily in that Kant's are essentially unchang-

ing whereas Fish's are never not changing—except at the precise moment of their description. But the similarity of their categories is more important than this difference: just as Fish conceives of the formal features of a text as a product of interpretation, not its cause, so Kant conceives of it as a datum of sense experience to be itself categorized. Kant argues this point in the *Critique of Pure Reason* (1781), trans. Norman Kemp Smith (London: Macmillan, 1929), sec. I ("Transcendental Doctrine of Elements"), bk. I, chap. 2, "The Deduction of the Pure Concepts of Understanding." The point is further emphasized in the much revised second edition (1787). Like Fish and Hirsch, Kant never explains how we know the categories (or "strategies," or "wholes") themselves, nor how we know which category is in force. The question of how to make philosophical assertions or, in terms of our discipline, how to begin critical argument is raised in the *Critique*, but left unanswered.

14. Karl Viëtor, "Die Geschichte literarischer Gattungen," in *Geist und Form* (Bern: A. Franke, 1952), pp. 292-309. See following note for Wellek. The "hermeneutic circle" problem is discussed at length by Claudio Guillén, *Literature as System: Essays toward the Theory of Literary History* (Princeton: Princeton University Press, 1971), essay 4, "On the Uses of Literary Genre," pp. 107-34, and by Gustavo Pérez Firmat (see below in text), whose discussion exposes the faulty analogy that engenders the problem. See also Allan Rodway, "Generic Criticism: The Approach through Type, Mode and Kind," in *Contemporary Criticism*, Stratford-upon-Avon Studies 12 (New York: St. Martin's Press, 1970). Rodway similarly sees the genre question as a phrasing of the "hermeneutic circle" problem and, like Hirsch, posits an inductive solution: "We escape, so to speak, by edging out, tacking from evidence to hypothesis to further evidence to renewed hypothesis" (p. 94).

15. René Wellek, *Discriminations: Further Concepts of Criticism* (New Haven: Yale University Press, 1970), p. 252.

16. Ibid., p. 252.

17. Firmat, "The Novel as Genres," p. 278.

18. E. D. Hirsch, Jr., "Stylistics and Synonymity," *Critical Inquiry*, 1 (1975); rpt. in *Aims of Interpretation* (Chicago: University of Chicago Press, 1976), pp. 50-73.

19. Maurice Blanchot, *Le livre à venir* (Paris: Gallimard, 1959), p. 293. See my theoretical introduction (no. 22 above) for further information.

20. Kenneth Burke, "Formalist Criticism: Its Principles and Limits," *Texas Quarterly* 9 (1966); rpt. in *Language as Symbolic Action: Essays on Life, Literature, and Method* (Berkeley: University of California Press, 1966), p. 489.

21. For a lucid and suggestive exposition of the infinitely regressive ground problem as it troubles literary studies, in particular literary history, see Michael McCanles, "The Authentic Discourse of the Renaissance," *Diacritics* 10 (1980): 77-87, discussed in my introduction.

22. Perhaps the strongest and most explicitly critical redefinition of *Joseph Andrews* is that of Sheldon Sacks, *Fiction and the Shape of Belief: A Study of Henry Fielding with Glances at Swift, Johnson and Richardson* (Chicago: University of Chicago Press, 1964), pp. 70-102. The genre is defined along Aristotelian lines, as an "action": "Actions . . . are works in which characters about whose fates we are made to care are introduced in unstable relationships which are then further complicated until the complication is finally resolved by the complete removal of the represented instability" (p. 24). Sacks is explicit about formulating a "Grammar of the Types of Fiction" (chap. 1) and about the purposefulness of that grammar: "The primary justification for establishing three classes—obviously others equally 'correct' are possible—is to formulate a meaningful general question, or possibly questions, about the relation between a novelist's beliefs and the forms of his novels" (p. 27). Sacks argues thus even as he quotes Howard Mumford Jones's observation: that *Joseph Andrews* is "the first English novel consciously fulfilling an aesthetic theory" ("Introduction" to *Joseph Andrews* [New York: Random House, Modern Library College Editions, 1950], p. vii; quoted by Sacks on p. 236). Only occasionally will a critic make explicit the typically determin-

ing criterion of the critical premise or model, namely, its worth in explanation. For an example from the interpretive history of the monologue, see Linda K. Hughes, "Dramatis and Private Personae: 'Ulysses' Revisited," *Victorian Poetry* 17 (1979): 192–203. In conclusion Hughes argues thus: "If this reading of the poem does not coincide exactly with Tennyson's own conception of scene and audience, it at least accords well with the movement of the poem. More important, this reading can perhaps answer to what is at best a minor criticism of 'Ulysses'—its apparent contradictions in setting, movement, and audience" (p. 203).

23. R. S. Crane, "Towards a More Adequate Criticism of Poetic Structure," in *The Languages of Criticism and the Structure of Poetry* (Toronto: University of Toronto Press, 1953), pp. 140–94. Further citations will be included in the text. For a searching critique of Crane's inductivism see Kenneth Burke, "The Problem of the Intrinsic," in *A Grammar of Motives* (Berkeley: University of California Press, 1969), pp. 465–84. See also W. K. Wimsatt, Jr.'s analysis of the inductive-deductive wavering of Richard McKeon's literary theory in Wimsatt, "The Chicago Critics: The Fallacy of the Neoclassic Species," *Comparative Literature* 5 (1953); rpt. in Wimsatt, *The Verbal Icon: Studies in the Meaning of Poetry* (Lexington: University of Kentucky Press, 1954), p. 43. For a recent "Chicago" statement on genre, see David H. Richter, "Pandora's Box Revisited: A Review Article," *Critical Inquiry* 1 (1974): 453–78.

24. R. S. Crane, "The Concept of Plot and the Plot of *Tom Jones*," in *Critics and Criticism: Ancient and Modern*, ed. R. S. Crane (Chicago: University of Chicago Press, 1952), pp. 616–47. The novel, like the dramatic monologue, has particularly attracted the attention of theorists of genre. The two genres are conceptually challenging for many of the same reasons: their deft interweaving of the spoken and written word, the designed blurring of borders between text and world, their tendency toward various kinds of calculated incompletion and polyvocality, what Bakhtin has called "heteroglossia." See M. M. Bakhtin, *The Dialogic Imagination: Four Essays*, ed. Michael Holquist, trans. Caryl Emerson and Michael Holquist (Austin: University of Texas Press, 1981). The first essay, "Epic and the Novel: Toward a Methodology for the Study of the Novel," exemplifies Bakhtin's never fully systematized notion of genre as both textually determining and itself determined by its socio-historical context.

25. R. S. Crane, "The Multiplicity of Critical Languages," in *The Languages of Criticism*, p. 13.

26. Northrop Frye, *Anatomy of Criticism: Four Essays* (Princeton: Princeton University Press, 1957), pp. 6–7. Further citations will be included in the text. Criticizing or "correcting" Frye is one of the three most frequent starting points for contemporary genre theories (the other two being Croce and Todorov). Among such corrections, that of Hazard Adams comes closest to mine: "My own objection to Frye's argument is that . . . I do not believe he can hold to the philosophical neutrality of his method" (*The Interests of Criticism: An Introduction to Literary Theory* [New York: Harcourt, Brace & World, 1969], p. 130). Frye's theory, Adams decides, is "neo-Kantian," and I agree. See also Murray Krieger, ed., *Northrop Frye in Modern Criticism: Selected Papers from the English Institute* (New York: Columbia University Press, 1966), particularly Krieger's introductory essay, "Northrop Frye and Contemporary Criticism: Ariel and the Spirit of Gravity." Elsewhere Krieger acknowledges "the practical impossibility of keeping criticism inductive . . . once we first concede—in post-Kantian manner—the constitutive role of our categories" ("Literary Analysis and Evaluation—and the Ambidextrous Critic," *Contemporary Literature* 9 [1968]; rpt. in Krieger, *Poetic Presence and Illusion: Essays in Critical History and Theory* [Baltimore: Johns Hopkins University Press, 1979], p. 307). And in his essay on Frye's *Anatomy* we find this footnoted but telling comment: "Originally I thought of using *systematics* instead of *schematics* here. But, as Frye points out . . . , his categories and modes might better be thought of as schematic rather than systematic creations" (p. 5).

27. For an elegant, historical, and schematic critique of the overly schematic theory from Plato and Aristotle onward, see Gérard Genette, *Introduction à l'architexte* (Paris: Éditions du Seuil,

1979). Discussing Frye's *Anatomy*, Genette comments that "on peut sans doute contester la procédure, mais non l'intérêt du résultat (p. 50). Hence Frye's power as a starting place.

28. Tzvetan Todorov, *The Fantastic: A Structural Approach to a Literary Genre*, trans. Richard Howard (Cleveland: Press of Case Western Reserve University, 1973). Further citations will be included in the text, the first page number referring to the English text, the second to the French (*Introduction à la littérature fantastique* [Paris: Seuil, 1970]). Howard's translation closely follows the original, so I will not give the French text here. I have, however, replaced the confusing punctuation of the passage beginning "no observation" with Todorov's own. Todorov's opening chapter is rapidly replacing Frye's *Anatomy* as *the* theory to "correct." See Firmat, "The Novel as Genres"; Richter, "Pandora's Box Revisited"; and Christine Brooke-Rose, *A Rhetoric of the Unreal: Studies in Narrative and Structure, Especially of the Fantastic* (Cambridge: Cambridge University Press, 1981), chap. 3, "Historic Genres/Theoretical Genres: Todorov on the Fantastic," pp. 55–71.

29. Hans Robert Jauss, "Theory of Genres and Medieval Literature," in *Toward an Aesthetic of Reception*, trans. Timothy Bahti (Minneapolis: University of Minnesota Press, 1982), pp. 76–109. Further citations will be included in the text.

30. Hans Robert Jauss, "Literary History as a Challenge to Literary Theory," in *Toward an Aesthetics of Reception*, particularly pp. 25–28. Further citations will be included in the text. The core of Jauss's definition is as follows: "The way in which a literary work, at the historical moment of its appearance, satisfies, surpasses, disappoints, or refutes the expectations of its first audience obviously provides a criterion for the determination of its aesthetic value. The distance between the horizon of expectations and the work, between the familiarity of previous aesthetic experience and the 'horizonal change' demanded by the reception of the new work, determines the artistic character of a literary work, according to an aesthetics of reception: to the degree that this distance decreases, and no turn toward the horizon of yet-unknown experience is demanded of the receiving consciousness, the closer the work comes to the sphere of 'culinary' or entertainment art [*Unterhaltungskunst*]" (p. 25).

31. Jauss's notion of "originality" is thoroughly Romantic and insufficiently complex. His aesthetics could not, for example, make the following discrimination concerning Mozart: '[He is] original in a different sense from Haydn, who astonished, amused, and charmed the people of his time by the freshness, wit, and insouciance of his ideas. Mozart seems never to want to exceed the bounds of convention. He wanted to *fulfill* the laws, not to violate them. Yet he constantly violates the spirit of the music of the eighteenth century—by his seriousness, his amiability (which was no longer the amiability of the *rococo* period), his artistry of combination" (Alfred Einstein, *Greatness in Music* [London: Oxford University Press, 1945], p. 153). Mozart's "conventional" greatness is perhaps best explained by Leonard B. Meyer, who, in his "Grammatical Simplicity and Relational Richness: The Trio of Mozart's G Minor Symphony," *Critical Inquiry* 2 (1976): 693–761, shows how the "unassuming, conventional means" of the Trio nevertheless can yield "rich" results. Not incidentally, Meyer's essay exemplifies many of the points I am making in this chapter and those following. He concentrates, as does Gombrich, on "relational results" rather than "material means," and emphasizes that when explaining these relationships "what seems crucial is that premises be made explicit and arguments from them consistent" (pp. 693, 759).

32. Hayden White, "The Value of Narrativity in the Representation of Reality," *Critical Inquiry* 7 (1980): 5–27.

33. Ibid., p. 24.

34. Ralph W. Rader, "Defoe, Richardson, Joyce, and the Concept of Form in the Novel," in *Autobiography, Biography and the Novel* (Los Angeles: University of California Press, 1973), p. 33.

35. Ralph W. Rader, "Fact, Theory, and Literary Explanation," *Critical Inquiry* 1 (1974): 245–46.

36. See Hans Vaihinger, *The Philosophy of "As If": A System of the Theoretical, Practical and Religious Fictions of Mankind*, trans. C. K. Ogden (London: Routledge & Kegan Paul, 1924), pp. 74-76, 313-18.

37. See Shelley, *A Defense of Poetry*, p. 503.

38. The aesthetic valuative criteria used in this study are most obviously manifest in formalist and deconstructionist criticism, the ethical criteria in reader-response criticism, particularly that of Stanley Fish. See Fish's *Self-Consuming Artifacts: The Experience of Seventeenth-Century Literature* (Berkeley: University of California Press, 1972), particularly chaps. 1 and 7. See Albert Camus, *La Chute* (Paris: Gallimard, 1956), for a "literary" inquiry into the powers and perfidies of judgment. By repeatedly manipulating its reader into judgments or readings that are repeatedly shown to be misjudgments or misreadings, the "récit" dramatizes even as it thematizes both the inevitability of judgment and its danger.

39. All generic explanations happen within the ongoing conversation that I am here calling the text's interpretive history. John Reichert initially seems to agree with this point: "the placing of a work in one genre can never rule out the interpretive questions raised by some other genre to which it may also belong" ("More than Kin and Less than Kind: The Limits of Genre Theory," in *Theories of Literary Genre*, ed. Joseph P. Strelka [University Park: Pennsylvania State University Press, 1978], p. 65). Reichert, however, argues on the assumption that a text may or may not *intrinsically* belong to a given genre or genres. My point is that a generic argument is convincing in part because it comprehends a text's previous generic definitions, whether by rebuttal, assimilation, or revision.

40. Paul de Man, "Introduction" to Jauss, *Toward an Aesthetic of Reception*, p. xiii.

41. Douglas Hofstadter, *Gödel, Escher, Bach: An Eternal Golden Braid* (New York: Random House, 1980), p. 15. Hofstadter's formulation of self-reflexivity, the "strange loop," is indebted to Gödel's Incompleteness Theorem, which states that in any sufficiently complex or powerful system there are true statements whose proof is beyond the resources of that system. These statements (which, for Gödel, were statements of number theory) can be understood on two different levels: as statements of number theory and as statements about those statements. This latter "level" analogizes with critical theory, the former with critical practice, and the formulation itself thereby offers an extremely suggestive if dizzying analogy for the fusion of theory and practice in our own discipline.

42. Vaihinger, *The Philosophy of "As If,"* p. 108.

43. See Jonathan Culler, *Structuralist Poetics: Structuralism, Linguistics and the Study of Literature* (Ithaca: Cornell University Press, 1975), particularly pp. 207-13.

44. See Paul Ricoeur, "The Metaphorical Process as Cognition, Imagination, and Feeling," *Critical Inquiry* 5 (1978): 143-59, for a challenging attempt to define in terms of metaphor the unity of cognitive, imaginative, and emotional processes. Ricoeur's notion of "predicative assimilation," defined as a "*making* similar, that is, semantically proximate, the terms that the metaphorical utterance brings together" (p. 148), is related to the notion of deductive genre as here defined. See also Hayden White's argument in *Tropics of Discourse* that "the model of the syllogism itself displays clear evidence of troping": "The move from the major premise (all men are mortal) to the *choice* of the datum to serve as the minor (Socrates is a man) is itself a tropological move, a 'swerve' from the universal to the particular which logic cannot preside over, since it is logic itself that is being served by this move. Every *applied* syllogism contains an enthymemic element, this element consisting of nothing but the *decision* to move from the plane of universal propositions (themselves extended synecdoches) to that of singular existential statements (these being extended metonymies)" (p. 3). See also Georg Wilhelm Friedrich Hegel, *The Logic of Hegel*, 2d rev. ed., trans. William Wallace (London: Oxford University Press, 1892), pp. 314-29.

45. Kenneth Burke, "Definition of Man," *Hudson Review* 17 (1963-64); rpt. in *Language as Symbolic Action*, p. 5.

46. Robert Langbaum, *The Poetry of Experience: The Dramatic Monologue in Modern Literary Tradition* (New York: W. W. Norton, 1957).

47. Burke, *Counter-Statement*, p. 160.

48. Chaim Perelman has observed that "everything that promotes perception of a device—the mechanical, farfetched, abstract, codified, and formal aspects of a speech—will prompt the search for a reality that is dissociated from it" (Chaim Perelman and L. Olbrechts-Tyteca, *The New Rhetoric: A Treatise on Argumentation*, trans. John Wilkinson and Purcell Weaver [Notre Dame: University of Notre Dame Press, 1969], p. 453). Perelman is speaking of argumentation generally, but we can usefully transfer his insight to genre criticism, wherein genre equals the "device" which, when foregrounded, prompts us to go beneath and behind in search of the textual reality it necessarily reduces and distorts. It is when the device is thoroughly exposed or used up through the sorites that we come face to face with citations from the poem itself, citations that I am here calling "hermeneutic detritus." Thus does the working of genre, by a paradoxical logic and by its yoking with the unique demands made of a *literary* explanation, finally depend upon the genre's *not* working in the more usual sense. For an explicit example of this process, see Avrom Fleishman, "*Wuthering Heights*: The Love of a Sylph and a Gnome," in *Fiction and the Ways of Knowing: Essays on British Novels* (Austin: University of Texas Press, 1978), pp. 37–51. Fleishman begins thus: "The premise stated in the title of this essay will require provisional justification, although its credibility can only gradually be gained" (p. 37). Fleishman then proceeds to this justification, reading the novel in terms of alchemical doctrines. When he has used up their explanatory power, he concludes by juxtaposing citations from both *Wuthering Heights* and alchemical texts, then remarking that "these doctrines may be related to *Wuthering Heights* in a sequence of declining specificity" and that "at this point, the theories of the alchemists begin to distinguish themselves sharply from the wider Gnostic tradition, and by the same token their application to the novel becomes increasingly problematic" (p. 50).

49. The most lucid and forceful statement of this point is Firmat's (in "The Novel as Genres"), which is phrased as a critique of Todorov's distinction, which, in turn, typifies that made by most theorists of genre:

> If one reviews Todorov's remarks, it becomes clear, first of all, that these two categories do not in fact designate two kinds of genres, but rather two ostensibly different ways of arriving at generic concepts. When he states that historical genres are "le fruit d'une observation des faits littéraires," while theoretical genres "sont deduits d'une théorie de la littérature," Todorov is in effect discriminating between inductive and deductive concept formation. The fact that he regards historical genres as subsets of complex theoretical genres bears out their essential likeness. Were the two categories qualitatively different, that is, were Todorov really defining two *kinds* of genres, this subordination would be impossible. . . . The two seem to be dissimilar only insofar as they were reached by different avenues. . . . What separates historical and theoretical geneology is simply an illusion, the illusion that one can form theories in a rigorously inductive manner." (Pp. 275–76)

Firmat refers us to Karl Popper's *The Logic of Scientific Discovery* (New York: Basic Books, 1959), as does Rader ("Fact, Theory, and Literary Explanation"). Popper's deductivism, his argument that induction necessarily leads to an infinite regress (p. 29), his definition of a theory's power in terms of its explanatory range—all make his theory seem readily transferable to literary studies. As in part it surely is. But we should keep in mind that Popper is explaining theories that would explain the world rather than texts, theories that, unlike literary theories or genres, can be falsified.

50. As I am arguing throughout, "insufficiently" and "sufficiently" are pragmatic and rhetorical criteria. They measure an explanation's success in terms of its function, purpose, and audience—terms that are open to change in time and, even at any given time, may be particularized in more than one way.

51. René Wellek and Austin Warren, *Theory of Literature* (New York: Harcourt, Brace & World, 1956), pp. 234–35.

52. Paul Hernadi, *Beyond Genre: New Directions in Literary Classification* (Ithaca: Cornell University Press, 1972), p. 184. For a "historical genre" study, which also proposes to be a theory of genre, see Alastair Fowler, *Kinds of Literature: An Introduction to the Theory of Genres and Modes* (Cambridge, Mass.: Harvard University Press, 1982). Fowler is primarily a historian of genre, interested in how genres evolve, die, and revive. He defines his theory against systematizing theories such as Frye's or Hernadi's. Finally, see Fredric Jameson, *The Political Unconscious: Narrative as a Socially Symbolic Act* (Ithaca: Cornell University Press, 1981), particularly chap. 2, "Magical Narratives: On the Dialectical Use of Genre Criticism." For the purposes of the present study, Jameson's most interesting point comes at the end of his lengthy and rigorous Marxist inquiry, where he notes that the "final moment of the generic operation, in which the working categories of genre are themselves historically deconstructed and abandoned, suggests a final axiom, according to which *all* generic categories, even the most time-hallowed and traditional, are ultimately to be understood (or "estranged") as mere ad hoc, experimental constructs, devised for a specific textual occasion and abandoned like so much scaffolding when the analysis has done its work" (p. 145). This "final axiom" is, in effect, my beginning premise.

Chapter 2. The Dramatic Monologue

1. The genre has most frequently been defined in terms of its combination of lyric and dramatic elements. (My definition does not reject this traditional beginning but, rather, tries for greater precision and power.) For a thorough exploration of this generic premise, see Donald S. Hair, *Browning's Experiments with Genre* (Toronto: University of Toronto Press, 1972). Like most genre critics, Hair uses his premise as an explanatory tool even as he "finds" it in history, speaking throughout of Browning's experimentation rather than of his own explanation. Browning, of course, being manifestly interested in genre, is a superb topic for such inquiry into the historical use of genre. But even in his case we do well to remember that the "dramatic monologue" is a critical invention, that however thoroughly we anchor it in history its critical value is a question not of its prior existence in a poet's mind but of its power to explain.

2. Ina Beth Sessions, "The Dramatic Monologue," *PMLA* 62 (1947): 503–16. The most comprehensive survey of poems in which the speaker is characterized is Benjamin Fuson's *Browning and His English Predecessors in the Dramatic Monolog*, State University of Iowa Humanistic Studies, ed. Franklin H. Potter (Iowa City: State University of Iowa Press, 1948). See also Fuson's later study, *The Poet and His Mask* (Parkville, Mo.: Park College Press, 1954). Robert Langbaum's *The Poetry of Experience: The Dramatic Monologue in Modern Literary Tradition* (New York: W. W. Norton, 1957), is the single most important study of the genre, but see also George T. Wright, *The Poet in the Poem: The Personae of Eliot, Yeats, and Pound* (Berkeley: University of California Press, 1962). Wright's study is suggestive, but his distinctions are obscured by his use of the term "persona" to refer to both the speaker and the implied poet, a practice that precludes discussion of the reader's shifting allegiance. W. David Shaw's *The Dialectical Temper: The Rhetorical Art of Robert Browning* (Ithaca: Cornell University Press, 1968) contains a superb unfolding of the *internal* rhetoric of the monologue, examining not the poem's suasive design on its reader but the speaker's suasive design on his auditor, which may include or be himself. Indeed, Shaw defines the genre in terms of this intramural drama (pp. 60–61). It is of theoretical interest to note that this definition is contained within a subsuming definition, stated in terms of Kierkegaard's three stages of development: the aesthetic, ethical, and religious. Shaw attaches "minimal importance . . . to the accidental historic fact that Browning and Kierkegaard were contemporaries" (pp. 62–63, note). He is "using Kierkegaard's analysis only as a heuristic device; much of it may be mere scaffolding, to be knocked away when Browning's own dialectical structures are in clearer view" (p. 63, note).

This notion of "heuristic device" closely resembles my notion of genre, and Shaw's critical practice thus exemplifies my theoretical thesis. However, by placing his definition in a footnote and by treating the heuristic as a way to visual revelation rather than as a way of reasoning, Shaw also illustrates the desire of contemporary genre criticism to conceal its inventionality.

Shorter studies (not including those mentioned below) that make significant generic distinctions are John Perry, "The Relationships of Disparate Voices in Poems," *Essays in Criticism* 15 (1965): 49–64; William Cadbury, "Lyric and Anti-Lyric Forms: A Method for Judging Browning," *University of Toronto Quarterly* 34 (1964): 49–67; A. R. Jones, "Robert Browning and the Dramatic Monologue: The Impersonal Art," *Critical Quarterly* 9 (1968): 301–28; K. P. Saradhi, "The Theatre of the Mind: Browning's Dramatic Monologues," *Genre* 8 (1975): 322–35. Ed Block, Jr., in his "Lyric Voice and Reader Response: One View of the Transition to Modern Poetics," *Twentieth-Century Literature* 24 (1978): 154–68, argues that the Victorian monologue called for a "less active reader involvement" than the modern lyric. My definition of the genre allows me to argue that reader involvement in the monologue and the lyric differs not so much in degree as in kind, an argument that upholds the monologue's heuristic power.

The important early definitions of the genre (not including those mentioned below) are W. L. Phelps, *Robert Browning: How to Know Him* (London: Smith, Elder, 1916); G. H. Palmer, *Formative Types in English Poetry* (Boston: Houghton, Mifflin, 1918); R. H. Fletcher, "Browning's Dramatic Monologs," *Modern Language Notes* 23 (1908): 108–11; S. S. Curry, *Browning and the Dramatic Monologue* (Boston: Expression Company, 1908); Claud Howard, "The Dramatic Monologue: Its Origins and Development," *Studies in Philology* 4 (1910): 31–88; M. W. MacCallum, "The Dramatic Monologue in the Victorian Period," *Proceedings of the British Academy* 11 (1924–25): 265–82.

3. Sessions, "The Dramatic Monologue," p. 508.

4. See Ralph W. Rader's argument for the pragmatic value of deductive rigor in "Fact, Theory, and Literary Explanation," *Critical Inquiry* 1 (1974): 245–72.

5. Park Honan, *Browning's Characters: A Study in Poetic Technique* (New Haven: Yale University Press, 1961), p. 22.

6. Ibid., p. 22. The mimeticism of Honan's language is clearly revealed on p. 3, where he values those monologues whose speakers seem to be autonomous, fully realized "portraits of character." My point is not that Honan's "definition" does or does not correspond to the way the poems really are but, rather, that he himself calls his definition by that name.

7. Robert Langbaum, *The Poetry of Experience*, pp. 77–78. Further citations will be included in the text. Obviously, Langbaum's study antedates Honan's. I use Honan's study to typify the *sui generis* argument that is compelled to generic definition by the interpretive history within which it is mounted.

8. E. H. Gombrich, *Art and Illusion: A Study in the Psychology of Pictorial Representation* (Princeton: Princeton University Press, 1960), p. 6. Further citations will be included in the text.

9. Ralph W. Rader, "The Dramatic Monologue and Related Lyric Forms," *Critical Inquiry* 3 (1976): 133, 150. For Elder Olson's conception of monologues and lyrics see "An Outline of Poetic Theory," in *Critics and Criticism: Ancient and Modern*, ed. R. S. Crane (Chicago: University of Chicago Press, 1952), p. 560; *The Poetry of Dylan Thomas* (Chicago: University of Chicago Press, 1954), pp. 30–33; "The Lyric," *Papers of the Midwest Language Association*, vol. I, ed. Robert Scholes (Iowa City: State University of Iowa Press, 1969), pp. 59–66. For Rader's further discussion of the genre and of genre per se see "The Concept of Genre and Eighteenth-Century Studies," in *New Approaches to Eighteenth-Century Literature*, ed. Phillip Harth (New York: Columbia University Press, 1974), pp. 91–96.

10. Rader's model is increasingly influential, as is shown by the number of recent explanations of the monologue, including the present one, that begin by reworking his definition. Among these, David Bergman's "Browning's Monologues and the Development of the Soul" (*ELH* 4 [1980]:

772–87) is of particular interest. Bergman faults Rader for not providing "criteria for distinguishing between a failed dramatic monologue and what he calls a 'mask lyric'" and for "fitting" his definition to only a small number of monologues (p. 773). Bergman accordingly expands the definition, treating the "realistic" characteristics of the monologue—"the specificity of the setting and the idiosyncrasy of the voice" (p. 781)—as symptoms of the speaker's rudimentary stage in "the development of the soul." His generic premise, like all such premises, is explicitly valuative: "In order to properly evaluate Browning's poems aesthetically, it is necessary to ascertain what level of spiritual development the speaker has attained and whether the poem's formal components properly reflect that level of spiritual attainment" (p. 786). But the premise, despite its explicit statement, is not presented *as* a premise or an explanatory tool but rather as a pattern that inheres in the poems themselves—or, more precisely, in their speakers. Many of the poems that for Bergman exemplify the higher stages of spiritual development are, not incidentally, what Rader (and I) would call mask lyrics—"Rabbi Ben Ezra," "Abt Vogler," "Saul," and "A Death in the Desert."

11. Wayne C. Booth, *A Rhetoric of Irony* (Chicago: University of Chicago Press, 1974), especially chap. 1. Booth argues for the *suasive* power of irony. Far from being an ornament on content, for Booth, as for I. A. Richards and Paul Ricoeur, the trope is instrumental to thought itself. Richards and Ricoeur focus on metaphor, but Booth has argued for the suasive and cognitive significance of both metaphor and irony. See his "Metaphor as Rhetoric: The Problem of Evaluation," *Critical Inquiry* 5 (1978): 49–72.

12. Browning's so-called doctrine of incompleteness is most eloquently expressed in his implicit yet devastating attack on the "flawless" Andrea del Sarto; in Fra Lippo Lippi's argument that "nature is complete:/Suppose you reproduce her—(which you can't)/There's no advantage!"; in the formalized skepticism of *The Ring and the Book*, where the rasping juxtaposition of speakers erodes the seeming completion of each; in the elaborated thesis of "Old Pictures in Florence" ("What's come to perfection perishes"). Consider also his repeated praise of Shelley in terms of his incompleteness: "I would rather consider Shelley's poetry as a sublime fragmentary essay"; "Such was the spheric poetical faculty of Shelley . . . radiating equally . . . through many fragments and occasional completion" ("Essay on Shelley" [1852], ed. Donald Smalley, in *The Complete Works of Robert Browning*, ed. Roma A. King, Jr. [Athens, Ohio: Ohio University Press, 1981], V, 151, 143). In the same essay Browning defines the "poet's function" in terms of his capacity to behold "the universe, nature and man, in their actual state of perfection in imperfection" and argues that "an absolute vision is not for this world" (p. 142).

For discussion of this doctrine see J. Hillis Miller, *The Disappearance of God: Five Nineteenth-Century Writers* (Cambridge, Mass.: Harvard University Press, 1963), p. 99, and Hoxie N. Fairchild, "Browning's Heaven," *Review of Religion* 14 (1949): 30–37. For a tracing of the development of the doctrine see Thomas J. Collins, *Robert Browning's Moral-Aesthetic Theory: 1833–1855* (Lincoln: University of Nebraska Press, 1967). Among earlier discussions see Henry Jones, *Browning as a Philosophical and Religious Teacher* (Glasgow: Maclehose, 1892); Solomon F. Gingerich, *Wordsworth, Tennyson, and Browning: A Study in Human Freedom* (Ann Arbor, Mich.: George Wahr, 1911); F. R. G. Duckworth, *Browning: Background and Conflict* (London: Ernest Benn, 1931). The most important recent study of the doctrine is Herbert F. Tucker, Jr., *Browning's Beginnings: The Art of Disclosure* (Minneapolis: University of Minnesota Press, 1980). Further citations will be included in the text. Tucker argues "that Browning's moral doctrine of incompleteness finds a clear aesthetic analogue in his poetics" (p. 5). He also argues—as I do in the present study—that both aesthetic and ethical value come into being as the reader completes and corrects the text he reads. As Tucker observes,

> Browning persistently explodes as illusory or cruel, as instinctively *wrong*, whatever presents itself as completion, triumph, or stability in the stories he tells or in the consciousnesses he imagines. His goals, once attained, are invariably disappointing and are often ruined by the

very act of attainment, so that they become in turn conditions of imperfection furnishing grounds for renewed desire and progress. The thoroughly provisional value of a Browning-esque goal consists not in the gratifying sense of possibility fulfilled, but in the more purposeful fulfillment that Browning discovers in the sense of possibility itself. (P. 5)

13. Stanley Fish, "Interpreting the *Variorum*," *Critical Inquiry* 2 (1976); rpt. in *Is There a Text in This Class? The Authority of Interpretive Communities* (Cambridge, Mass.: Harvard University Press, 1980), p. 159. Fish elaborates this "language" throughout his books on Milton, Herbert, and the seventeenth-century's "self-consuming artifacts," but for its definition see "Literature in the Reader: Affective Stylistics," *New Literary History* 2 (1970); rpt. in *Is There a Text in This Class?* pp. 21–67.

14. Walter Bagehot, "Wordsworth, Tennyson, and Browning; or Pure, Ornate, and Grotesque Art in English Poetry" (1864); rpt. in *Collected Works*, ed. Norman St. John-Stevas (Cambridge, Mass.: Harvard University Press, 1965), II, 353.

15. Hazard Adams, *The Contexts of Poetry* (Boston: Little, Brown, 1963), pp. 151–52.

16. For examples see Fuson's studies as well as Alan Sinfield, *Dramatic Monologue* (New York: Barnes & Noble, 1977), chap. 5. Consider also such early and less than memorable productions of the major Romantics as Wordsworth's "The Complaint of a Forsaken Indian Woman" and Coleridge's "The Complaint of Ninathoma."

17. Southey called these poems "monodramas." The term "dramatic monologue" did not come into general use until late in the century (see discussion below in text). A. Dwight Culler has explored the historical and rhetorical distinctions among monologues, monodramas, and prosopopoeia ("Monodrama and the Dramatic Monologue," *PMLA* 90 [1975]: 366–85). For discussion of the monologue's relationship to the stage see Philip Hobsbaum, "The Rise of the Dramatic Monologue," *Hudson Review* 28 (1975–76): 227–45.

18. See J. Hillis Miller's argument, which follows Nietzsche's, that the reader masters the text ("Tradition and Difference," *Diacritics* 2 [1972]: 12). Miller later argues the reverse, in "Theory and Practice: Response to Vincent Leitch," *Critical Inquiry* 6 (1980): 611, and in *Fiction and Repetition: Seven English Novels* (Cambridge, Mass.: Harvard University Press, 1982): "Each good reader of *Wuthering Heights* is subject to the text, coerced by it" (p. 52). Norman Holland is primarily a defender of the reader: what is important is whether "the reader has achieved a concept of the work which gave him a sense of personal mastery" (*Poems in Persons: An Introduction to the Psychology of Literature* [New York: W. W. Norton, 1973], p. 148). But he intermittently implies the power of the text, particularly his own—he is able to "influence" our reading "by adding to what the poet gave, my own comments on the work" (p. 150)—and at times he treats the reader *as* a text, replete with all its old or "new critical" power: "*Identity* is the *unity* I find in a *self* if I look at it as though it were a *text*" ("Unity Identity Text Self," *PMLA* 90 [1975]: 815). Stanley Fish champions the reader over the text in his early work (see particularly "Literature in the Reader," his most polemical statement), but even there, as he himself later observes, the text gradually becomes "more and more powerful," the reader "more constrained," until the charge of "solipsism and anarchy" is once more finessed by announcing "the constraints imposed on readers by the text" (*Is There a Text in This Class?* p. 7). Wolfgang Iser collapses the reader-text agon, carefully balancing interpretive power between the two: "the term 'implied reader' . . . incorporates both the pre-structuring of the potential meaning by the text, and the reader's actualization of this potential through the reading process" (*The Implied Reader: Patterns of Communication in Prose Fiction from Bunyan to Beckett* [Baltimore: Johns Hopkins University Press, 1974], p. xii). Reading these and other theorists of the last decade raises the suspicion that the master-slave relationship of reader and text, however the power is phrased, is less inherent than strategic, that it is a rhetorical tool for mounting a polemical offensive against whichever the critic chooses to be the second member of the pairing.

19. See the following readings, which despite their differences similarly exemplify the equation between explaining Cleon's failure and explaining the poem: Roma A. King, Jr., "Browning's 'Mage' and 'Maker'—A Study in Poetic Purpose and Method," in *Robert Browning: A Collection of Critical Essays*, ed. Philip Drew (New York: Houghton Mifflin, 1966), pp. 189–98, and Young G. Lee, "The Human Condition: Browning's 'Cleon,'" *Victorian Poetry* 7 (1969): 56–62.

20. Honan, *Browning's Characters*, p. 165.

21. William C. DeVane, headnote to "Cleon" in *Major British Writers* (New York: Harcourt, Brace & World, 1959), II, 521. DeVane's *A Browning Handbook*, 2d ed. (New York: Appleton-Century-Crofts, 1955), gives the biographical genesis and interpretive history of the monologues here discussed. For a discussion of the historical connection between "Cleon" and "Empedocles" see A. W. Crawford, "Browning's 'Cleon,'" *Journal of English and German Philology* 27 (1927): 485–90. According to Arnold himself, Browning was responsible for the republication of "Empedocles" in 1867. One might also posit a connection between Arnold's thesis, taken from Schiller— "All art is dedicated to joy"—and the importance of "joy" for Cleon. For further discussion of the poem in terms of its epigraph and Arnoldian context see G. W. Spence, "Browning's Cleon and St. Paul," *Studies in Browning and His Circle* 6 (1978): 25–31, and Antony H. Harrison with Samia Dodin, "Cleon's Joy-Hunger and the Empedoclean Context," *Studies in Browning and His Circle* 9 (1981): 57–68. See also Ian Jack, *Browning's Major Poetry* (Oxford: Clarendon Press, 1973), pp. 239–43.

22. I here use "match," as I will throughout, in Gombrich's sense: the attempt to conflate one thing with another in specifically "as if" fashion. Gombrich is talking of paintings and their topics, I of readers and the "others" textualized in the monologue, whether the speaker or the implied poet.

23. For discussion of the term "narratee" see Gerald Prince, "Introduction à l'étude du narrative," *Poétique* 14 (1973); rpt. as "Introduction to the Study of the Narratee," in *Reader-Response Criticism*, ed. Jane Tomkins (Baltimore: Johns Hopkins University Press, 1980), pp. 7–25.

24. George Santayana, "The Poetry of Barbarism," in *Robert Browning: A Collection of Critical Essays*, ed. Philip Drew (New York: Houghton, Mifflin, 1966), p. 30.

25. From a letter to Ruskin, published in *The Works of John Ruskin*, ed. E. T. Cook and Alexander Wedderburn, vol. 36 (London: George Allen, 1909), p. xxxiv. See chap. 3 of the present study (n. 22) for the full passage as well as Ruskin's remarks.

26. H. P. Grice, "Logic and Conversation," in *Speech Acts: Syntax and Semantics*, ed. Peter Cole and J. L. Morgan, vol. 3 (New York: Academic Press, 1975), especially p. 45. See also Grice's "Utterer's Meaning and Intention," *Philosophical Review* 78 (1969): 147–77.

27. Mary Pratt, *Toward a Speech Act Theory of Literary Discourse* (Bloomington: Indiana University Press, 1977), especially chap. 5, "Literary Cooperation and Implicature."

28. See Bergman, "Browning's Monologues," pp. 782–86; Langbaum, *The Poetry of Experience*, p. 98; Joseph Solimine, Jr., "A Note on Browning's 'An Epistle from Karshish,' " *Studies in Browning and His Circle* 6 (1978): 73–75; Shaw, *The Dialectical Temper*, pp. 170–77.

29. The two rhetorics have grown increasingly separate since Ramus in the sixteenth century, and contemporary literary theory characteristically assumes their distinctness. See, for example, Northrop Frye, *Anatomy of Criticism: Four Essays* (Princeton: Princeton University Press, 1957), p. 21, and Paul de Man, "Semiology and Rhetoric," in *Textual Strategies: Perspectives in Post-Structuralist Criticism*, ed. Josué V. Harari (Ithaca: Cornell University Press, 1979), p. 125. The "rhetoric" of the dramatic monologue, however, can only be fully explained by invoking both rhetorics. The implication is that the division between the two rhetorics may not only not be "natural," it may impede critical explanation.

30. Tzvetan Todorov has in several places discussed this opacity, which results from the collapse of levels of discourse or, put otherwise, from figuration. See "Poetics and Criticism" and "How to Read" in *The Poetics of Prose*, trans. Richard Howard (Ithaca: Cornell University Press, 1977), pp. 28–41, 234–46.

31. See n. 12 above for a discussion of Tucker, *Browning's Beginnings*.

32. T. S. Eliot, "Tradition and the Individual Talent" (1919), in *T. S. Eliot: Selected Essays* (New York: Harcourt, Brace & World, 1964), p. 4.

33. The quoted passages are from John Keats, "Ode on a Grecian Urn."

34. Roma A. King, Jr., *The Bow and the Lyre: The Art of Robert Browning* (Ann Arbor: University of Michigan Press, 1964), p. 52. Further citations will be included in the text.

35. John Ruskin, *Modern Painters* (London: Smith, Elder, 1873), IV, 379.

36. The allusions made by Browning's speakers assist their seeming reality by connecting them to the reader's world, but they also pose potential problems for the critic. For example, in l. 95 of "The Bishop Orders His Tomb," the Bishop, in alluding to the Sermon on the Mount, confuses the female Saint Praxed with Christ. Browning, who repeatedly had to announce that his speaker's mistakes were not his, explained the Bishop's confusion thus: "the blunder as to 'the sermon' is the result of the dying man's haziness; he would not reveal himself as he does but for that" (*Select Poems of Robert Browning*, ed. William J. Rolfe and Heloise E. Hersey [New York: Harper & Brothers, 1894], p. 195). The editors had questioned Browning on this and other points of confusion, and he answered them in a letter, dated 10 July 1886, which contained the explanation here quoted.

37. See Aristotle's *Poetics* for the seminal statement of the "men in action" model and Elder Olson's "An Outline of Poetic Theory" for its neo-Aristotelian elaboration (Olson takes "The Bishop Orders His Tomb" as his generic paradigm). Literature that readily coincides with this model seems realistic not simply because it uses illusionistic strategies but because the model has been so thoroughly assimilated. It is, in effect, a generic metaphor that has "died." See Northrop Frye's observation in *Anatomy of Criticism*: "An original painter knows . . . that when the public demands likeness to an object, it generally wants the exact opposite, likeness to the pictorial conventions it is familiar with" (p. 132). Tzvetan Todorov ("Introduction to Verisimilitude" in *The Poetics of Prose*) argues similarly: that verisimilitude is in large part a matter of a text's correspondence to generic conventions. See also chap. 1 ("Literary Genres") of Todorov's *The Fantastic: A Structural Approach to a Literary Genre*, trans. Richard Howard (Cleveland: Press of Case Western Reserve University, 1973).

38. Kenneth Burke, "Formalist Criticism: Its Principles and Methods," *Texas Quarterly* 9 (1966); rpt. in *Language as Symbolic Action: Essays on Life, Literature, and Method* (Berkeley: University of California Press, 1966), p. 499.

39. Elder Olson, "William Empson, Contemporary Criticism, and Poetic Diction," in *Critics and Criticism*, p. 80.

40. Harold Bloom, *A Map of Misreading* (New York: Oxford University Press, 1975). Further citations will be included in the text.

41. Samuel Taylor Coleridge, *Biographia Literaria*, ed. John Shawcross (London: Oxford University Press, 1907), I, chap. 13, 202.

42. Ibid., p. 202.

43. Sören Aabye Kierkegaard, *Repetition: An Essay in Experimental Psychology*, trans. Walter Lowrie (Princeton: Princeton University Press, 1946), pp. 3-4.

44. David J. DeLaura, "The Context of Browning's Painter Poems: Aesthetics, Polemics, Historics," *PMLA* 95 (1980): 381.

45. See Glen Omans, "Browning's 'Fra Lippo Lippi': A Transcendentalist Monk," *Victorian Poetry* 7 (1969): "Browning was certainly using Fra Lippo to express to his own age his own theory of poetic technique" (p. 141). See also DeLaura: "Lippo's quarrels with his viewers and superiors are parallel to Browning's struggles to gain a sympathetic readership, and the doctrine advanced is a partial rationale of Browning's own art and indeed of his own multitudinous mode of expression" (p. 380). Richard Benvenuto, in "Lippo and Andrea: The Pro and Contra of Browning's Realism," *Studies in English Literature, 1500-1900* 13 (1973): 643-52, gives a superbly subtle analysis of the ways in which the aesthetics of Andrea, Lippo, and Browning concur and differ, reminding us in

conclusion that there is no such thing as "Browning's theory of art," that a somewhat different "theory" or, as we might say, implied author seems to authorize each poetic inquiry into "realism." For a detailed grounding of these "painter poems," both in their own time and in Browning's, see Jacob Korg, *Browning and Italy* (Athens: Ohio University Press, 1983).

46. See Tucker, *Browning's Beginnings* (see n. 12 above), pp. 201–8. Many critics have discovered an ambivalence towards Lippo—see the survey by Susan Hackett and John Ferns, "A Portrait of the Artist as a Young Monk: The Degree of Irony in Browning's 'Fra Lippo Lippi,'" *Studies in Browning and His Circle* 4 (1976): 105–18. See also W. O. Raymond's *The Infinite Moment* (Toronto: University of Toronto Press, 1950). Raymond argues that Browning is seduced by the casuistry of his own speakers. But Fra Lippo seems more than usually seductive, for, as DeLaura observes, "None of the other casuists, with the possible exception of Blougram at points, presents such important doctrine that goes so relatively uncriticized" (p. 387).

47. Alexander Cozens, *A New Method of Assisting the Invention in Drawing Original Compositions of Landscape* (1785), quoted by Gombrich, *Art and Illusion*, p. 183.

48. Edward FitzGerald, quoted by Christopher Ricks in his annotated edition, *The Poems of Tennyson* (New York: W. W. Norton, 1969), p. 542.

49. See Fuson, *Browning and His English Predecessors* (pp. 44–45) for an exhaustive list of poems spoken by animals and inanimate objects.

50. Miller, *The Disappearance of God* (see n. 12 above), p. 87.

51. Virtually all critics of the monologue, including the present one, feel the need at some point in their arguments to narrate the history of the term "dramatic monologue." This narration is typically used to validate and substantiate the intrinsicality of the genre. My purpose is precisely the opposite.

Chapter 3. The Mask Lyric

1. See Douglas R. Hofstadter, *Gödel, Escher, Bach: An Eternal Golden Braid* (New York: Random House, 1980), especially p. 15. Further citations will be included in the text.

2. Ezra Pound, *The Letters of Ezra Pound: 1907–1914*, ed. D. D. Paige (New York: Harcourt, Brace & World, 1950), pp. 3–4.

3. T. S. Eliot, "Ezra Pound," *Poetry* 68 (1946); rpt. in *Ezra Pound: A Collection of Critical Essays*, ed. Walter Sutton (Englewood Cliffs, N.J.: Prentice-Hall, 1963), p. 20.

4. Aside from the stylistic kinship between the two poets and their similar interest in things and persons historical (for discussion of which see Jacob Korg, "The Music of Lost Dynasties: Browning, Pound and History," *ELH* 31 [1961]: 20–40), we also find more particular links. Pound's "Scriptor Ignotus" explicitly proclaims its intertextual origin in Browning's "Pictor Ignotus," and Pound in his criticism explicitly admires the poems in *Men and Women*, calling them the "most interesting poems in Victorian English" ("T. S. Eliot," *Literary Essays of Ezra Pound*, ed. T. S. Eliot [New York: New Directions, 1935], p. 419). Yet even here Pound tells us that he is doing something different. His speaker is a "scriptor," an announced self-writer. And even as he admires *Men and Women*, Pound faults their maker, implicitly correcting the monologic schema for his own more lyric use: "Browning included a certain amount of ratiocination and of purely intellectual comment, and in just that proportion he lost intensity" ("T. S. Eliot," pp. 419–20). But perhaps the most intriguing and explicit instance of such correction is Pound's address to Browning in an early draft of Canto I (*Poetry: A Magazine of Verse* 10 [1917]: 114–15):

> To set out so much thought, so much emotion;
> To paint, more real than any dead Sordello,
> The half or third of your intensest life
> And call that third *Sordello*;
> And you'll say, "No, not your life,

He never showed himself,"
Isn't worth the evasion, what were the use
Of setting figures up and breathing life upon them,
Were't not *our* life, your life, my life, extended.

See also Pound's "Mesmerism," addressed to Browning, and T. S. Eliot's early definition of Browning's influence in "Ezra Pound: His Metric and Poetry" (1917), in *To Criticize the Critic* (New York: Farrar, Straus & Giroux, 1965), pp. 162–82. Eliot began the tradition of naming Yeats and Browning Pound's two "fathers" (p. 167). For a more general study of Browning's influence, see Betty S. Flowers, *Browning and the Modern Tradition* (London: Macmillan Press, 1976).

5. N. Cristoph de Nagy, *The Poetry of Ezra Pound: The Pre-Imagist Stage* (Bern: Franke, 1960), p. 132; Hugh Witemeyer, *The Poetry of Ezra Pound: Forms and Renewal, 1908–1920* (Berkeley: University of California Press, 1969), p. 60. Further citations will be included in the text.

6. Walter Bagehot, "Wordsworth, Tennyson, and Browning; or Pure, Ornate, and Grotesque Art in English Poetry" (1864); rpt. in *Collected Works*, ed. Norman St. John-Stevas (Cambridge, Mass.: Harvard University Press, 1965), II, 353.

7. J. P. Sullivan, "Pound's *Homage to Propertius*: "The Structure of a Mask," *Essays in Criticism* 10 (July 1960); rpt. in *Ezra Pound*, p. 143.

8. Ezra Pound, *Gaudier-Brzeska: A Memoir* (1916; rpt., New York: New Directions Books, 1970), p. 85.

9. Hugh Kenner, *The Pound Era* (Berkeley: University of California Press, 1965), pp. 265–66.

10. M. L. Rosenthal, *The Modern Poets: A Critical Introduction* (New York: Oxford University Press, 1965), p. 55.

11. The Victorians tended to endorse either the past over the present or the present over the past. These endorsements, obviously antithetical, are also profoundly similar in origin and purpose: both arise from the increasing awareness of an immense difference between *then* and *now*; both define the past by the needs of the present. Whether arguing for progress or decadence—the poles that magnetized Victorian thought—the concept of historical time was the same: ineluctably linear and unashamedly strategic. I am here discussing the shift in historical consciousness that happened around 1900 in terms of a generic displacement, but this was only one of the many shifts that, together, undid the nineteenth century's notions of reality, knowledge, and language. Heisenberg's uncertainty principle and Gödel's Incompleteness Theorem formalized the conceptual unease generated by a universe whose newly revealed curvature and randomness were moving it beyond the ken of Euclidean geometry and Kantian teleology. In a more "human" sphere, Virginia Woolf announced that "in or about December, 1910, human character changed" (*Collected Essays* [New York: Harcourt, Brace & World, 1967], I, 320). And D. H. Lawrence wrote to Edward Garnett on 5 June 1914 that "you mustn't look in my novel for the old stable *ego* of the character" (*Selected Letters of D. H. Lawrence*, ed. Diana Trilling [New York: Farrar, Straus and Cudahy, 1958], p. 75). For further discussion see Adena Rosmarin, "The Historical Imagination: Browning to Pound," *The Victorian Newsletter* 61 (1982): 11–16; Jerome Hamilton Buckley, *The Triumph of Time: A Study of the Victorian Concepts of Time, History, Progress, and Decadence* (Cambridge, Mass.: Harvard University Press, 1966); and Hofstadter's study, *Gödel, Escher, Bach*, which displays the consequences of these shifts for contemporary thought and, through the example of Escher, for contemporary vision.

12. T. S. Eliot, "Tradition and the Individual Talent," in *Selected Essays* (New York: Harcourt, Brace & World, 1932; new ed., 1964), p. 4.

13. Ezra Pound, *The Spirit of Romance: An Attempt to Define Somewhat the Charm of the Pre-Renaissance Literature of Latin Europe* (New York: E. P. Dutton, 1910), p. vi. See also Pound's later remarks in "Praefatio~aut tumulus cimicium," *Active Anthology* (London: Faber and Faber, 1933): "Mr. Eliot and I are in agreement, or 'belong to the same school of critics,' in so far as we

both believe that existing works form a complete order which is changed by the introduction of the 'really new' work" (p. 9). This belief, as Pound wrote in his preface to *The Spirit of Romance*, requires "a literary scholarship, which will weight Theocritus and Yeats with one balance . . . " (p. 8). Pound's intertextualism precedes Harold Bloom's by over half a century.

14. Robert Langbaum, *The Poetry of Experience: The Dramatic Monologue in Modern Literary Tradition* (New York: W. W. Norton, 1957), pp. 94–95. Further citations will be included in the text.

15. Ezra Pound, "How I Began," *T. P.'s Weekly* 21 (6 June 1913): 707.

16. E. H. Gombrich, *Art and Illusion: A Study in the Psychology of Pictorial Representation* (Princeton: Princeton University Press, 1960), p. 73. Further citations will be included in the text.

17. Wayne C. Booth, *A Rhetoric of Irony* (Chicago: University of Chicago Press, 1974), pp. 5–6.

18. Cleanth Brooks, "The Heresy of Paraphrase," in *The Well Wrought Urn: Studies in the Structure of Poetry* (New York: Harcourt, Brace & World, 1947), p. 214.

19. Robert Penn Warren, "Pure and Impure Poetry," *Kenyon Review* 5 (1943); rpt. in *Critical Theory Since Plato*, ed. Hazard Adams, (New York: Harcourt, Brace & Jovanovich, 1971), p. 992.

20. Cleanth Brooks, "Irony as a Principle of Structure" (1949); rpt. in Adams, *Critical Theory*, p. 1043. See also I. A. Richards, *Principles of Literary Criticism* (New York: Harcourt, Brace & Jovanovich, 1925). Standing behind Richards' notion of synthesis is, of course, Coleridge's notion of the imagination as a synthetic power—as Richards himself acknowledges.

21. Hans Vaihinger, *The Philosophy of "As If": A System of the Theoretical, Practical and Religious Fictions of Mankind*, trans. C. K. Ogden (London: Routledge & Kegan Paul, 1924), p. 108.

22. Robert Browning, quoted in *The Works of John Ruskin*, ed. E. T. Cook and Alexander Wedderburn, vol. 36 (London: George Allen, 1909), p. xxxiv. Browning is replying to Ruskin's letter of 2 December 1855, for the text of which see David J. DeLaura, "Ruskin and the Brownings: Twenty-five Unpublished Letters," *Bulletin of the John Rylands Library* 54 (1972): 324–27. Ruskin had been reading *Men and Women*:

> Your Ellipses are quite Unconscionable: before one can get through ten lines, one has to patch you up in twenty places, wrong or right, and if one hasn't much stuff of one's own to spare to patch with! You are worse than the worst Alpine Glacier I ever crossed. Bright, & deep enough truly, but so full of Clefts that half the journey has to be done with ladder and hatchet.

Browning replied:

> I cannot begin writing poetry till my imaginary reader has conceded licences to me which you demur at altogether. I *know* that I don't make out my conception by my language, all poetry being a putting the infinite within the finite. You would have me paint it all plain out, which can't be. . . .

See also Herbert F. Tucker's discussion of this exchange (*Browning's Beginnings: The Art of Disclosure* [Minneapolis: University of Minnesota Press, 1980]) and of the paradox involved in using "a style that acknowledges its own insufficiency" (p. 15). The paradox, not incidentally, expresses in critical terms my theoretical thesis concerning genre.

23. Brooks, "Irony as a Principle of Structure," p. 1043.

24. Schlegel's definitions and elaborations of the notion of romantic irony are primarily found in *Friedrich Schlegel's Lucinde and the Fragments*, trans. Peter Firchow (Minneapolis: University of Minnesota Press, 1971), and *Dialogue on Poetry and Literary Aphorisms*, trans. Ernst Behler and Roman Struc (University Park: Pennsylvania State University Press, 1968). Only recently has critical attention turned to the explanatory possibilities of this notion. See Clyde de L. Ryals, *Becoming*

Browning: The Poems and Plays of Robert Browning, 1833-1846 (Columbus: Ohio State University Press, 1983), Anne K. Mellor, *English Romantic Irony* (Cambridge, Mass.: Harvard University Press, 1980), and Lilian R. Furst, *Fictions of Romantic Irony* (Cambridge, Mass.: Harvard University Press, 1984.) E. Warwick Slinn, in *Browning and the Fictions of Identity* (London: Macmillan Press, 1982), reads Browning's monologues as self-conscious self-dramatizations, wherein the "self" is more or less aware of its fictions or strategies. Slinn does not tie his analyses to the tradition of Romantic irony or to Vaihinger, nor does he make the generic distinctions I am making. Nevertheless, it is no accident that he finds "Childe Roland" to be the "quintessential Browning poem, despite the way it differs from more orthodox monologues" (p. 162). It is precisely this difference that "fits" the poem to the critical language Slinn is using, making it the paradigmatic case.

25. See Friedrich Schlegel, *Critical Fragments* from *The Athenaeum* (1798-1800), in *Lucinde and the Fragments*, no. 121, in which irony is defined as the "absolute synthesis of absolute antitheses, the continual self-creating interchange of two conflicting thoughts." Schlegel's dialectic, in other words, is not Hegelian. It is not progressive and transcendental but, rather, paradoxical and endlessly self-perpetuating. The clearest laying out of this distinction is found in Murray Krieger's *The Classic Vision: The Retreat from Extremity in Modern Literature* (Baltimore: Johns Hopkins University Press, 1971), pp. 24-27. Krieger does not mention Schlegel, but his "tragic vision," as he says, "thrives on the rejection of Hegelian synthesis" (p. 24). Like Schlegel, he argues that "what converts reconciliation into unyielding tension is the refusal of a polar extreme to melt into its antagonist by way of synthesis" (p. 24).

26. See Friedrich Schlegel, *Critical Fragments* from *The Lycaeum*, in *Lucinde and the Fragments*, no. 37.

27. Friedrich Schlegel, *Literary Notebooks, 1797-1801*, ed. Hans Eichner (London: Athlone Press, 1957), no. 506.

28. Alfred, Lord Tennyson, quoted by Christopher Ricks in his annotated edition, *The Poems of Tennyson* (New York: W. W. Norton, 1969), p. 1113. For an analysis of how Tennyson revised "Tithon" into "Tithonus," see Mary Joan Donahue, "Tennyson's 'Hail, Briton!' and 'Tithon' in the Heath Manuscript," *PMLA* 64 (1949): 385-416. Compare as well a poem of 1830, "The Grasshopper." Linda K. Hughes, in another examination of Tennyson's revisions, argues that "Tithonus" is superior to "Tithon," a judgment with which I concur, but the reasons given for this aesthetic superiority—it is a "less personal, more detached vision of death and immortality" in part because Tithonus, unlike Tithon, refers to his past self as "he," in part because the added lines (11-23) give motivation to his predicament—clash with her conclusion: that "Tithonus" is therefore a better *dramatic monologue* than "Tithon" (*Philological Quarterly* 58 [1979]: 82-89). Because the revisions make our judgment of Tithonus less likely by making him both more sympathetic and self-distanced, they indeed make the poem better—but only if read as a mask lyric. See also W. David Shaw, "Tennyson's 'Tithonus' and the Problem of Mortality," *Philological Quarterly* 52 (1973), 274-85. Shaw argues that Tithonus comes to a transcendent insight by the end of the poem, an insight shared by the speaker of "Ode on a Grecian Urn": that immortality divorced from "sensuous immediacy" is a doom. This insight is here discounted no more than it is in Keats's poem, which is to say not at all, and the poem accordingly remains lyric, despite its "mask."

29. James R. Kincaid, *Tennyson's Major Poems: The Comic and Ironic Patterns* (New Haven: Yale University Press, 1975), p. 45.

30. Ibid., pp. 46-47.

31. See Seymour Chatman, *Story and Discourse: Narrative Structure in Fiction and Film* (Ithaca: Cornell University Press, 1978), and his "What Novels Can Do That Films Can't (and Vice Versa)," *Critical Inquiry* 7 (1980): 121-40. Chatman's distinction between story-time (the sequence of plot events) and discourse-time (the sequence of reading events) is most commonly applied to

novels. The distinction, however, is fundamental to any attempt to tell a story "regardless of medium" ("What Novels Can Do," p. 122), and Tithonus, like all mask-lyric speakers, is telling a story, specifically the story of his life.

32. Murray Krieger, *Theory of Criticism: A Tradition and Its System* (Baltimore: Johns Hopkins University Press, 1976), p. 11.

33. Hallam, Lord Tennyson, *Alfred Lord Tennyson: A Memoir* (New York: Macmillan, 1898), I, 459.

34. Ibid., p. 196.

35. James Knowles, "Aspects of Tennyson, II (a Personal Reminiscence)," *Nineteenth Century* 33 (1893): 182.

36. Ralph W. Rader, "The Dramatic Monologue and Related Lyric Forms," *Critical Inquiry* 3 (1976): 142. Further citations will be included in the text. Rader's definition of the mask-lyric concentrates on the relationship of the poet to the speaker (as does his definition of the monologue) rather than, as here, on the reader-critic's attempt to make a reasoned and aesthetic sense of that relationship. For a history of the critical controversy see John Pettigrew, "Tennyson's 'Ulysses': A Reconciliation of Opposites," *Victorian Poetry* 1 (1963): 27-45. See also the opening pages of Linda K. Hughes, "Dramatic and Private Personae: 'Ulysses' Revisited," Victorian *Poetry* 17 (1979): 192-203.

37. E. J. Chiasson, "Tennyson's 'Ulysses'—A Reinterpretation," *University of Toronto Quarterly* 23 (1954): 402-9; John Perry, "The Relationship of Disparate Voices in Poems," *Essays in Criticism* 15 (1965): 55. Among the most interesting of recent "negative" or monologic readings is that of Arthur D. Ward, " 'Ulysses' and 'Tithonus': Tunnel-Vision and Idle Tears," *Victorian Poetry* 12 (1974): 311-19. Ward argues that Ulysses' fault is that of "tunnel-vision" or "narrow ruthlessness" joined to "madness."

38. Chiasson, "Tennyson's 'Ulysses,' " p. 405.

39. Perry, "Relationship of Disparate Voices," p. 56.

40. W. H. Auden, "Introduction," in *Tennyson: An Introduction and a Selection by W. H. Auden* (London: Phoenix House, 1946), p. xix.

41. Henry Kozicki, *Tennyson and Clio: History in the Major Poems* (Baltimore: Johns Hopkins University Press, 1979), p. 43. Kozicki defines the critical challenge of "Ulysses" as "finding a vantage point that will unite simultaneous yet contradictory perceptions of social and individual imperatives" (p. 42).

42. In Harvard University Library Tennyson Papers, Notebook 16 (Houghton Library).

43. Jerome Buckley, in *Tennyson: The Growth of a Poet* (Cambridge, Mass.: Harvard University Press, 1960), argues that including the Telemachus episode moves the poem "from a personal description of what the poet felt" to "the full sense of character" and "fine balance of rhetoric" that make the final version "memorable" (p. 61).

44. P. F. Baum, *Tennyson, Sixty Years After* (Chapel Hill: University of North Carolina Press, 1948), p. 303.

45. See Aristotle's *Rhetorica*, trans. W. Rhys Roberts, in *The Works of Aristotle*, ed. W. D. Ross (Oxford: Clarendon Press, 1966), XI, 1366b.

46. See, for example, "Anthony to Cleopatra" and "The High Priest to Alexander" in *Poems by Two Brothers*. See also A. Dwight Culler's "Monodrama and the Dramatic Monologue," *PMLA* 90 (1975): 366-85.

47. For an example of Tennyson's philosophy of gradualism, which alone should suffice to rebut Auden's charge and show, as most critics recognize, that the poem is indeed concerned with "extramural" values, see "You ask me, why," in particular, the following lines:

> Where faction seldom gathers head,
> But, by degrees to fullness wrought,

The strength of some diffusive thought
Hath time and space to work and spread.

For "virtuous" readings of Telemachus see A. Dwight Culler, *The Poetry of Tennyson* (New Haven: Yale University Press, 1977), pp. 95–96, and Mary Saunders, "Tennyson's 'Ulysses' as Rhetorical Monologue," *The Victorian Newsletter* 60 (1981): 20–24. Saunders recognizes the rhetorical cast of Ulysses' discourse but sees it as depending upon the presence of an actual audience, whom Ulysses is trying to persuade to action. This reading, which does not consider the use of rhetoric in the self's dialogue with itself, requires Saunders to argue against the generic definition of the mask lyric—Childe Roland and Prufrock, after all, have no audience—and to posit another genre, wherein the reader comes to share the speaker's opinion through persuasion. In this sense, however, all mask lyrics are "rhetorical." They always persuade the reader to match with the speaker, and the presence of an audience, as in "Tithonus," is incidental to this effect. Like others who attack Ulysses for his "rhetoric" (see also L. M. Findlay, who reads the poem as a monologue in part because of Ulysses' "accents of self-persuasion" ["Sensation and Memory in Tennyson's 'Ulysses,' " *Victorian Poetry* 19 (1981): 146]), Saunders assumes that self-deliberation signifies the absence of argumentation. Persuasion of the self, however, is a special case of persuasion, in which the "other" that is being persuaded is an exalted version of the self, much like the "soul" in Yeats's "A Dialogue of Self and Soul." Persuasion of this idealized audience has traditionally been considered veridical. See, for example, René Descartes, "Preface to the Reader," *Meditations on the First Philosophy*, in *The Philosophical Works of Descartes*, trans. Elizabeth S. Haldane and G. R. T. Ross (Cambridge: Cambridge University Press, 1973): "I shall first of all set forth in these Meditations the very considerations by which I persuade myself that I have reached a certain and evident knowledge of the truth, in order to see if, by the same reasons which persuaded me, I can also persuade others" (p. 139). The tradition of treating self-persuasion as a stylus with which we write knowledge extends back to Isocrates and forward to Tennyson's contemporary, John Stuart Mill (see *A System of Logic* [1843; rpt., New York: Harper & Brothers, 1859], p. 3). See also the discussion of "self-deliberating" in Chaim Perelman and L. Olbrechts-Tyteca, *The New Rhetoric: A Treatise on Argumentation*, trans. John Wilkinson and Purcell Weaver (Notre Dame: University of Notre Dame Press, 1969), pp. 40–45.

48. Aristotle, p. 1366b. That Tennyson also knew Pope's translation of the *Odyssey* (Hallam, *Memoir*, I, 11) is interesting in light of Pope's footnoted discussion of Ulysses' artful use of rhetoric, a deftness admired by the ancient rhetoricians.

49. Aristotle, p. 1366b. Ricks tells us that "the first version of this line included an approving comment on Telemachus which made it clear that Ulysses was not here scornful of him" (*Poems*, p. 564, note to l. 43). (The comment, as Ricks explains in his preface [p. xix], may not be quoted due to restrictions placed on the manuscript when presented to Trinity College, Cambridge.) The Harvard manuscript, by showing the Telemachus passage to be a deliberate addition, implicitly makes the same point.

50. Aristotle, p. 1367b.

51. Percy Bysshe Shelley, *A Defense of Poetry*, in Adams, *Critical Theory Since Plato*, p. 502. For a full discussion of Romantic "sincerity," see David Perkins, *Wordsworth and the Poetry of Sincerity* (Cambridge, Mass.,: Harvard University Press, 1964).

52. Shelley, *Defense of Poetry*, p. 500.

53. I am indebted to Culler for the observation that "of the twenty names mentioned in the 1832 version of *The Palace of Art* (there were many fewer in 1842) all but four appear in the *Defence of Poetry*" (Culler, *The Poetry of Tennyson*, p. 71).

54. Dante Alighieri, *The Divine Comedy*, The Carlyle-Wicksteed Translation (New York: Random House, 1950), p. 141.

55. The visionary and perpetual nature of Ulysses' quest, which is what, as I am arguing, makes

that quest redemptive and life-giving, has not surprisingly occasioned many of the "negative" or monologic readings in the poem's interpretive history. Clyde de L. Ryals argues that Tennyson meant for his readers to notice that the poem deviates from the *Odyssey*, that, in particular, the mariners are all dead, and that this "notice" is what makes the poem ironic ("Point of View in Tennyson's *Ulysses*, *Archiv* 199 [1962]: 232–34). Arthur Ward picks up on this suggestion in " 'Ulysses' and 'Tithonus,' " using it to argue that Ulysses is divorced from reality and hence mad (p. 316). Commenting on Ulysses' allusion to the mariners with whom he has "toiled, and wrought, and thought," L. M. Findlay argues in "Sensation and Memory in Tennyson's 'Ulysses' " that "one might expect 'fought' instead of 'thought' here; the cerebral substitution is uneasy, like all such references in the poem" (p. 143). Because Findlay is reading in monologic terms, the repeated substitution of mental for physical action is interpreted as damning Ulysses. But perhaps the most interesting argument along these lines is that of Elizabeth K. Helsinger, who places Tennyson's Ulysses midway in the nineteenth century's radical shift in notions of selfhood and time: "Tennyson's Ulysses is already slow to depart. Pater gives up the voyage entirely, turning from Ulysses' mode of self-exploration to Penelope's, 'that strange, perpetual weaving and unweaving of ourselves' " ("Ulysses to Penelope: Victorian Experiments in Autobiography," in *Approaches to Victorian Autobiography*, ed. George P. Landon [Athens: Ohio University Press, 1979], p. 4). Ulysses' "slowness" is not damning here but, rather, dooming: "The Victorians know what Wordsworth never quite admitted: that self-discovery has become not the prelude to an active life but an inadequate substitute for it" (p.5). Helsinger's argument meshes with the preachings of the Victorians, but their poetic practice, like that of the Romantics, argues quite otherwise: that self-discovery is itself an act, specifically the act of writing the self in words, and could hardly be more consequential, whether in societal terms ("Ode to the West Wind") or personal terms ("Tintern Abbey"). Ulysses' critics equate healthy action with physical action: hence the ironic or monologic reading. This equation is in part a consequence of the traditional notion of "self-discovery," which assumes that an essential self can be "found," but nineteenth-century writers practiced—even if they did not preach —assumptions that our century has labeled "existentialist": that the self is made rather than found and that this making is a kind of writing, which is perpetually open-ended and, for this reason, life-perpetuating. It is precisely "that strange, perpetual weaving and unweaving of ourselves," then, that saves us from our urns and tombs. For discussion of prose self-writing see Avrom Fleishman, *Figures of Autobiography: The Language of Self-Writing in Victorian and Modern England* (Berkeley: University of California Press, 1983). For discussion of Browning's "existentialism" see Norton B. Crowell, *The Convex Glass: The Mind of Robert Browning* (Albuquerque: University of New Mexico Press, 1968), chap. 5.

56. Harold Bloom, *A Map of Misreading* (New York: Oxford University Press, 1975), p. 19.

57. Gaston Bachelard, *The Poetics of Space*, trans. Etienne Gilson (Boston: Beacon Press, 1969), pp. 183–84.

58. Ibid., p. 195.

59. Ibid., p. 203. Tennyson, not incidentally, wrote a long poem called "The Day-Dream."

60. Harvard Notebook 16.

61. Leo Bersani, *A Future for Astyanax: Character and Desire in Literature* (Boston: Little, Brown, 1976), p. 58.

62. Langbaum, *The Poetry of Experience*, p. 91; Culler, *The Poetry of Tennyson*, p. 97.

63. Culler, *The Poetry of Tennyson*, p. 97. Charles Mitchell perceives that Ulysses is questing for an infinite goal ("The Undying Will of Tennyson's 'Ulysses,' " *Victorian Poetry* 2 [1964]: 91). In response to Mitchell, Arthur Ward argues in " 'Ulysses' and 'Tithonus' " that Ulysses' "quest is infinite only in that it is insatiable" (p. 313, n. 4). My point is that Ulysses keeps himself alive by keeping himself unfinished, by aiming at the infinite. The worth of this strategy is a pragmatic question: Does it work?

64. "Childe Roland" is typically read as a quest-poem: see Langbaum, *The Poetry of Experience*, pp. 192–98; Donald S. Hair, *Browning's Experiments with Genre* (Toronto: University of Toronto Press, 1972), pp. 85–86; Harold Bloom, *Poetry and Repression: Revisionism from Blake to Stevens* (New Haven: Yale University Press, 1976), chap. 7 ("Browning: Good Moments and Ruined Quests") and *A Map of Misreading*, chap. 6; Ian Jack, *Browning's Major Poetry* (Oxford: Clarendon Press, 1973), pp. 179–94. Jack's reading is of particular interest, being composed largely of readings of the poem's complex literary and interpretive histories.

65. "Childe Roland" is typically discussed in terms of nightmare. For example, see Barbara Melchiori, *Browning's Poetry of Reticence* (New York: Barnes & Noble, 1968), chap. 6.

66. Rosenthal, *The Modern Poets*, p. 84.

67. Elisabeth Schneider, *T. S. Eliot: The Pattern in the Carpet* (Berkeley: University of California Press, 1975), p. 24. See also Carol T. Christ, "T. S. Eliot and the Victorians," *Modern Philology* 79 (1981): 157–65. Christ's argument, with which I agree, is that Eliot's announced break with his Victorian fathers is a polemical move, a strategy aimed at creating "a climate of appreciation" for his poetry and, we might add, Pound's. Christ goes on to trace the close ties of these two poets with Tennyson and Browning respectively, focusing on their adaptations of the monologue. Although continuing to call the monologue-like poems of all four poets "dramatic monologues," Christ nevertheless makes distinctions within the genre that at points concur with my distinctions between the genres:

> The profoundest poetic influence of the Victorian period on Eliot I would argue to be Tennyson. Unlike Pound, who learned much about persona, the dramatic monologue, and even about the possibilities of difficult and contorted syntax from Browning, Eliot learns his use of the dramatic monologue from Tennyson. Browning most frequently uses the dramatic monologue to portray eccentric characters with extraordinary intellectual or moral positions in dramatic and self-revealing situations. Tennyson, on the other hand, more frequently uses mythological or literary figures to express a mood far more general, far less dependent on particular personality or dramatic situation. T. S. Eliot shares not only the mood of Tennyson's poetry, a mood of despairing impotence, of longing for oblivion, but the technique Tennyson uses to evoke that mood. Both poets use character not for its dramatic potential but as a way of providing a unifying focus, a skeleton on which to hang lyrical, often fragmentary evocations of mood, a mood often expressing deeply felt personal emotion. Character thus enables both poets to objectify and control the personal. At the same time, the mythological status of character—and for Eliot the dense tissue of mythological and literary reference with which he surrounds character—gives mood a symbolic resonance. (Pp. 162–63)

68. Barbara Herrnstein Smith, *Poetic Closure: A Study of How Poems End* (Chicago: University of Chicago Press, 1968), pp. 26–27.

69. William Wordsworth, "Preface to the Second Edition of *Lyrical Ballads*" (1850 edition), in *The Prose Works of William Wordsworth*, ed. W. J. B. Owen and Jane Worthington Smyser (Oxford: Clarendon Press, 1974), p. 140. For an intriguing unfolding of James Wright's Romanticism, in particular the continuity of his poetry with Wordsworth's and their common discontinuity with Ben Jonson's, see Leonard Nathan, "The Private 'I' in Contemporary American Poetry," *Shenandoah* 22 (1971), 80–99.

70. Gregory Corso, "Some of My Beginning . . . and What I Feel Right Now," in *Poets in Poetry*, ed. Howard Nemerov (New York: Basic Books, 1966), p. 172. See also Samuel Taylor Coleridge, *Biographia Literaria*, ed. John Shawcross (Oxford: Oxford University Press, 1907), II, chap. 14, 12: "What is poetry? is so nearly the same question with, what is a poet? that the answer to the one is involved in the solution of the other."

71. Simon O. Lesser, *Fiction and the Unconscious* (London: Peter Owen, 1960), p. 203.

72. Pound, *Letters*, p. 50.

73. Edith Wharton, *A Backward Glance* (New York: D. Appleton-Century, 1934), p. 173.

Epilogue

1. Virginia Woolf, *To The Lighthouse* (New York: Harcourt, Brace, & World, 1927), pp. 255–56.

2. This particular point was, for example, argued by Helen Regueiro Elam in a paper ("Repetition and Vision in Stevens, Ammons, and Ashbery") delivered on 30 August 1980 at a meeting of the English Institute, Harvard University. But even the "negative" hermeneuticist occasionally argues the affirmative power of these denials. See Geoffrey H. Hartman, *Saving the Text: Literature/Derrida/Philosophy* (Baltimore: Johns Hopkins University Press, 1981): "Cordelia's 'Nothing' proves to be sadly prophetic. It exhibits the power of words in seeming to deny them" (p. 130). Hartman, following a suggestion of Theodor Reik, also speculates "that silence is always, to some degree, deathlike" (p. 104, note). Such silence, as this study has argued, is the logical fulfillment of representational desire: hence Cleon in his urn. But as long as Cleon speaks his silence, like Cordelia's speaking "Nothing," he "exhibits the power of words." In other words, he remains alive, or, what Browning's doctrine would argue is the same, vitally imperfect and unfinished.

3. Dante Alighieri, *The Divine Comedy*, The Carlyle-Wiksteed Translation (New York: Random House, 1950), p. 380.

4. Vergil, *Aeneid*, bk. II, ll. 52–53: "The womb thus stricken, the hollows groaned with the sound of hollowness" (my translation).

5. See "Bless," *The Compact Edition of the Oxford English Dictionary* (Oxford: Oxford University Press, 1971), for the full etymological story. See also Hartman's last chapter in *Saving the Text* ("Words and Wounds"). Hartman concludes that "Literature . . . moves us beyond the fallacious hope that words can heal without also wounding. They are homeopathic, curing like by like in the manner of Spenser's "myrrh sweet bleeding in the bitter wound" (pp. 122–23). But Hartman, despite his "homeopathic" conclusion, actually seems to be arguing, as we are here, the case for curing like by *unlike*, for allopathy rather than homeopathy. His example from Spenser is telling.

6. Walter Bagehot, "Wordsworth, Tennyson, and Browning; or Pure, Ornate, and Grotesque Art in English Poetry" (1864); rpt. in *Collected Works*, ed. Norman St. John-Stevas (Cambridge, Mass.: Harvard University Press, 1965), II, 353.

7. Hazard Adams, *The Contexts of Poetry* (Boston: Little, Brown, 1963), pp. 151–52.

8. See Samuel Taylor Coleridge, *Biographia Literaria*, ed. John Shawcross (London: Oxford University Press, 1907), I, chap. 13, 202.

9. See Ralph W. Rader, "The Dramatic Monologue and Related Lyric Forms," *Critical Inquiry* 3 (1976): 140–41.

10. Samuel Taylor Coleridge, "On the Principles of Genial Criticism Concerning the Fine Arts," originally published in *Felix Farley's Bristol Journal* (August, September 1814); rpt. in *Criticism: The Major Texts*, ed. Walter Jackson Bate (New York: Harcourt, Brace & World, 1952), p. 373.

11. Immanuel Kant, *Critique of Judgment*, 2d rev. ed., trans. J. H. Bernard (London: Macmillan and Co., Ltd., 1914), p. 77.

12. George Eliot, from an unsigned review of *Men and Women*, *The Westminster Review* 65 (January 1856): 291.

13. E. H. Gombrich, *Art and Illusion: A Study in the Psychology of Pictorial Representation* (Princeton: Princeton University Press, 1960), p. 314. Gombrich's claim for the heuristic power of "matching" finds its "ethical" ancestor in Shelley's equation of heuristic and moral power. See

particularly the following passage, taken from Percy Bysshe Shelley, *A Defense of Poetry*, in *Critical Theory Since Plato*, ed. Hazard Adams (Harcourt, Brace & Jovanovich, Inc., 1971), p. 503:

The great secret of morals is love; or a going out of our own nature, and an identification of ourselves with the beautiful which exists in thought, action, or person, not our own. A man, to be greatly good, must imagine intensely and comprehensively; he must put himself in the place of another and of many others; the pains and pleasures of his species must become his own. The great instrument of moral good is the imagination; and poetry administers to the effect by acting upon the cause. . . . Poetry strengthens the faculty which is the organ of the moral nature of man, in the same manner as exercise strengthens a limb.

Consider also the well-known observation by Friedrich von Schiller: "man only plays when he is in the fullest sense of the word a human being, and he is only fully a human being when he plays. This proposition, which at the moment may sound like a paradox . . . will . . . prove capable of bearing the whole edifice of the art of the beautiful, and of the still more difficult art of living" (fifteenth letter, *Letters on the Aesthetic Education of Man, in a Series of Letters*, ed. and trans. Elizabeth M. Wilkinson and L. A. Willoughby (Oxford: Clarendon Press, 1967), pp. 107–9. I would add only that the proposition *is* a paradox and that it is capable of doing what Schiller says it can precisely because it is.

Index

Index

193

Adena Rosmarin is an associate professor of English at the University of Texas at Austin. She received her Ph.D. in 1978 at the University of California at Berkeley and in 1980–81 was an Andrew W. Mellon Fellow at Harvard University. She is currently a fellow at the Stanford Humanities Center. Rosmarin's articles on literary theory and interpretive history have appeared in *Critical Inquiry*, *ELH*, *PMLA*, and the *Journal of Aesthetics and Art Criticism*.